American Iron MAGAZINE Presents

1001

HARLEY-DAVIDSON FACTS

TYLER
GREENBLATT

COVERS
1903 TO
PRESENT

CarTech®

CarTech®, Inc.
838 Lake Street South
Forest Lake, MN 55025
Phone: 651-277-1200 or 800-551-4754
Fax: 651-277-1203
www.cartechbooks.com

Edit by Wes Eisenschenk
Cover art by George Trosley

ISBN 978-1-61325-296-3
Item No. CT575

Library of Congress Cataloging-in-Publication Data Available

Written, edited, and
designed in the U.S.A.

Printed in China
10 9 8 7 6 5 4 3 2 1

DISTRIBUTION BY:

Europe
PGUK
63 Hatton Garden
London EC1N 8LE, England
Phone: 020 7061 1980 • Fax: 020 7242 3725
www.pguk.co.uk

Australia
Renniks Publications Ltd.
3/37-39 Green Street
Banksmeadow, NSW 2109, Australia
Phone: 2 9695 7055 • Fax: 2 9695 7355
www.renniks.com

CONTENTS

DEDICATION

This book is dedicated to my grandfather, Don Stroika, who passed his life-long love of anything with an engine on to me. We never had much in common until I was 16 and got my first car, a Cadillac DeVille, which is what he had been driving since he was 16 and bought a 1929 Caddy as his first car.

Our relationship grew tremendously when I started working in the Harley-Davidson industry and bought my first Harley. He loved getting his *American Iron Magazine* subscription and usually called with every issue to talk about it, especially if there was something related to his Super Glide. We finally got to ride together when I pitched a Northern Wisconsin tour story, flew to Milwaukee to pick up a factory Street Glide, and then rode up north for a couple days of riding with him.

A couple years later, our monthly calls occurred more and more frequently as he started chemotherapy and talking about Harley-Davidsons on the phone was the best way I could think of to help take his mind off it. After his passing, at his funeral, we displayed copies of the tour story for people to read and I was sure to wear my Harley-Davidson tie! Although we had a lot of great times over the years, the absolute best memory I have from our time together will always be that one Harley ride.

Opposite: Buzz Kanter is the publisher and editor-in-chief of American Iron Magazine *and* American Iron Garage, *both based in Stamford, Connecticut. A dedicated enthusiast, Buzz competed in the first three Motorcycle Cannonball coast-to-coast endurance rides on Harley-Davidsons (1915 twin, 1929 JDH, and 1936 VLH) and often rides his classic Harleys to work and for fun.*

FOREWORD

by Buzz Kanter, Editor-In-Chief,
American Iron Magazine

It would be a tough call to think of any topic that is so studied or argued about than the history of Harley-Davidson. Okay, sports and politics rank up there for friendly bar bets. But, after that, you'd be hard pressed to match the obsession and passion for Harley-Davidson history and trivia.

Most enthusiasts can tell you the company started out in a small shed in 1903. And that a band of dedicated ex-AMF executives rescued The Motor Company from extinction mere hours before it was too late. Others can share years of manufacture by model (such as the Knucklehead from 1936 to 1947) or when specific engine changes were made (the last Iron-head Sportster was 1985, and 1986 gave us the new Evo-powered Sportster). And then there are the H-D badged oddities including the AMF golf cart or Italian-built single-cylinder motorcycles. Along with more than a century of known facts related to Harley-Davidsons, there is also lots of Harley trivia mis-information that is seldom challenged.

For example, do you know what the first production electric-start Harley-Davidson motorcycle was? If you think it was the 1965 Panhead, you'd be wrong, and need to read this book more carefully (it was the 1964 Servi-Car). After reading this book by Tyler Greenblatt, you can go win a few friendly bar bets with your riding buddies.

I have been riding, racing, and rebuilding motorcycles since the 1970s and have been editor-in-chief of *American Iron Magazine* (AIMag.com) since 1991. In all those years I have read everything I can about Harleys and their amazing history. I have written extensively on the subject, and I'm fortunate to have ridden a large and wide variety of motorcycles. I feel Tyler has done an outstanding job researching and pulling together a wide range of Harley-Davidson–related facts and data for this book.

ABOUT THE AUTHOR

Tyler Greenblatt has been passionate about cars and motorcycles since day one. His parents hooked him on internal combustion when they had a jump seat installed in the back of their 1966 Sting Ray coupe so that a baby seat could be secured back there. The roar of a high-revving small-block V-8 and the distinctly American smell of vinyl and gasoline had a lasting effect that led to considerably more time being spent researching cars, ATVs, motorcycles, and snowmobiles than doing schoolwork. After high school, Tyler majored in print journalism at the University of Wisconsin– Milwaukee, a town where Miller and Harley-Davidson reign supreme, although he could only afford one of those brand names at the time.

His first real experience with Harley-Davidson came when he interned at TAM Communications, the publisher of *American Iron Magazine*, after his junior year and was offered a full-time job as Assistant Editor upon graduation. His love and passion for the Bar & Shield grew exponentially from there as he moved up the ranks to Associate Editor and then as Editor of *American Glory: 110 Years of Harley-Davidson*, a high-end special issue released for The Motor Company's 110th anniversary in 2013. He continues to serve as Associate Editor of *American Iron Magazine* and as Editor of *American Iron Garage* and various special one-off publications.

He lives in Madison, Wisconsin, with his wife, Danielle. His regular rides are a 2010 Nightster and a 2015 Street Bob, and he's currently working on a 1932 RL custom project.

ACKNOWLEDGMENTS

As this is my first published book, my list of thanks goes back many years to every person who encouraged me to write as a career, those who taught me how to do just that, and those who supported me throughout this journey, of which I hope this is but an early step.

First, thank you to my wife, Danielle, who makes everything I do worth doing. Thank you for your understanding for all the nights and weekends spent working on this book and for when I travel around the country for weeks at a time attending rallies and press launches (I'm writing this on my way to Los Angeles to test the new Low Rider S, as you dig out from another Wisconsin snowstorm).

Thank you to my parents, who have supported my writing for as long as I can remember and who encouraged me to actually consider and pursue it as a career. They came through with motivational text messages and phone calls throughout this writing on those late nights where the amount of work left seemed endless. To my godfather, Uncle Denny, and his wife, Aunt Shirley, for being some of the earliest supporters of my writing and also some of the biggest to this day. Uncle Denny was my first and only paying advertiser when I published a monthly family newspaper when I was about ten, and he even paid up front for a book that I started writing and never finished. I hope a copy of this one will make up for it. Of course, all my family and friends have encouraged or supported me in one way or another over the years. However, a special thank you has to go out to my uncle, Ron, who is partially to blame for getting me hooked on anything with an engine since he put my name on his race car when I was a little kid, then helped me fix my "hot rod" tractor, and then kept my truck running in college (as he still does to this day).

Professionally, I've had nothing but the greatest experience working in the motorcycle industry and getting to know the awesome, and occasionally crazy, people who make it up. First and foremost I have to thank Buzz Kanter, who hired me into this wild world straight out of college and whose friendship and mentorship has taught me so much over the years. He's given me opportunities over the years that were above and beyond what I expected, including recommending me to write this book. You never know how starting up a conversation with a stranger on an old Harley will turn out! I'd also like to thank the other past and current editors at *American Iron Magazine* who have taught me the ins and outs of the Harley-Davidson world and have only succeeded in making me more enthusiastic about it, including Dain Gingerelli, Joe Knezevic, Chris Maida, and Steve Lita. Thanks to those at The Harley-Davidson Motor Company with whom I work regularly and who also helped on this project; a special shout-out goes to museum curator Jim Fricke.

A huge thank you goes to Dale Walksler, curator of Wheels Through Time museum, and his fiancée, Trish Davis, for getting me hooked on old Harleys and continuing to further that interest every time I visit the museum. Also to Matt Walksler for providing a fresh perspective on vintage motorcycling to the next generation and for the great times we've had around old bikes together. I'd also like to thank the following people for influencing not only my writing but my love for Harley-Davidsons new and old: Jim Babchak, Bob Bishop, Pete and Maureen Minardi, Kevin McKay, Cris Sommer Simmons, Pat Simmons, Sam Whitehead, and Roger Williams.

Thank you to the readers who perhaps have been reading my work in *American Iron Magazine* over the years and enjoyed it enough to pick up this book, or are new readers who are seeing my name for the first time here. I love hearing from you on social media and meeting you and talking Harleys at rallies around the country or local events in the Wisconsin area.

Thank you to the folks at CarTech, especially my editor, Wes Eisenschenk, for this unique Harley-Davidson book concept. There are a lot of the same old Harley-Davidson books out there (I know because I've read most of them) and I'm honored to be a part of a fresh new take on the genre. Thank you for giving me this opportunity to not only learn more than I ever thought I could about my favorite motorcycles, but to be able to write about it and share it with others. This is a dream come true, but it will be nice to have my nights and weekends back so I can actually ride the bikes that I'm writing about.

INTRODUCTION

Riding a Harley-Davidson isn't just about basic two-wheel transportation. Although there are many motorcycles out there that attempt to copy the look of a Harley-Davidson, many times for half the price, none can give a rider that same feel. It's an experience that pleasures all the senses: the smell of leather and gasoline, the feel of the hot, torquey engine trying to shake free of its cradle, the sound of the unmistakable exhaust rumble, the classic look that's crossed over multiple generations, and most importantly, the mouth-watering taste of freedom that allows for even brief escapes from the norm.

I remember when I got hooked on Harley-Davidsons. I was probably somewhere around the age of five, living in a Manhattan apartment with my parents. To this day, I can remember the sound of roaring engines echoing through the canyons of high-rises. I have no doubt we heard a lot of motorcycles, but, more than 20 years later I remember that sound like it was yesterday. And that's where my Harley-Davidson experience began.

But what exactly is "the Harley-Davidson experience?" You're likely already familiar with the emotional experience that comes with riding a Harley, and you may have even attended a rally or two, but the full "Harley-Davidson experience" comes when you fully immerse yourself into the company's history and the people and machines that paved the way. Harley-Davidson is a company that takes incredible pride in its Milwaukee, USA, roots and has time and time again supported its country in times of war and in peace. It's a company that has been beaten down so badly that recovery seemed impossible, yet it overcame and prospered twice. It's a company whose harshest critics are its biggest supporters. But most importantly, it's a company about family. I've attended several events with Willie G. Davidson (grandson of founder William A. Davidson), his wife, Nancy, and their son, Bill, and daughter, Karen, who are both executives with The Motor Company. No matter how many people this real Harley-Davidson family meets, each one is greeted with open arms and a smile.

Consider this book a history lesson on your Harley-Davidson family from the first time young Bill Harley and Arthur Davidson are known to have seen a motorcycle to 2016 when their 113-year-old company produces 41 different models of world-class machines. My goal with this book was to include facts that appeal to the broad spectrum of Harley-Davidson owners and enthusiasts. It's not a technical, nuts-and-bolts encyclopedia, although you'll find many technical details and year-by-year changes.

You'll find many great facts and stories about The Motor Company itself inside, but I've made no effort to sugarcoat any of it, and I know you'll learn much more than is readily distributed.

Though it's not as big today as it was in the early days, The Motor Company's history with racing and the military is enormous, and I hope that besides the raw facts, you'll get a better understanding of our country's history as well. Something that is often seen today (although preferably not in your rearview mirror) is a motor officer on a Harley-Davidson. The Thin Blue Line has long been supportive of the American brand, and has received unparalleled support by The Motor Company in return, but there's a lot more that goes into a duty bike than what meets the eye.

Harley-Davidson has always been a cultural icon enjoyed by unique individuals from around the world, and I hope you'll enjoy reading about not just the pop culture references to the Bar & Shield, but about the amazing people who've done incredible things with their Harley-Davidsons over the years, most of whom you've likely never heard of. In an effort to cover the entire spectrum of Harley-Davidson, you'll find that some facts are more along the lines of legends and rumors that are based on hard fact, but that have never been officially confirmed or denied. These were some of my favorites to write about, and I hope you'll enjoy reading them as they're intended and making up your own mind about their likelihood.

As with any work that dates back more than 50 years, truth can only be based on what previous historians have written. I strived to use only the most reputable of sources in my research, although I uncovered quite a few occasions where information differed between them, which required further digging for the truth. I hope I found it, and I sincerely hope you enjoy reading and learning from *American Iron Magazine Presents 1,001 Harley-Davidson Facts*.

Chapter 1

Early Era
1915 and earlier

THE MOTOR COMPANY

 While the timing of Fact No. 1 occurs toward the very end of this chapter, there's something revealing and inspiring about the Harley-Davidson Motor Company in the way that it preserves its legendary past for the enjoyment and discovery of current and future generations. In 1915, the founders began the tradition of saving one or two motorcycles directly from the factory every year. To backfill the archive with previous models, they placed newspaper ads seeking to purchase earlier motorcycles. The effort even kept up during the Great Depression, World War II, AMF ownership, and near bankruptcy. Because of the incredible foresight of the founders, and the continuing of the tradition, the Harley-Davidson Museum is able to share the company's legacy with visitors and storytellers from around the globe. Without this pivotal action taken so early on by the founding partners, much of the company's history might be lost today.

Arthur Davidson and Bill Harley grew up as neighbors in Milwaukee and spent most of their spare time in Arthur's father's basement workshop building things and thinking of new ideas. The boys were avid fishermen and often took their poles to the lake via bicycle, sometimes instead of going to school. Ever the thinkers and

The men whose dedication, ingenuity, and perseverance made possible The Motor Company that we know and love are, from left to right: Arthur Davidson, Walter Davidson, William Harley, and William Davidson

Although there were three Davidson brothers. Harley's name comes first because he was the engineer and designer of the first motorcycle. (Photo Courtesy Harley-Davidson)

inventors, one of their first big ideas was to install motors on their bicycles so that they could get to the fishing hole faster and have a little more fun on the way. Although their first motorcycle was still years away, they never lost sight of the dream of making a faster bicycle.

 Arthur and Bill received help from all over Milwaukee to make their motorized bicycle dream come true. Anyone who's ever attempted to start his own company can attest to the fact that there's usually not a whole lot to start with. The boys needed two things: knowledge and tools. They sought knowledge from a fellow employee at Barth Manufacturing, where they both worked, named Emil Kroeger, who was familiar with the French de Dion single-cylinder, four-stroke engine that had taken the internal combustion world by storm. Bill even took a summer job at the Meiselbach bicycle factory in Milwaukee to learn about frames. Then, they received assistance from another neighborhood friend, Henry Melk, who had a lathe in his basement and allowed them to machine parts on it. Harley-Davidson is more of a Milwaukee company than you may have even thought.

 Friends and business partners Arthur Davidson and Ole Evinrude made a pact before either of them actually developed their namesake product, promising that they would never encroach on each other's market. That pact is honored to this day, on purpose or by default. Evinrude never built a motorcycle engine and Harley-Davidson has never built a water product. The latter is surprising because The Motor Company owned, bought, or built just about everything else from snowmobiles to golf carts.

 While home in Milwaukee for William A. Davidson's wedding, Walter Davidson, a skilled mechanic, helped Arthur and Bill successfully put together all the parts they had crafted to build their motorized bicycle. When the three were done, Walter hopped on and took the machine for a ride, making that the first ever ride on a Harley-Davidson motorcycle.

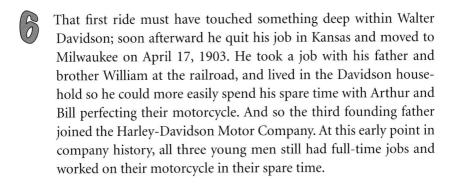 That first ride must have touched something deep within Walter Davidson; soon afterward he quit his job in Kansas and moved to Milwaukee on April 17, 1903. He took a job with his father and brother William at the railroad, and lived in the Davidson household so he could more easily spend his spare time with Arthur and Bill perfecting their motorcycle. And so the third founding father joined the Harley-Davidson Motor Company. At this early point in company history, all three young men still had full-time jobs and worked on their motorcycle in their spare time.

In 1903, Bill and Walter's mother, Margaret Davidson, finally had enough of the three boys tracking dirt and grease throughout her house and the constant working in the basement. In truth, their father, William C., encouraged their entrepreneurship, but he liked to build furniture in his spare time and also wanted his basement woodworking studio back. And so, the day after Margaret had finally let the world know she had had enough, William C. bought some lumber and set to work building a 10 x 15–foot shed in the backyard. This shed became the first Harley-Davidson "factory."

The first Harley-Davidson was sold to the founders' friend, Henry Meyer, in 1903. In 1913, a company researcher was tasked with tracking down that first motorcycle and looking at its maintenance history. After Henry Meyer, four others owned it and put a cumulative 83,000 miles on the machine and none ever had to replace the engine bearings. In a 1913 advertisement, the company bragged that this was a testament to the durability and longevity of its motorcycle. Serial Number One, as it's affectionately called, is on display at the Harley-Davidson Museum.

Before the founders knew the advantages of using a bank, they stored their sales proceeds in a canning jar and hid it in the Davidson family's pantry. Unfortunately, the maid, hired by Margaret Davidson to clean up the boys' dirt and grease, discovered the small stash and stole it. They quickly learned their lesson and began keeping the company's earnings in the bank while sister Bessie kept the books. She was responsible for the company's financial records in the early years, and her brothers rewarded her by paying for her college education.

10 By 1904, the Harley-Davidson Motor Company had sold about ten motorcycles, so the boys doubled the size of the backyard shed to handle the additional capacity. But the shed wasn't going to last much longer for the burgeoning company, and there were no funds to open a real factory yet. That's when help came from the Davidson brothers' "Honey Uncle," James McLay. The land he owned is now known as Picnic Point, a beautiful spit of land on Lake Mendota in Madison, Wisconsin. Uncle James kept bees there and lived off the land, hence his nickname. He was intrigued with his nephews' motorcycles and loaned his life's savings to the young company. As you might imagine, he was paid back many times over.

11 With the money from their Honey Uncle, Bill Harley and the Davidson brothers purchased some land on Chestnut Street in Milwaukee, where, in 1906, they built the first Harley-Davidson factory. It measured 28 x 80 feet, not exactly large by factory standards, but the additional space allowed the company to produce motorcycles on a much grander scale. Apparently, they accidentally built part of the building on railroad-owned land so, to remedy the problem, all of the employees gathered outside and lifted the building and moved it a foot and a half. Soon after, Chestnut Street was renamed Juneau Avenue, which is where Harley-Davidson's corporate headquarters exists today.

12 Harley-Davidson hired its first outside employee in 1905 and production increased from 3 motorcycles a year to 7. In 1906, things really took off for the fledgling company. It hired 5 more employees that year, and production increased to 50 motorcycles.

13 In 1907, Harley-Davidson produced 150 motorcycles and it was clear that The Motor Company was destined for great things. After only about a year at the Juneau Avenue factory, it was rebuilt with cream-colored brick and mortar to 40 x 60 feet, with a second floor. This allowed production to skyrocket to 410 motorcycles in

1908. The new factory had two doors, one for management and one for employees. However, because the doors were next to each other, everyone simply used the convenient door and this helped promote a family atmosphere at the company, which still exists.

14 The Harley-Davidson Motor Company officially incorporated on September 17, 1907, and all 17 employees opted to purchase stock in the company. Walter Davidson became the first company president, Bill Harley became chief engineer and treasurer, and Arthur Davidson took on the role of secretary and general sales manager. After the company incorporated, the oldest Davidson brother, William, decided to leave his job at the railroad and join the company as the works manager.

15 Arthur Davidson insisted that the company must advertise its product, even though it was already struggling to keep up with demand and all of its money was going into meeting that demand. Arthur convinced his friend, Walter Dunlap, a partner at a new advertising firm, to publish a Harley-Davidson catalog on credit. This was a big risk, but the catalog was a success and The Motor Company retained Dunlap's advertising firm as its exclusive agency well into the 1950s.

16 The first official Harley-Davidson dealer, C. H. Lang, opened in Chicago in 1904; it sold one of the first three motorcycles that the company produced.

17 The distinctive Bar & Shield logo was seen for the first time on 1908 model toolboxes. It featured the words "Harley-Davidson" in a bar across the middle in front of a shield that showed "Motor" on the top and "Cycles" on the bottom. However, it didn't see widespread use until 1910 when it appeared on a variety of company literature and packaging. Technically, The Motor Company officially trademarked the logo on May 6, 1910, leading many to believe that 1910 was the first usage.

18 By 1914, less than a decade after hiring its first employee, Harley-Davidson employed 1,570 workers. That year, 16,284 motorcycles were produced, which means that one was completed every 5-1/2 minutes. Not long before, the average was one motorcycle every four months. During this same time period, more than 100 other motorcycle manufacturers had come onto the scene in the United States and gone out of business.

19 Harley-Davidson was Milwaukee's largest user of gas and electricity in the 1910s, perhaps because it was the city's only company using an electric furnace. The same General Electric transformer powered the Juneau Avenue factory from 1913 right through the 1990s. Then it continued service as a backup power unit until 2011, when the 8-foot-tall 8,000-pound unit was moved to the lobby area of the Harley-Davidson Museum where it is currently displayed.

20 The first Parts & Accessories department is formed in 1912 and officially becomes its own division of the business. In that same year, the first P&A catalog, which features parts and riding clothes, is distributed. I'm sure Harley owners then, just as today, waited anxiously for the local dealer to receive the new year's P&A catalog.

21 When the Harley-Davidson Motor Company incorporated on September 17, 1907, the total value of company stock was $14,200. That's a little over $350,000 in today's dollars.

22 On August 14, 1915, Harley-Davidson held its first company picnic at Army Lake in East Troy, Wisconsin. More than 150 employees and their families attended the company outing where they enjoyed games, music, and other festivities. In attendance was L. C. Rosenkrans, the company's staff photographer, who took several pictures of that first event, which disappeared until they were discovered in 2012. Interestingly, East Troy is the hometown and headquarters of Buell, Harley's future sportbike division.

23 Harley-Davidson begins selling H-D branded oil for the first time in 1909. I don't know about you, but I find something very reassuring about filling my bike with Harley-Davidson oil today! As you'll read, Harley-Davidson oil has been given great credit over the years for helping adventure riders achieve successes once thought to be impossible.

24 Although Harley-Davidsons were sold overseas early on, it wasn't until 1913 that The Motor Company sent Export Manager H. C. "Doc" Garner on a six-month tour of Europe to gauge the desire and the market for the Milwaukee brand. Upon his return, he noted that the British motorcycles proved to be tough competition throughout Europe, but that many Europeans wanted to ride an American Harley-Davidson. Immediately following his exploratory trip, The Motor Company began opening dealerships across the continent.

25 In 1908, when most of the country was still using horses as transportation, Harley-Davidson began using automobiles to transport parts. Brush built the first truck in use by The Motor Company. It was little more than a pickup-type bed on a chassis with a couple seats and a steering wheel in the front. Without the steering wheel, it was indistinguishable from a horse-drawn carriage.

THE CHASSIS

26 After spending a summer working at the Meiselbach Bicycle factory in Milwaukee, Bill Harley learned all about bicycle construction and deduced that the traditional triangle frame wouldn't be strong enough for motorized use, even though, in 1901, most motorcycle companies used them. So Bill set to work designing a strong, loop-style frame specifically for use with a motor. That frame design worked so well that it remained in use into the 1950s when production of the WL ceased.

27 Before 1909, H-D oil tanks were fitted on top of the gas tank and to the frame's backbone by a pair of nickel-plated steel bands. Because of this design, the earliest motorcycles are called "straptanks."

The early strap-tank Harley-Davidsons built from 1903 through 1908 carried 1-1/2 gallons of fuel in the large tank underneath and two quarts of oil in the flat tank on top. Janet Davidson's handiwork is evident on the pinstripes and lettering on this 1906. However, someone else added the Bar & Shield logo at a later date; this logo wasn't used until 1910.

28 Harley-Davidson offered its first sidecar for sale in 1914 to compete with the numerous other motorcycle companies that offered a "sidehack" option. Rogers, a notable sidecar company, built the company's first sidecar, but H-D began producing and selling its own sidecar in 1915. Sidecars added a major dose of practicality and usability to any motorcycle, especially for the workingman's cycle. For the average family, automobiles were still far in the future, but a whole family could fit on a motorcycle and enjoy trips and adventure never before imagined. The sidecar remained a staple accessory for Harley-Davidson's civilian, commercial, police, and military functions until production ceased abruptly in 2011.

29 The first Harley-Davidson prototype motorcycle used a basic triangular bicycle frame design, but Walter's first ride quickly revealed that the design did not support a four-stroke engine well. Following that ride, Bill Harley designed a loop-style frame that cradled the engine and allowed a more secure mounting. The first handful of motorcycles remains relatively unchanged between 1903 and 1905; they featured rudimentary bicycle-style seats and handlebars, and had no suspension. A coaster brake stopped the 178-lb. machine (plus rider), which was spread out over a 51-inch wheelbase. All machines up until 1905 were black and had gold pin-striping with red and gold Harley-Davidson lettering, all applied by Janet Davidson.

30 The first suspension appeared on a Harley-Davidson in 1907 in the form of a Sager-Cushion leading-link front fork, which was the precursor to the famous Harley-Davidson springer fork. The two rear legs of the fork mounted solidly to the motorcycle's frame neck on the top; a pivoting bracket on the bottom connected to the wheel and another set of tubes. The forward set of tubes had springs inside; they compressed as the wheel hit a bump, which then actuated the pivoting bracket.

By 1907, Harley-Davidsons were painted the traditional Renault Gray and featured a higher level of polish (overall) than previous models. This motorcycle is equipped with the standard Sager-Cushion leading-link front fork and all-white tires, which help define the look of that era. The gas tank lettering is much straighter and more consistent than previous years; although it was still hand-rendered, a more scientific process had been developed.

31 The 1909 Harley-Davidson took a major leap forward from its strap-tank predecessors with a more durable frame, front end, and chassis layout. The new frame used a twin backbone design to mount the new, longer, one-piece gas/oil tank, which is tapered at the front and rear for a streamlined look. The new frame's wheelbase was 56-1/2 inches, which made room for the molded and painted compartment that sat behind the rear downtube, in front of the rear wheel. It could house tools, gear, and the battery if so equipped. A stronger and more effective front fork was used, as was better seat suspension.

32 In 1909, Harley-Davidson began offering diversified models to its customers with different equipment at different price points. The previous year, the company began naming its machines based on their production pedigree. The 1908s are Model 4s, while 1909s are Model 5s. The most popular model in 1909, with 1,030 sold, was the Model 5, which had the standard 28-inch wheels and a battery, and was priced at $210. The 5A, of which only 54 were built, featured a Bosch magneto and a $250 price tag. B and C models were also available, which matched the 5 and 5A, respectively, but used 26-inch wheels for shorter riders. 27 individuals opted to purchase the $325, twin-cylinder machine in 1909, designated the 5D. Single-cylinder Model 5s weighed in at 235 pounds, a significant jump from previous years; it was a number that only kept increasing.

33 Electric headlights weren't available on Harleys until 1915. Before that, owners or dealers had to mount their own acetylene headlamps to the handlebars. Illumination came from mixing carbide pellets in a water reservoir underneath the lamp, which created the acetylene gas that could be lit; it burned with a relative amount of efficiency and control. They were used for lighting the road, but functioned better at making the motorcycle visible at night. Most acetylene headlamp models had red and green colored glass gems on either side, which also alerted vehicles approaching from the side. A chimney sat on top and released the burnt gas. Many also used an adjustable knob that could control the brightness of the flame. I have an acetylene headlamp produced by Twentieth

Century Manufacturing Company that uses a rounded, magnified glass in front to increase the flame's brightness. These are beautiful pieces that have an incredible amount of design and detail in such a small package. However, these lamps could also potentially set your motorcycle on fire if you hit a big bump or fell over.

34 With the addition of a powerful twin to its lineup, and the single becoming more potent with each year, Harley-Davidson introduced a new frame for the 1911 Model 7s that used a straight front downtube. This new tube was stronger than the curved downtube it replaced, and placed the engine closer to the ground. The wheelbase stayed the same but a new seat with better suspension moved the rider forward a few inches toward the center of the wheelbase. A new, larger gas and oil tank now held 2-1/2 gallons of fuel and one gallon of oil.

35 For the 1912 model year, the company redesigned what can best be described as its rear suspension to a system that was used right into the early 1970s. Instead of using just the small front and rear springs on the seat, which did very little to cushion the rider from impact, Model 8s saw the addition of a 9-inch-long spring inside the frame's rear downtube, on which the seat post sat. This provided about 4 inches of suspension travel for the rider in addition to helper springs on the seat. The Motor Company called this new setup the Ful-Floeting Seat.

36 Some worthwhile changes were made to the frame in 1912 that show a change toward the Harley-Davidson motorcycle's future shape. The rear downtube was shortened, dropping the seat slightly into the middle of the motorcycle; the top backbone was curved down in the back to meet it. The rear of the gas tank was also curved down to match the curve in the frame and the handlebars now stood taller than the seat to create a more comfortable riding style. To protect the rider and engine better from debris and water, a skirted front fender was used for the first time.

37 By 1914, almost all models could hit more than 60 mph. This excluded the singles, which were produced in low quantities. Both speed and weight increased every year after that first motorcycle was built in the woodshed, but the coaster brake in the rear hub remained almost unchanged. A new internal expanding band rear brake was introduced in 1914. A precursor to the drum brake, the more powerful rear brake could be applied by reversing the pedals (as on some children's bicycles), or by using a brake pedal connected to the rear hub by a linkage. The first footboards were introduced along with the new brake pedal, which made long-distance cruising and short jaunts much more comfortable for the rider.

38 Now officially made by Harley-Davidson, the 1915 sidecars received an updated chassis and longer body. Automobiles were now accurately seen as the future of transportation and motorcycles were viewed as enjoyment. The Motor Company advertised the sidecar as a practical way for a whole (small) family to travel economically and enjoyably. A pair of leaf springs on either side of the sidecar made it a remarkably comfortable ride by 1915 standards. Even so, the automobile was tough competition.

39 The Harley-Davidson motorcycle, with the addition of a sidecar, had proven itself a valuable asset to businesses. In 1913, the company expanded its commercial offerings with the Model G Forecar. The Forecar was based on the standard V-twin frame, except that it had a subframe in front to hold a large storage box, which was flanked by a pair of wheels. Two outriggers under the steering head controlled the wheels with a regular handlebar. It used the automobile-style point and go method instead of the motorcycle's countersteer method. The G was built for only three years, likely because it was difficult to operate and the air-cooled engine became extremely hot from the lack of airflow around it. Some Forecars were even produced with skis on the front and a spiked tire in the rear for use in the snow. It's believed that only approximately 330 were built. One beautifully restored Forecar makes regular appearances at Harley-Davidson Museum events, and always draws a good crowd.

40 What's the most important feature that motorcyclists look for in a tire? Because the loss of traction can be disastrous, most likely you'll want a tire that doesn't slip, slop, or skid during maneuvers. Throughout the 1910s, Firestone, the primary supplier of tires to The Motor Company, wanted to make this necessary feature of its tires known. Instead of using what are today called traction grooves, Firestone simply used the words "NON SKID" across the tread. What could be safer than that?

41 Just about everyone should already be familiar with the braking system on the early Harley-Davidsons. Just like on your first bicycle, Harleys used a coaster brake that applied braking force to the back wheel when the rider backpedaled! This system worked well enough until a more powerful drum brake replaced it in 1914. Originally, H-D's coaster brake system was supplied by Thor, which made many different parts for small motorcycle manufacturers.

42 Just because the early Harleys look like there's nothing to them, don't be fooled; they're just good at hiding all the ugly parts. The single-speed bikes, including those made in 1915, had enough space between the engine and rear fender to position a large metal case along the rear of the frame's center downtube. It follows the curvature of the fender in the back and blends in seamlessly; but its aesthetic and practical use doesn't stop there. The compartment housed the motorcycle's tool kit, spare parts, and, if applicable, battery and associated wiring; they were safe from the elements and from thieves. It also keeps the bike looking simple and clean.

43 In 1914, with the addition of the 2-speed rear hub with chain drive and the subsequent changes in the pedals, the rear storage compartment changed shape and became a little smaller. When the 1915 model with a big 3-speed gearbox was introduced, the size of the rear compartment was nearly halved. Even more wires and equipment were left outside to support the needs of the big V-twin.

44 Until 1909, all H-Ds came with a battery-powered ignition system; after that, the dependable magneto ignition system was an extra option. You'd just run the dry-cell battery until it stopped producing spark and then stop at the store for a new one. Dry-cell batteries can't be recharged, so there was no way of reusing them once drained. Early ads place battery mileage at around 1,500 miles. And anyway, and trickle chargers weren't available back then.

45 The earliest image of a Harley-Davidson motorcycle comes in the form of a line drawing believed to be by Bill Harley, which appeared in the April 1905 issue of *Cycle and Automobile Trade Journal*. The motorcycle in the drawing uses a small seat and low handlebars, which indicate a racing machine, unlike stock bikes that had a large seat and handlebars that looped farther back. This marks the first known advertisement for a complete Harley-Davidson motorcycle.

46 That first advertisement described the 138-pound motorcycle's special features, which included a low-hung engine for a well balanced, easy ride (something Harleys still make a point of) and large gasoline and "lubricating" oil tanks. By using the grip throttle control, the rider could adjust speed between 5 and 50 mph. The frame was listed as being 21-1/2 inches, presumably using bicycle-style measurements, with a 51-1/2-inch wheelbase. The 2-inch tires were included with the motorcycle although the buyer could upgrade to a 2-1/4-inch set. The cost was $175.

47 The earliest known photo of a Harley-Davidson appears in the April 1905 issue of *Automobile Review*. It differs from the line drawing in *Cycle and Automobile Trade Journal* in several respects, giving credence to the idea that these bikes were being improved with each new construction. Taller handlebars and a larger, sprung seat indicate a true street machine, although the lack of fenders suggests that The Motor Company still wasn't producing fenders yet. The other big differences are the locations of the coil and battery box. In the drawing, the coil is mounted below the seat and the battery box is beneath the gas tank. However, the photograph shows the coil underneath the gas tank and the battery box mounted on top of the frame's rear tube, above the tire.

48 The first use of fenders, or mudguards as they were called, was in 1905. Prior to a photograph of racer Perry Mack in the June 12, 1905, edition of the *Milwaukee Journal*, there is no evidence of a Harley-Davidson using mudguards (or fenders). Mack's H-D, which had just won a major race the week before, breaking a Wisconsin speed record in the process, is clearly seen equipped with front and rear fenders. A photograph taken in 1906, of a 1905 model delivered in April, also shows that model with a front fender (the rear fender is hidden from view).

49 Although the Harley-Davidson loop-style frame looked nearly identical to that of the Merkel motorcycles being built across town, Bill Harley and Bill Davidson made one key improvement to strengthen the frame. The Merkel's exhaust system ran through the frame tubes to hide what is generally considered an ugly necessity. Harley-Davidson firmly believed that drilling holes, regardless of the heat's effects, greatly weakened the frame. Although it looked good, H-D was more focused on durability and serviceability than good looks, and pointed out this major difference in a brochure sent to potential customers in late 1905.

50 Harley-Davidson discovered the importance of a strong frame neck early on; so much of the force imparted on the front end found its way to the frame. In 1906, it began using a new one-piece frame head that was cast as one part instead of several parts that were then brazed together. It made the frame much more durable. A strong steering head and neck is the hallmark of a Harley-Davidson frame today.

THE POWERTRAIN

51 Bill Harley's first known detailed plans for a motorcycle engine are dated July 20, 1901. They contain the specifications for the very first Harley-Davidson engine, which include the use of 4-inch flywheels. The plans are labeled "Details of 2 x 2-1/4–inch bicycle motor." It gives some idea of the boys' early intentions for their engines.

52 Bill Harley and Arthur Davidson created their first engine in 1901 with help from their coworker Emil Kroeger, who was familiar with French motor bicycle engines. The first single-cylinder, four-stroke, de Dion–type engine was first put into a chassis in 1903 and ridden by Walter Davidson. Some dispute exists regarding the dimensions of that first engine because an early source mentions it having used a 2-1/8-inch bore, a 2-7/8-inch stroke, and 5-inch flywheels, which displaced 10.2 ci; this differs from the first detailed plans that exist today. Arthur Davidson and Bill Harley made two key discoveries with that first test ride: the frame had to be stronger and the engine needed to be more powerful. The first motorcycle was effective on flat ground, but any type of incline required the rider to use the pedals, which defeated the purpose of the machine.

53 Arthur and Bill's second engine dwarfed the first, and performed satisfactorily in The Motor Company's first machines. It displaced 24.74 ci by using a 3-inch bore and 3-1/2-inch stroke, and hefty 8-inch flywheels. The additional 1 horsepower (approximately) gained from the new engine allowed the motorcycle to achieve speeds up to around 35 mph. Milwaukee's hills were no longer of any concern.

54 While not a "clutch" in the technical sense, Harley-Davidson motorcycles began using a spring-loaded belt tensioner in 1906. A lever mounted to the left side of the gas tank controlled the tensioner. It allowed the rider to place enough tension on the drive belt so that the engine couldn't overcome the resistance. The engine continued to run, but the belt remained stationary, as did the rear wheel. When the rider wanted to go again, he simply pushed the lever forward and the bike started to move. The system was far from perfect, and had trouble working if it was wet or greasy, but it laid the groundwork for what became the modern clutch. An increased displacement of 26.8 ci on the 1907 single brought the horsepower count to 4; the Harley-Davidson could now achieve 45 mph.

55 Harley-Davidson produced its first prototype V-twin engine as early as 1907, although the first public appearance of a V-twin was in 1908. It used the same de Dion design as the single, but it was fitted with a beefed-up bottom end. This intake over exhaust (IOE) engine displaced 49 ci (810 cc) and made about 7 hp. Despite its 65-mph top speed, The Motor Company's first V-twin had a few drawbacks in addition to its hefty price tag. It didn't come with a chain tensioner as the singles did, making it difficult for city use and requiring riders to have to pedal-start a large-displacement engine every time they had to start going again. This might not have been such a big deal except that starting the thing was a pain unto itself. The engines still used an atmospheric valve system that used cylinder vacuum to actuate the valve, which was made difficult by the V-twin's high crankcase pressure. This engine was used in a production model for the first time in 1909, but was dropped for 1910; it was not considered a viable option until 1911 when mechanical valves were introduced.

56 Most customers opted for the single-cylinder motorcycle in 1909, which, in addition to chassis upgrades, saw numerous improvements to the drivetrain and controls. A quick glance at a 1909 model reveals a lack of the usual linkages, chains, and levers that adorned strap tank models. Now, the throttle control and spark advance grips used cables that ran through the handlebar. The 1909 twin lacked a chain tensioner; the single used an improved tensioner with a spring-loaded thumb release and a notched gate on the gas tank for solid engagement. The tensioner pulley was moved closer to the engine pulley to put more pressure on the belt, ensuring more effective clutching. The Model 5's single-cylinder was bored up to 3.31 inches to displace 30.16 ci, which made it good for 4.3 hp.

57 Other than the 6E racer, Harley-Davidson didn't offer any twins for sale. The thinking must have been to take the year and perfect it before bringing it back to the public, an approach that is typical of

The overall shape and design of the Harley-Davidson V-twin has remained relatively unchanged through the years from the first 45-degree engine with Y-shaped manifold and carburetor in between the cylinders. In 1912, the magneto was moved to behind the rear cylinder. However, the gearcase on this original 1911 resembles that of a modern Sportster more closely, except that the oil filter would be where this magneto is located.

The Motor Company to this day. So, in 1911, they reintroduced the Model 7D V-twin to the motoring public. Displacement remained at 49 ci, which was all that was necessary to propel the 6-1/2-hp 295-pound machine to 60 mph. Although it was a superior engine, compared to the offering from two years earlier, it wasn't all that special when compared to the competition. With a $300 price tag, motorcyclists of the day could opt for a competitor's machine, which made more power for less money. And four-cylinder motorcycles had also begun to make their powerful presence known.

58 Starting the 7D engine was made easier thanks to mechanical intake valves; they required an additional pushrod on each cylinder. The dual pushrod design on a brand-new Harley began back in 1911 and, even though it has changed considerably since then, all air-cooled and Twin-Cooled (air and oil cooling) Harley-Davidsons still have a pair of parallel pushrods on the right side of each cylinder.

59 Up until 1910, Harley-Davidson engines had horizontal fins from the bottom of the cylinder all the way up to the spark plug. To many folks, this makes the cylinders look like a beehive, leading collectors and restorers to call pre-1911 engines "beehives." These single-direction fins did a good enough job when engines were only making a few horsepower, but as power increased, so did heat. For 1911, the fins on the top of the cylinder, from just below the intake manifold and up, became vertical. This allowed for more fins, and better cooling, at the top of the cylinder where combustion occurred. Vertical fins are found on all 1911 and later F-head cylinders, as well has Flathead and K-model cylinder heads.

60 The competition's advantage in the engine department didn't last long. Harley-Davidson unleashed a new, more powerful V-twin engine option and wholly modern drivetrain on the public in 1912. With a 3-1/2-inch bore and 3.31-inch stroke, the Model X8E under-square engine displaced 60.32 ci, almost 1,000 cc. The 8 hp produced by the larger twin could bring the motorcycle up to 65 mph.

61 In addition to the honkin' new twin engine, the new Model X8E had two other drivetrain features that combined to make it one of

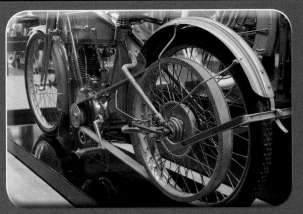

The Free Wheel Control clutch built into the rear hub in 1912 added a whole new dimension to the viability of the motorcycle as a machine for everyday transportation. After it was started, a rider simply operated a lever to engage and disengage power to the rear wheel, allowing the motorcycle to sit at idle and not have to be pedaled (and therefore restarted) away from every stop. Although chains were first used on twins in 1912, singles, such as this one, didn't have a chain-drive option until 1913.

the best motorcycles that money could buy in 1912. The X designation meant that the bike had a real mechanical clutch, dubbed Free Wheel Control by its inventors Bill Harley and his old buddy Henry Melk, who had the lathe down the street. Clutches were available for an extra $10 on the twins, which included the 8-hp version instead of the 6-1/2-hp version.

62 The top dog Model X8E took performance a step further by using the first chain-drive system to drive the rear wheel. Actually, it used two chains. The engine transfers power to a primary chain, which spins a set of gears that operate the final drive chain, which fits around a gear on the rear wheel hub. This was a first, as was the first use of the traditional primary chain cover. A slotted gear on the left side of the crankshaft oiled the primary chain as well as the drive chain. Represented by the E designation, both twin options could be ordered with a chain or a belt, while singles weren't offered with a chain until 1913.

The defining look of the left side of a Harley-Davidson came to fruition in 1912 with the first appearance of a chain-driven rear wheel. The belt drive connected the engine pulley directly to the rear wheel. However, the chain-drive used a series of sprockets at the engine and the pedals, and at the rear wheel. Look at any new Big Twin and you'll see that it uses the exact same pattern, albeit with a belt instead of a chain.

63 The 1913 Harley-Davidson Model 9A was the only motorcycle in the United States still available with a belt drive and was the last Harley available with a leather belt drive. This is actually pretty surprising, even for Harley-Davidson; not only had the new V-twins outsold singles in 1912, but the single-cylinder engine was now larger and produced even more power. This time, the size grew by increasing the stroke from 3-1/2 to 4 inches. Displacing 34.47 ci and pushing 4-1/2 hp, the Model 9 earned the nickname "5-35" for its approximate power and displacement figures. The single-cylinder 5-35, which was produced until 1918, could hit 50 mph. The 9A and 9B (both chain-drive) were available standard with the rear hub clutch and both retailed for $290. Also for 1913, The Motor Company began the practice of balancing the flywheel, rod, and piston as a single assembly, which made the engine longer lasting and smoother to operate.

64 The 1914 Model 10-F is the only model to feature H-D's first transmission. Patented by William S. Harley, it features two speeds located in the rear hub. It added yet another dose of rider friendliness to the early machines. At least, that was the idea. The bicycle-style epicyclical rear hub was so revolutionary, and had such tight tolerances, that many riders found it difficult to operate. A company service bulletin was published that reminded 10F owners not to force the shifter into gear when the machine wasn't running, which could cause the shift lever to bend. The 10-F also saw the first use of floorboards and a pedal-operated drum brake in the rear.

65 The Harley-Davidson motorcycle took a major stride forward with the 1915 11-F and the introduction of the 3-speed, sliding-gear transmission that sits behind the engine. The new 3-speed featured large ball bearings to secure the main shaft; two special, heavy-duty roller bearings allow the jackshaft to spin smoothly. The jackshaft transmits power in low and intermediate gear while the transmission is essentially free running in high gear. For extra durability, the engineers made sure not to include any small parts that could potentially break or wear out, and the 3-speed proved to be extremely reliable. The transmission is controlled with a

The Motor Company's 1915 model 11-F set the stage for every Big Twin to follow with its durable 3-speed transmission, a powerful V-twin, and an automatic oil pump, which is visible on the gearcase. By using a separate engine and transmission, linked only by the primary chain, this setup would last for another 80 years on some Big Twin models.

foot-operated rocker clutch and a gated shift arm on the tank. With 9,855 produced, 3-speed H-Ds made up 75 percent of that year's total motorcycle production. The 1915 11-F is, like the 10-F before it, a one-year-only design thanks to its using bicycle-style pedals to start the engine.

66 In addition to the new 3-speed transmission, Harley-Davidson completely redesigned its 61-ci IOE engine for 1915. It now used larger intake valves that now entered the heads at a 45-degree angle instead of a 60-degree angle. The engine used new cylinders and a larger intake manifold to increase airflow. To handle the power increase, engineers used heavier flywheels with a 1-inch crankpin (previously 7/8 inch). The new Harley-Davidson–made bearings are 3/8 inch wider than on the previous engine. A newly designed, more efficient muffler was used and, while it produced significantly less backpressure, it also made less noise.

67 The engine lubrication system was also completely reimagined in 1915, beginning with the oil tank's relocation from underneath the seat to the left side of the gas tank; it now displaced 2-1/2 quarts. A new, automatic oil pump, visible on the cam cover on the right side of the engine, ensured precise lubrication at any speed and crank pressure. Occasionally, when running flat out, or powering up a steep incline, the rider had to pump in extra oil via the auxiliary hand pump that sat atop the oil tank.

68 Harley-Davidson claimed exactly 29 engine improvements, leading the 1915 models to put out an advertised 31 percent more power at 2,500 rpm and a whopping 47 percent more power at 3,000 rpm. The Motor Company guaranteed that the 11-F was capable of achieving 65 mph. My friend and colleague, Cris Sommer Simmons, can vouch for that claim; she rides her 1915 11-F regularly (and rode it more than 3,000 miles on the 2010 Motorcycle Cannonball).

69 In 1915, The Motor Company guaranteed the 61-ci V-twin to produce 11 hp. Solid output on these early machines, no doubt, but just because the company guaranteed it, didn't make it so. In fact, in typical Harley fashion, 11 hp was a modest figure, and many of its street engines actually produced up to 16 hp on the dynamometer thanks to larger intake and exhaust ports, which lead to larger valves and carburetors.

70 With the sliding-gear transmission in 1915 also came the first use of the gated shift lever on the left side of the gas tank. The gate is labeled with the different gear positions so the rider can easily and confidently put his motorcycle into the correct gear. The 1915 gate is mounted to the left-side oil and gas caps and is notched to make it more difficult to go back a gear by mistake.

71 Some riders today have trouble stopping and starting on a hill. So imagine what it was like for riders in 1915 when they were learning to use a clutch and transmission for the first time, and didn't have a front brake to hold. To alleviate this issue, a rider could engage and disengage the clutch with his or her left hand using a lever attached to the clutch pedal linkage. The rider kept the left foot on the ground to stabilize the bike with the right foot on the pedal brake. Then he (or she) used the throttle with the right hand as usual while releasing the clutch with the left hand. Off and away!

72 Although readers of this book probably like to argue that Harley-Davidson built (and still builds) the best motorcycle engine available, it wasn't the first. All early motorcycle engines stemmed from a single design created by Frenchmen Albert de Dion and Georges Bouton in the 1890s. Every other IOE motorcycle engine produced at the time, whether by Indian, Harley-Davidson, or Merkel used a nearly identical design as the de Dion-Bouton engine. This is important to The Motor Company's history because without the de Dion-Bouton, motorcycling might have gotten off to a later and less successful start.

73 If you measure the rear belt drive pulley on a modern Harley, you'll find it's about 9 inches in diameter and, as you already know, supplies a solid mix of off-the-line acceleration and on-highway cruising performance. In Harley-Davidson's early days, before transmissions and when belt-drives were still a leather strap with no teeth, the rear wheel pulley measured 20 inches in diameter. It provided enough force to get the single-cylinder machine moving. As with many drive belts today, the original leather belt was 1.25 inches wide on the singles and 1.75 inches wide on the twins.

74 Today's spark plugs are so small and inexpensive that many riders opt to keep a spare set in their tool kit at all times. But when the first Harley-Davidson was built, spark plugs were much larger (like a doorknob), and much more expensive. The first motorcycle used a spark plug that took up much of the cylinder head, and cost $3, or approximately $80 in today's money. Considering that the earliest machines sold for about $200, that single spark plug was nearly 2 percent of the cost!

75 Some folks may wonder exactly how the early atmospheric valve system worked on the early Harleys. Keep in mind that the IOE design positioned the intake valve at the very top of the engine and the exhaust valve on the side. A camshaft and pushrod operated the exhaust valve, but the early H-D engines had no such pairing for the intake valve. Instead, as the piston went down in the cylinder on the intake stroke, that vacuum caused the valve to be pulled down into the cylinder head, allowing air and fuel to enter. Then, on the compression stroke, the upward motion of the piston forced the valve shut. The explosion on the power stroke created enough pressure to keep the valve closed; on the exhaust stroke, the piston forced pressure back up again.

PEOPLE AND POP CULTURE

76 Janet Davidson, the older sister of the brothers, was responsible for the famous hand-painted "HARLEY-DAVIDSON MOTOR CO." on the front door of the famous backyard woodshed where the first motorcycles were built. She's also responsible for the lettering and pinstriping on the early motorcycles. In the very early days, their other sister, Elisabeth, was in charge of the company's bookkeeping.

77 Although the first Harley-Davidsons were painted black, Henry Ford quickly laid claim to that color, and the founders wanted their machines to stand apart from other machines. Renault Gray was chosen as their official color because it blended in so easily with the streets and surroundings of the early 1900s. Black was still available until 1910. And most riders, especially H-D's target customer (the working man), didn't want anything flashy or showy. Early Harleys also had the reputation of running more quietly than other brands, which furthered its practicality because it didn't startle horses, pedestrians, or wake the neighbors. These attributes earned it the nickname of *The Silent Gray Fellow*, a name that stuck until World War I, when gray ceased to be used.

78 Dudley Perkins opened his Harley-Davidson dealership in San Francisco in 1914. Today, it's the oldest dealership in the world still owned by the original family. However, the oldest continuously operating dealership is A. D. Farrow Co. Harley-Davidson in downtown Columbus, Ohio, which began operations in 1912.

79 Harley-Davidson didn't introduce its V-twin engine to the public until 1909, when only 28 were sold. However, one appeared mysteriously in 1908 at the Algonquin, Illinois, hillclimb races. Harvey Bernard rode his Harley-Davidson V-twin, stuffed into a single-cylinder frame with 1908-style gas/oil tanks, to victory in July 1908. No other information on this strange phenomenon exists, and The Motor Company has denied any involvement with Mr. Bernard. The most likely scenario is that Bernard added a second cylinder onto a single, which is essentially what The Motor Company did to achieve its first twin.

80 Crystal Haydel was Harley-Davidson's first full-time female employee. Hired in 1907, she was the only office employee at the time and eventually became the office manager. In 1925, she was promoted to assistant secretary of the company, and also filled the role of assistant treasurer. She worked as Walter Davidson's right-hand woman, and the two even shared an office. She was a shareholder in the company and was involved in nearly every aspect of running the business.

81 1903 was a big year in the United States for transportation inventors. On June 6, one of Harley-Davidson's biggest competitors, Henry Ford and the Ford Motor Company, incorporated. On December 7, a whole new future of human transportation dawned when Orville and Wilbur Wright flew their first motorized aircraft across Kitty Hawk, North Carolina.

82 Many Harley-Davidson historians credit the Davidson boys' sister Janet with designing the first Bar & Shield logo. She proved to be not only to be a good artist, but a remarkable designer. Her design ranks with brands such as Chevrolet, McDonald's, and Starbucks. It wasn't until 1922, however, that the color scheme was changed to the orange on black that we're familiar with today.

83 In 1915, Harley-Davidson published Theodore J. Werle's *Camping Hints when Touring with a Motorcycle*. This 24-page book provided tips from nature-lover Werle on the best ways to break free from society and live in the wilderness. He wrote, "Touring on a motorcycle and living by the way is a glorious sport. If one finds pleasure living close to nature, if one wishes to go about in a rugged, manly way, let him pack his tent aboard a motorcycle and live in the open."

84 Early motorcycle pioneer Della Crewe left her home in Waco, Texas, astride a Harley-Davidson with sidecar on July 24, 1914, in search of adventure. She got it, too; her trip covered 5,378 miles. Originally from Racine, Wisconsin, she made her way north to Milwaukee and then east to New York City. She arrived in New York in mid-December and had to wear four layers of clothing just to stay warm. As she traveled, she stopped at Harley-Davidson dealerships along the way and stayed with locals at their farmhouses wherever she could. She recorded her journeys aboard her *Silent Grey Fellow* in a series of articles, each one touting the durability and effectiveness of a Harley-Davidson with sidecar and the friendly people she met at dealerships. Della Crewe didn't travel alone, though, her dog, Trouble, tagged along in the sidecar!

85 After the concrete work was completed on the renovation of the factory in the summer of 1912, workers hoisted a Christmas tree to the top of the construction elevator, signaling that their part of the project was finished. According to company lore, they finished exactly 15 minutes before the deadline, which meant that they had earned free beer. Supposedly, Walter Davidson obliged, and provided beer for the workers.

86 Harley-Davidson's massive use of electricity was a great marketing campaign for the Milwaukee Electric Railway and Light Company. It placed a massive lit sign on top of its building that read "Electric Power Is Best – Ask Harley Davidson," with a 70-foot-long arrow pointing to the Juneau Avenue factory. The sign itself was 68 feet long and 40 feet high. Historic photography shows it standing in 1913; it was likely there in 1912 as well.

87 Massachusetts was the first state to require a visible registration tag on both cars and motorcycles in 1903 in the form of what we now call a "license plate." Massachusetts' plates were made of iron and covered with enamel porcelain that was painted dark blue with white numbers. "MASS. AUTOMOBILE REGISTER" was printed across the top and the plates differed in size to meet the necessary amount of characters. Approximately 500 motorcycles were in use in the state at the time of the first required plate, which were the same for both automobiles and motorcycles. The only difference was that motorcycle plates' identification began with the letter Z. Most states required visible license plates by 1914.

88 Crystal Haydel was not just an employee at Harley-Davidson, she was a rider, too! In fact, she's recognized as the first woman in Wisconsin to register a motorcycle for road use, which she did in 1911.

89 Part of the Harley-Davidson mystique surrounding the company throughout its 100-plus years involves the actual year of its first production and the year of the first commercial sale. Even though 1903 is the generally accepted first year of production, and the one reported by The Motor Company itself, varying evidence has come to light through the years that places the first motorcycle as early as 1901 and as late as 1905. To make matters even more confusing, Harley-Davidson never acknowledged its first year until the 1954 model line and, by then, none of the founders were still alive to discuss or confirm the company's timeline. One of the most interesting pieces of evidence is an advertisement from the factory in 1910 that says "eight years ago we placed on the market the first model of the Harley-Davidson motorcycle." This suggests that a motorcycle was built and sold in 1902, although it could also mean 1903.

90 Evidence also exists that puts Harley-Davidson's first real motorcycle and sale at a later date; that's C. H. Lang's 1914 testimony as part of a patent infringement lawsuit. As you know, the accepted history is that C. H. Lang sold his first Harley-Davidson in 1903. However, in his testimony he says that he became familiar with the H-D motorcycle in the autumn of 1904 and became an official dealer in 1905. Most of the conspiracies regarding the first year of manufacture can be attributed to misspeak, or confusing and generalizing language that rounded up years rather than giving an exact time. As unlikely as any of the alternative start years might be, it's still a fun and interesting debate.

91 Harley-Davidson produced its first advertisement in the January 1905 issue of *Cycle and Automobile Trade Journal.* That ad touted only the part of the bike that really makes a Harley-Davidson a Harley-Davidson: the engine. Although many motorcycles were being produced at the time, it was a far greater task to build an entire motorcycle (with the engine) than it was to build just an engine. Therefore, marketing the engine as a stand-alone product that included mounting equipment for a bicycle made good business sense, and it was a great start to promoting the company's name. The ad showed a picture of the single-cylinder engine and advertised 3-1/4 bhp (brake horsepower). It also listed the company's address at 315 37th Street in Milwaukee, the famous backyard shed.

92 *The Enthusiast,* first published in 1916, is often mistaken as The Motor Company's first print publication. However, in 1912, the company began publishing *Harley-Davidson Dealer,* which was sent out to dealerships. Although the content was focused more on the business aspect of the company, the magazine contained good maintenance tips and H-D model information that just about any owner would find valuable. It's likely that enough owners started asking for it, which led to the creation of *The Enthusiast.*

93 In the early years of motorcycling, hundreds of marques sprang up and then quickly disappeared. Many of them, including Milwaukee-based Merkel (later known as Flying Merkel), beat Harley-Davidson to its frame design and the use of a V-twin engine. However, Flying Merkel's last motorcycle was built in 1915, after the company relocated to Ohio. During Harley-Davidson's first decade, more than 75 American motorcycle companies went out of business; some only managed to build a handful of bikes.

94 In the earliest days of his motorcycle company, Bill Harley attended the University of Wisconsin in Madison and studied engineering; his focus was internal combustion engines. Because he was not from a family of means, he waited tables at a fraternity house to pay for tuition. In later life, he became one of the wealthiest men in Wisconsin.

95 In 1915, Carl Peterson and his wife (whose name is unknown) took their Harley-Davidson to Europe to enjoy a tour of the continent, beginning in Scandinavia. Unfortunately, World War I had erupted in Europe the year before. As they were about to head to Germany from Sweden, they were advised to return home to the United States. Carl said that the Swedish riders were extremely impressed with the power of his motorcycle and, although the trip didn't end as he would have liked, the Harley-Davidson "performed perfectly."

96 In 1901, Bill Harley and Arthur Davidson attended a performance by French stage performer and singer Anna Held at Milwaukee's Bijou Theater. As part of her performance, Held rode a shiny French motor-powered bicycle across the stage. The 20-year-olds were likely the only men in the audience who paid more attention to the vehicle than the performer. This is the earliest recorded instance of Harley and Davidson actually seeing a motorcycle, although it's believed that they had seen at least one previous demonstration in their home city.

97 Legend has it that when Arthur and Bill built a carburetor for their first experimental engine, they crafted the body from a tomato soup can. According to historian Herbert Wagner, it's more likely that the carburetor simply resembled a tomato can and was therefore given that nickname. Perhaps not surprisingly, they had trouble getting the fuel to flow properly, so they took it to a close friend, Ole Evinrude. At the time, Ole was a friend who had to row his boat out to his favorite fishing spot, just like everybody else. It was on one of these rows that Arthur and Ole thought up the idea for a small engine to power a rowboat. The idea was similar to Arthur and Bill and their need for a motorized bicycle.

98 The March 31, 1914, edition of the *Milwaukee Journal* featured an article titled "Harley-Davidson Motor Co.: Its Marvelous Growth and Development, Hum Of Wheels Spins Romance – True Tale Reads Like Fiction." This is one of the earliest pieces of writing that examines the history of Harley-Davidson and uses direct quotes from the founders; these quotes have been used repeatedly in articles since then. Much of the company's early history, correct or not, has been based on his writing.

99 A letter that Steven J. Sparough wrote, dated April 15, 1912, has become one of the most instrumental tools for historians to piece together The Motor Company's early history. In his letter, Sparough says that his Harley-Davidson, which had 51,000 miles on it when he bought it, was the first Harley-Davidson motorcycle ever built. He says it was built in 1903 and sold in 1904 to Henry Meyer. The bike was then transferred through several Chicago area owners: Geo. W. Lyon, Dr. Webster, and Louis Fluke. Sparough bought the

This is the only known photograph of a pre-1905 Harley-Davidson and it is believed to be the very first motorcycle that the company built. That's Steven J. Sparough standing behind it, the man whose surviving 1912 letter was pivotal in tracing The Motor Company's early history. (Photo Courtesy Harley-Davidson)

machine in 1907 after the previous owners managed all those miles, which makes his 1903 year of manufacture seem very likely.

100 On April 30, 1905, Arthur Davidson set off from Milwaukee to Cambridge, Wisconsin, to deliver a motorcycle to his friend, postal carrier Peter Olson. The 50-mile trip took Arthur 5-1/2 hours according to the *Cambridge News*, and officially made Olson one of the earliest (possibly the second) owners of a Harley-Davidson motorcycle.

MILITARY, POLICE AND RACING

101 After performing well at the Milwaukee Motordrome in 1914, Harley-Davidson racing manager Bill Ottaway invited Leslie "Red" Parkhurst to become the first member of The Motor Company's race team. Parkhurst piloted the new racebike to victory in most of the initial regional races in which he competed; then they decided to take on a big national race. Parkhurst and five other racers went to Dodge City, Kansas, to compete in the July 4, 1914, Dodge City 300. The H-Ds ran fast, but by the end of racing on the 2-mile track, only two of the six were still running. Nevertheless, Harley-Davidson had entered the world of professional racing, and Parkhurst went on to be one of its biggest stars.

102 Harley-Davidson's first recorded championship race win was on October 5, 1914 at the 1-hour Federation of American Motorcyclists (FAM) Birmingham race. Of course, riding a Bill Ottaway-prepped factory 11-K racer was none other than Red Parkhurst. On lap 33, Parkhurst entered the pits with a fuel problem. While there, he tried to clean the dirt and oil from his goggles, but his handkerchief was so dirty that he asked for help from a spectator with a clean hankie. Parkhurst reentered the race and won. An official protest was filed shortly after the race ended, claiming that Parkhurst received illegal aid from a spectator. In the interest of safety, the protest was denied, and Parkhurst was given the championship title.

103 The first Harley-Davidson sold specifically for police use went to the Detroit Police Department in 1908. At the time, the United States had less than 200 miles of paved roads, and automobiles were still very expensive. The only logical solution to the horse was the iron horse, and Harley-Davidson was proving itself dependable, so it was an easy decision. Today, police bikes are separate models from civilian models and have a variety of different equipment. However, the first police bikes differed little from their civilian counterparts. They still offered incredible duty performance in terms of speed, longevity, and the cost of purchase and operation.

104 Initially, three of the four founders wanted no part in racing their motorcycles. They were designed for practicality and durability, not speed and performance. Walter Davidson, the pro-racing founder, began campaigning his personal motorcycle in local events in 1905. He won a handful of Milwaukee-area races, including a hillclimb event over the next couple of years.

105 In 1908, Walter decided that he and his motorcycle could handle much stiffer competition, and headed to New York to

Walter Davidson stands beside his trusty 1908 single; this motorcycle earned him first-place awards at both endurance and fuel mileage events. It's difficult to believe that this early contraption could be so reliable, but The Motor Company built them that way then, and now! (Photo Courtesy Harley-Davidson)

compete in the FAM Endurance and Reliability Contest, which covered 365 miles from the Catskills, around Long Island, and ended in New York City. And this was a challenge with very few roads. Unlike his competitors who had automobiles filled with mechanics and spare parts, Walter rode alone with no spare parts. When the dust settled, Walter won the race handily; he earned a perfect score on both days of the event, something never before achieved. In fact, he was awarded an additional five bonus points over his perfect 1,000 for the impeccable consistency of his riding abilities and his motorcycle.

106 Fresh off his win at the FAM Endurance Run, Walter competed in the FAM Economy Run a week later. Competitors were tested on how far they and their motorcycle could travel on 1 gallon of gas. Walter finished far ahead of the competition, achieving 188.234 mpg on his stock bike. With these back-to-back FAM wins, Harley-Davidson quickly became known as one of the premier motorcycle manufacturers in the country. And these two wins showed off the exact attributes of the H-D motorcycle that the founders wanted to portray to their buyers. Even so, Walter remained the only founder intent on pursuing factory racing.

107 In 1914, Harley-Davidson could no longer sit on the sidelines as its rival Indian continued to win races around the country, including motordrome boardtrack races in Milwaukee. And so, Bill Harley, by now very much a proponent of racing, established a racing department at the company and hired William "Bill" Ottaway to take charge. Bill Ottaway had one of the greatest minds in racing, and he set to work developing a racer that could take on Indian and the rest.

108 While it certainly wasn't the first Harley-Davidson to go racing, or even the first racing V-twin, the 6E stock racer brought to market in 1910 was the first factory race bike from Harley-Davidson. This V-twin model retailed at $275, and was only sold to customers who were established racers. How many were produced is unknown, but it's thought to be no more than four.

109 A pair of privateer racers on 6Es took a 1-2 finish at the treacherous Denver to Greeley road race. The 60-mile route wasn't paved, and with the speeds that twins were capable of at the time, the motorcycle itself had to be durable to take that kind of beating. The Harley-Davidson's win in these conditions served as yet another example of the everyday value its motorcycles provided. In addition to their first and second finishes, the 6Es beat the next fastest twin-cylinder entry by almost 10 minutes.

110 Police departments weren't the only ones who discovered the numerous advantages of using a motorcycle in the line of duty; early motorcycles became popular among rural postal service employees. In 1907, rural mail delivery regulations were adapted to allow the use of motorcycles to deliver mail, as long as packages remained free from damage or loss, as they did with the standard horse-drawn carriage. By 1914, the U.S. Postal Service was using nearly 5,000 motorcycles for mail delivery. Harley-Davidson ran an ad describing how a rural postman could complete his route

This 1916 Package Truck made the life of a rural mail carrier easier, more economical, and a whole lot more fun. A Harley-Davidson could do the same route as a horse and wagon in a third of the time at the cost of about ten cents a day.

quickly in the morning and then go on trips with his wife in the afternoon. The ad quoted a rider who said he was able to complete his 25-1/2 mile route on poor rural roads in 1 hour 15 minutes.

111 Bill Ottaway introduced his first factory racer in 1914, dubbed the 10-K. Based on the 1914 10E with a 61-ci chain-driven powertrain, it was meant to be a stopgap model designed mostly for testing. It was also a way to start competing with Indian immediately. Harley-Davidson sold only a handful of the untested K models in 1914, which was a good thing because they had some teething issues. Even though they were as fast as any of the competitors, the Ks suffered engine and other powertrain failures when they pushed for distance.

112 The Motor Company proved its dedication to racing in 1915, when 8 of the 17 models available that year were factory race bikes. The 11-K racer, which was said to produce 20 hp, cost $250 in 1915. That was less than other street-going V-twins built that year and only $10 more than a magneto-equipped 60-ci twin.

113 The first known order of a Harley-Davidson specifically for military duty was in 1912 when the Japanese Army ordered a small handful of machines.

114 On July 3, 1915, Harley-Davidson factory racer Otto Walker broke the speed records at the Dodge City, Kansas, 200- and 300-mile races. He finished the 200 in 2 hours 32 minutes 58 seconds for an average speed of 78.4 mph. He ran the 300 in 3 hours 5 minutes 45 seconds with an average speed of 76.27 mph. Walker was the previous record holder for the Dodge City 300.

115 One of Harley-Davidson's first known race wins and records occurred on June 3, 1905, at the Wisconsin State Fair Park. Perry Mack, one of the first men to race a Harley-Davidson, won the race. He set a new record in the process, completing 1 mile in 1 minute 16 seconds, for an average speed of 47.35 mph. Mack later developed his own brand of motorcycles, with a strong emphasis on racing.

116 A. W. Stratton set the 90-mile road race world record on May 30, 1912, aboard a Model 8-E Harley-Davidson in the Colorado Springs to Pueblo to Colorado Springs race. Producing only about 7–8 hp, Stratton's twin completed the trip in 1 hour 54 minutes with an average speed of 47.4 mph. He also reported reaching speeds of almost 65 mph in some sections. Only 5 of the original 13 machines in the twin class managed to finish that race. Moreover, Harley-Davidson also won the single-cylinder class, as well as third place in both classes, totaling four of the six podium spots.

117 1915 is considered the end of The Motor Company's early era. By this time, Harley-Davidsons were achieving consistent speeds that were only dreams just 10 years earlier. On April 12, 1915, Roy Artley piloted his Harley to a win at the 1-hour Bakersfield, California, race, and managed a top speed of 68.7 miles in that hour. He averaged speeds that, even just a few years earlier, could only be hit at maximum throttle, on a smooth road, and with a tail wind. Artley, naturally, set the track record that day.

118 One year before Harley-Davidson began its official race program, Ben Torres and Ray Watkins set a world record on their H-D by riding 346 dirt-track miles in just 7 hours on December 8, 1913. Their 8-hp, single-speed twin ran open headers for exhaust and used a low seat with dropped handlebars for speed and rider aerodynamics. For the entire record-setting run in San Jose, California, they didn't have to make a single repair or adjustment on the bike. They finished 17 miles ahead of the second-place competitor, proving outright Harley-Davidson's dominance as a durable and powerful motorcycle.

119 In September 1907, Walter Davidson competed in a two-day, 414-mile endurance race from Chicago to Kokomo, Indiana. Of the 23 riders to start, Walter was one of only three to finish the event with perfect scores. This race was before his better-known endurance races in 1908, which launched The Motor Company's motorcycles into their position among the country's best machines.

120 Walter Davidson, who pushed for racing involvement in the earliest days of The Motor Company, competed in his first recorded race of any kind in 1896 at age 20. The race was the first annual bicycle road race put on by railroad shop employees where his father and brother Walter worked. The thrill of two-wheeled competition certainly stuck with him and fueled his desire to build a faster two-wheeler.

121 A September 8, 1904, *Milwaukee Daily News* article listed the names of riders expected to race in an upcoming event that month at the Wisconsin State Fair. Among the names listed was A. Davidson; no makes were listed, and it's unknown if this is actually the Arthur Davidson. In the September 9 edition of the *Milwaukee Sentinel*, Walter Davidson's name is listed as a rider in the upcoming event. This race was the first known instance of a Harley-Davidson being used in competition

122 September 9, 1904, not only marked the first recorded race of a Harley-Davidson motorcycle, but also the first undisputed evidence of one actually running. Motorcycle racing was quite uncertain back then and no one was ever sure who would actually show up to compete with a running machine. The most reliable information I have that the Harley-Davidson on September 9 actually ran is from a *Milwaukee Journal* article that lists the identities of the racers and the make of their motorcycle. That article lists Edward Hildebrand as the rider. This seems to make the company's early history even more confusing because neither a Harley nor a Davidson is listed as a racer. Hildebrand finished sixth in the 2-mile race and fifth in the 5-mile race. It's not clear if the machine was supplied by the young factory or simply brought out by Hildebrand, one of its earliest customers.

123 Peter Olson of Cambridge, Wisconsin, received a 1905 Harley-Davidson delivered directly from Arthur Davidson, and became the first postal carrier to use a Harley-Davidson. Upon delivery of his motorcycle, Olson mounted baskets to the front end and rear frame to carry mail on his deliveries. If he wasn't the fastest man in Cambridge, he was certainly the fastest mail carrier.

124 Walter Davidson's first motorcycle race win came at the Wisconsin State Fair on June 2, 1905. He beat Henry Zerbel, who rode a Merkel, by an eighth of a mile. The *Milwaukee Sentinel* wrote, "Walter Davidson demonstrated the superiority of the larger motor. Davidson led all the way." The following day, he finished second to Perry Mack, also aboard a Harley-Davidson.

125 Walter Davidson and Perry Mack swept another race weekend, this time in the nationally recognized Fourth of July races in Chicago. In the 15-mile race, Mack took the checkered flag in the heavyweights class followed closely by Walter, who placed second. In the 10-mile race held next, Walter won after Mack hit a dog that had roamed onto the track and was hurt badly in the ensuing crash. This race was a turning point in The Motor Company's history. It had become clear that a profitable business could be built around motorcycles and that the machines themselves were top notch when compared to the competition.

Chapter 2

F-Head Era
1916–1929

THE MOTOR COMPANY

126 *The Enthusiast* is published by Harley-Davidson for the first time in 1916 and provides H-D owners with a real, personal connection to the brand. It also provides The Motor Company with a marketing tool to showcase the latest products and accessories directly to its increasingly loyal consumers. *The Enthusiast*, distributed only to registered owners and dealers, was an immediate hit and, in 1919, it became a monthly publication. *The Enthusiast* bears the title of the longest continuously produced motorcycle magazine in the world.

127 Following the success of the Quartermasters School during World War I, Harley-Davidson changed the name to the Service School, and authorized dealership employees were invited to attend. The Service School succeeded on the civilian side as well, bringing dealership techs from all over the country up to date on mechanical procedures and motorcycle operation. The Service School exists today as Harley-Davidson University.

Harley-Davidson has instructed hopeful technicians in the intricacies of its motorcycles for 100 years. Uniform and consistent repair procedures and knowledgeable techs have helped make the purchase of a Harley-Davidson stress-free. Shown here is the small Service School in operation in 1920. (Photo Courtesy Harley-Davidson)

128 Most motorcycle brands at the turn of the century began as bicycle manufacturers. They transitioned into bicycles with motors fixed to their frames, which finally gave way to the full-fledged motorcycle. Harley-Davidson did things the opposite way, starting first as a motorcycle company and then, in 1917, launching a line of foot-pedal bicycles. It commissioned the Davis Machine Company in Dayton, Ohio, to build its bicycles, hoping to bring more customers to the brand and then to eventually sell more motorcycles. Three models were available including the standard diamond frame version for men, a step-through version known as the Ladies Standard, and a youth model called the Boy Scout. Sales were disappointing and production ceased in 1923.

129 By 1920, Harley-Davidson was the largest motorcycle manufacturer in the world with more than 2,000 dealerships in 67 countries. It took the brand just 17 years after selling its first motorcycle to achieve this status.

130 Remember that young advertising executive, Walter Dunlap, who helped his friends publish their first catalog on credit when they didn't have any cash available? The Harley-Davidson Motor Company was now one of the largest advertisers in the country with an annual budget of $250,000, all going to Dunlap's firm.

131 Although its origin is from racing, the term Hog has become synonymous with the Harley-Davidson motorcycle as well as the Harley Owners Group (H.O.G.) and the New York Stock Exchange ticker symbol. The name was first used in 1920 when the H-D factory race team became known as the Hog Boys. It wasn't just their farming background that garnered the nickname; they actually brought a live pig to events as their mascot. After each of their frequent victories, the winning rider put the hog on his bike and took a victory lap.

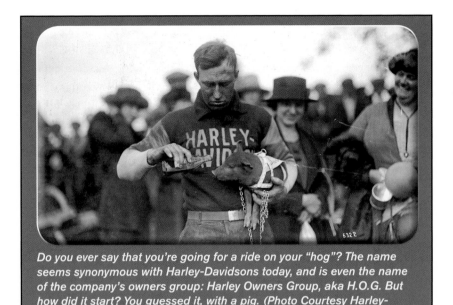

Do you ever say that you're going for a ride on your "hog"? The name seems synonymous with Harley-Davidsons today, and is even the name of the company's owners group: Harley Owners Group, aka H.O.G. But how did it start? You guessed it, with a pig. (Photo Courtesy Harley-Davidson)

132 By the end of 1917, motorcycling was clearly in favor of the V-twin. Of the total 18,522 motorcycles that The Motor Company sold, only 730 were singles.

133 Unfortunately, even with its incredible engineering, the W Sport Twin didn't sell well, and production ceased in 1923. Several factors have been attributed to the demise of the well-engineered machine including its price, which was only 10 percent less than that of a full-size twin. It just never caught on with the younger riders for whom it was designed. The nail in the coffin may have been the 1920 launch of the Indian Scout that was faster, more comfortable, and had a traditional design.

134 In 1919, Harley-Davidson was hit by a legal blow that could have easily destroyed a poorly managed company. The Eclipse Company sued H-D for infringing on the patent of its clutch design. Eclipse was awarded a $1.1 million settlement that had to be paid within two weeks. Fortunately, The Motor Company had enough money stashed away in government bonds to meet its obligation.

135 The first Harley-Davidson dealers' convention was held November 13–15, 1919. The convention, which has been held every year since, provided a convenient way for dealers to meet and discuss company business with H-D executives. It also has always functioned as a way for corporate staff to find out about trends and concerns occurring at the dealership and consumer levels. In addition, these conventions allow dealers to have the first look at the motorcycles for the upcoming model year. Today, two meetings are held each year, but they're now called Dealer Meetings, possibly to clarify to the IRS that it falls under the business category.

136 In 1928, Harley-Davidson sent a notice to the dealerships that a great way of encouraging customers to take advantage of the maintenance and repair services at the dealership was to equip technicians with bright white "service coats." The coat, which more closely resembled something that a doctor might wear rather than a Harley-Davidson mechanic, had the Bar & Shield logo on the left chest and Harley-Davidson script stitched on the back. The Motor Company informed its dealers that wearing these coats made it clear to customers that the dealer shop was a factory-affiliated facility.

137 The Harley-Davidson headquarters was not always at the now-famous Juneau Avenue address; it was originally on Chestnut Street. Prior to 1926, the one street had two names: it was Chestnut Street east of the Milwaukee River and Division Street west of the Milwaukee River. The City of Milwaukee thought this was too confusing. It wanted to name a significant street after Milwaukee's founder and first settler, Solomon Juneau. "Avenue" was more fashionable than "street," and so Chestnut/Division Streets became Juneau Avenue.

138 By 1916, Harley-Davidson had so many dealers and was producing so many motorcycles that it became impossible for Arthur Davidson to maintain successful contact with all of them. Therefore, he divided the country and global markets into regions, each with its own representative. Arthur continued to maintain personal relationships with individual dealerships; he also oversaw the factory representatives who provided more in-depth contact with the dealers in their region. This is the same way that The Motor Company's dealer network is set up today, albeit with many more regions.

139 During World War II, Harley-Davidson, like every other automotive company, halted all civilian production to focus on the war effort. During World War I, however, The Motor Company continued to build and sell civilian models. Indian took a different approach and relied solely on the military for its income during the war years. Although Indian didn't go out of business until much later, many people believe that those years of not building any machines for the public sent a significant amount of business to Harley-Davidson, a decision from which Indian never fully recovered.

140 In late 1918, construction began on a massive 600,000–square-foot factory at Juneau Avenue to keep up with the incredible demand for motorcycles. The L-shaped structure was divided into 96 unique departments; it had enough room for 2,400 full-time employees. Upon completion of the new factory, Harley-Davidson's company was now physically larger than Indian's and had a greater production capacity.

141 In 1923, a secret meeting took place between the three major motorcycle brands: Harley-Davidson, Indian, and Excelsior. By today's standards, its legality was questionable. This meeting led to the agreement that dealerships should be required to represent only one brand. The different manufacturers could no longer influence dealers to sell motorcycles from different companies. Consumers didn't like the new organizational strategy because they couldn't study different makes side by side or test several makes at a time to find the one best suited to their needs. This strategy, whether intentional or not, essentially wiped out all of the small-time motorcycle manufacturers that could no longer effectively maintain a dealership network.

142 Amid the economic downturn of the early 1920s, Harley-Davidson cut output by almost two-thirds and laid off half of its employees. Arthur Davidson knew that the dealerships would play a pivotal role in keeping the entire operation in business. He sought to improve brand loyalty through the new dealership strategy. He also implored dealers to host rides, meetings, and competition events to increase the amount of fun that people had on their motorcycle and to encourage others to take up the sport. In addition, it was at about this time that a new pay-as-you-ride program began, now known as Harley-Davidson Financial.

143 Harley-Davidson produced nearly three times fewer motorcycles for the U.S. government during World War I than Indian. But the fact that it did supply army bikes gave The Motor Company the opportunity to advertise its part in supporting the war effort.

144 Racing is expensive at any level and sponsors weren't as engrained in the sport in first half of the 20th Century as they are now. To give you an idea: Harley-Davidson spent only $250,000 on the 1920 race season. If The Motor Company had kept and maintained its old race bikes through the years, it could have proven quite profitable. Factory racers from the 1920s have sold at auction for up to $420,000, and private sales often fetch far more than that!

145 In 1920, $250,000 was a lot of money, even for mighty Harley-Davidson. However, it had sold only 11,000 motorcycles in 1920, so at the end of the 1921 season, it cancelled the racing program. The team found out about the disbanding only after the races in Phoenix, Arizona. The Motor Company gave everyone money only to cover food and hotel expenses, but no salary or money for the trip home. Only the mechanics received their salaries and trip money to Milwaukee, with the understanding that they would take the motorcycles, tools, and any other equipment back with them. Legend has it that the racers had to borrow money from the local Harley-Davidson dealer to get home.

146 Many people know about the wartime production restrictions during World War II, but did you know that the United States used similar measures during World War I? In addition to Harley-Davidson's military contracts, it was allowed to continue producing civilian models as well, which were seen as efficient modes of transportation for industrial and government workers. Bill Harley was a member of the Motorcycle War Service Board and pushed to give two-wheelers a B-4 classification, meaning that it was an essential industry.

147 Harley-Davidson assisted the war effort by supplying thousands of motorcycles to the U.S. army and its allies' armies, and 312 H-D employees volunteered and served in the military. Three made the ultimate sacrifice for their country. At the war's end, The Motor Company invited every employee who served to return to their jobs at the same standing that they had before they left.

148 To introduce the 1924 models, Harley-Davidson released an advertisement that featured images of President Walter Davidson and Bill Harley enjoying a sidecar-equipped JD in a variety of ways. Each photo was captioned describing the activity and showed how the founders used their products in much the same way as those who bought them. Walter penned a personal letter for the ad in which he invited the reader to step into the nearest dealership to explore the new machines. Interesting, the letter states, "Bill Harley and I and my brothers have ridden motorcycles, built them, and lived with them for 21 years." Because the ad was released for the 1924 models, Walter's letter suggests that the first motorcycle was built in 1903.

149 By the early 1920s, Harley-Davidson had developed its first complete line of branded clothing and riding accessories. The line included sweaters, jerseys, gloves, goggles, and waterproof gear. It wasn't until 1928, however, that a leather jacket made its first appearance in the H-D clothing line. 1929 was the first year for decorative accessories and jewelry intended for off- and on-motorcycle use, a concept that has continued to present.

150 Headwear appeared in Harley-Davidson's parts and accessories catalog as early as 1915 with the introduction of riding goggles that kept dust and wind out of a rider's eyes at high speeds. Following that, the catalog featured knit caps, hats, and a Tourist Hood that provided protection for long, fast rides. It wasn't until 1921 that the first "protective" headwear became available through the catalog: the $8 Leather Touring Helmet and the $3 Tourist Helmet. They are advertised as a way to keep wind and dirt out of the rider's hair without losing the shape.

THE CHASSIS

151 Harley-Davidson beefed up its frames for 1916 so they were better suited for sidecar use and also to handle the additional power output of the V-twin. A new front fender featured more curve to match the 28-inch wheel and more protection for the rider and machine. The fender used front and rear flat mounting struts that are body colored and bolted to the underside of the fender. The old fender used a basic round metal bracket in the rear only; the fender had a tendency to shake around. A wider front end and larger steering head bearings were added to handle the added width and weight. The wheelbase was lengthened to 59.5 inches.

152 The 1916 models received a more-rounded, larger gas tank to go with the updated frame. It now carried oil and gas on the left side, but still only gas on the right side. Fuel capacity increased to 2.75 gallons but oil capacity was cut from 4 quarts to 5 pints. The color changed from Renault Gray to Harley-Davidson Gray for the 1915 and 1916 models; 1916 was the last year of the traditional gray paint scheme.

153 By 1916, Harley-Davidson's model naming system had become confusing. The model numbers trailed the year by four, and after 13 years in business, those new to the brand couldn't figure out why. Because of this, The Motor Company changed the system to match the model number with the year, meaning that 1916 model numbers started with "16." The year was stamped into engine numbers until the mid-1970s, but the practice of using the year in the model name soon ended.

154 Even though The Motor Company offers numerous paint options today, that wasn't the case during the company's first 30 years. Customers were limited to the company's choice of color. Beginning in 1917, because so many of its machines were serving military duty, the official color became Military Drab, which is basically Olive Green. Rumor has it that this color remained even after the war because The Motor Company had a massive oversupply that it didn't want to waste.

155 One of the most popular options in the early years was a luggage rack that mounted above the rear axle and to the front of the rear fender. It allowed for the easy mounting of throwover saddlebags or any type of equipment. The retail price of the rack in 1921 was $6. Today, an original luggage rack is worth about $900.

156 Even though the Olive Green paint was changed to the darker Brewster Green in 1922 and 1923, Harley-Davidson didn't offer multiple color options until the 1926 model year. The standard color went back to Olive Green, but buyers could opt for white or cream paint.

157 The timeless form of the Harley-Davidson motorcycle first appeared in 1925. The seat height was reduced 3 inches to provide the rider with the "in the bike feel" that separates cruisers from other machines today. The huge reduction in seat height provided a massive feeling of control and additional comfort to the rider while also lowering center of gravity for ease of handling. Even though the seat was now 3 inches lower, engineers actually managed to increase the length of the spring inside the seat post from 9 to 14 inches for a cushier ride. A new frame brace underneath the engine, between the downtube and seat post, held the engine lower and more solidly.

158 Because of the lower seat height, which would have impeded the 1924's gas tank, H-D introduced a streamlined, teardrop tank, the basic style of which is used today. To go with the lower seat height and the increasing sportiness of its machines, The Motor Company stopped using the straight pullback handlebars in favor of bars that stayed tighter to the front end and curved down slightly; they resemble modern handlebars. A pair of smaller 27-inch wheels with wide 3.85-inch tires also helped to modernize the appearance and performance of the 1925s. Tipping the scales at just over 400 pounds, the redesigned J models needed the extra load-bearing ability.

159 Did you know that Harley-Davidson produced an opposed Flathead twin for public use in 1919? Many fans know of the XA produced for use in World War II, but The Motor Company actually experimented with an opposed twin more than 20 years earlier. The 19W Sport Twin weighs only 257 pounds, has a low center of gravity, and vibrates much less than its V-twin counterparts. It was advertised as a dependable commuter, targeted at women and younger riders. The 19W's goal was to compete for sales with Indian's Model O and it succeeded with twice the engine capacity and only 25 percent more weight. Its effectiveness was proven when professional racer Hap Scherer set two endurance records on it: Canada to Mexico and New York to Chicago.

160 Harley-Davidson's first use of a dashboard and ignition key was in 1926, although it used two keys, not just one. The left-side key provided the simple on/off ignition connection while the right key controlled the electric headlight and taillight with positions for on, off, and dim.

The dash on this 1928 H-D is the same one used since 1926 and is branded with a Bar & Shield logo with the proud proclamation of "MADE IN U.S.A." The company idiot-proofed its new dash by labeling positions on the top and bottom of the switches. This view also shows the oil tank cap and pump, as well as the two gas caps.

161 Although H-Ds had been in production for more than two decades, it wasn't until 1928 that a front brake was included as part of the motorcycle. By this time, the bikes were heavy and powerful enough that a front brake was necessary to provide sufficient stopping power. It's also possible that the addition of a front

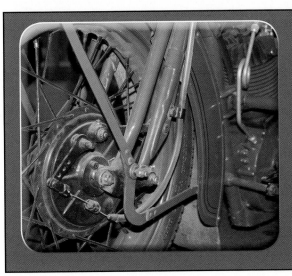

Riders can be thankful that The Motor Company has updated the brakes through the years. In 1928, this first drum brake operated with a leather-sheathed cable. This motorcycle has obviously been ridden, based on the wear of the newer Avon tires and the dirt on the inside of the fender.

brake was timed with the launch of the high-performance two-cam engines, also in 1928.

162 The 1929–1930 Harley-Davidsons sported a lean, sporty-looking pair of 4-1/2-inch headlights, which lowered the bike's overall height while providing additional lighting capability. However, riders of these models discovered the drawback to this design the hard way. At night, the headlights looked like automobile headlights that were a quarter-mile away. It went back to its single headlight setup for 1931.

163 With the handful of electrics now on their motorcycles, Harley riders needed a way to monitor the electrical current. For 1929 models, an ammeter was included as part of a redesigned, rounded dash with the gauge tucked between the two switches. The ammeter used a needle to show either a charge or discharge up to 10 amps in either direction. A small update from the 1926 dash is the word "park" instead of "dim" on the right light switch.

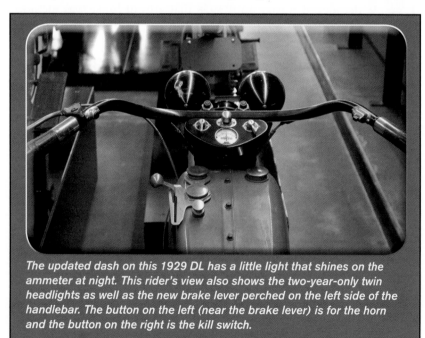

The updated dash on this 1929 DL has a little light that shines on the ammeter at night. This rider's view also shows the two-year-only twin headlights as well as the new brake lever perched on the left side of the handlebar. The button on the left (near the brake lever) is for the horn and the button on the right is the kill switch.

164 Harley-Davidson began its special color program in February 1927, even though colors other than the usual Olive Drab were rarely ordered. For a surcharge of between $6 and $13, depending on the model, a new owner could have his (or her) motorcycle painted Azure Blue, Maroon, Police Blue, or Coach Green. In addition, pin-striping and a two-tone option of Fawn Grey or Cream could be added. Actually, special paint finishes were technically available in 1926, but dealers were instructed not to publicize it. In 1928, colors other than Olive Drab were available as standard fare, and special combinations and colors were still available for a surcharge.

165 Throughout the years, Harley-Davidson kept improving the cushioning effect provided by the springer front fork. From 1916 until the redesigned, I-beam springer on the Flatheads, H-D springers used 41 feet of tempered steel spring wound up inside the fork legs.

166 The first Harley-Davidson to use external fork springs was the Model W Sport in 1919. The overall girder-style design was actually closer to the style that Indian was using, except that The Motor Company tightened up its version by using a very short leaf spring for compression and a large single coil spring for rebound. In 1922, H-D added a pair of external springs to the center of the forks.

167 What would you do if it was 1916, and your motorcycle broke down at night, with no streetlights or cell phone lights? The answer is easy if your bike had electric lights. On H-Ds with an electric system, the rear taillight was easily detachable from its housing and could be used as a roadside emergency light. The long wire allowed the light to reach anywhere on the bike.

168 In 1926, Harley-Davidson made roadside wrenching a little easier by using a hinged rear fender. The rear section of the fender could be unbolted from its stay and swung up and over the main section so that the wheel could simply slide out the back while the bike was on the rearstand. Previously, the rear of the bike had to be lifted higher than the rearstand allowed to drop the wheel out from under the bike. To riders' delight, hinged fenders were used on varying models until 1980, when once again, changing a wheel required lifting the entire bike up.

169 To provide the largest possible space for fuel, Harley-Davidson began using a "cutout" gas tank in 1915. Remember the pocket valves that sat on top of the engine? The rocker arms and grease fittings actually protruded high above the cylinder head and into part of the space that could be occupied by a fuel tank. It was an easy fix for the designers to form rounded cutouts on the right side of the gas tank; the rocker arms tucked into these cutouts. This allowed the gas tank to sit low above the cylinder heads, but it still allowed room for the intake valve to function properly. This design was used through 1929, although the cutouts were updated through the years as gas tank styles changed. What was certainly a practical measure at the time is today a classic and defining feature of Harley-Davidson's F-head motorcycles.

170 In the early days of motorcycling, long before the buddy seat, how did riders carry passengers without having to bolt a huge sidecar to the side of their bikes? Harley-Davidson had them covered then, just as it does now. A complete passenger seat attachment sat above the rear fender. Using a series of mounting brackets, the passenger seat, which was nearly identical to the rider's seat, was mounted directly to the bike's frame rails and axle plates. Like the rider's seat, it, too was sprung, except that it used a pair of reverse-coiled springs on either side of the fender. Some of the earliest examples actually had a small handlebar for the passenger to hold; later models use a grab rail at the front. With this setup, two people could more easily and comfortably enjoy motorcycling.

171 Because Harley-Davidsons and other motorcycle brands were used primarily as transportation in the early years, they were used year-round, regardless of weather. Nothing hampers the ability to use a motorcycle like ice and snow, so a popular modification for owners who lived in snow country was to attach stabilizing skis to either side of the frame. The skis kept the motorcycle upright and going straight but they were just high enough so they wouldn't scrape if the ground were dry.

172 Before Harley-Davidson developed separate front and rear braking systems, Commonwealth countries and territories required motorcycles to be equipped with a dual rear brake system. The rear brake had to be controlled by the standard right-side brake pedal but also by a lever on the right side of the handlebar. Presumably, this was to aid in stopping and starting on hills. Many export models that show up at auctions and shows today retain their originally handbrake, although it takes most viewers a few moments to realize that there's no front brake!

173 The Troxel Mfg. Co., based in Elvira, Ohio, supplied Harley-Davidson's seats beginning in the 1917 model year. Two versions were offered. The Jumbo was the more popular because of its large, comfortable size; the Wizard was smaller and more closely resembled a racing or bicycle seat.

174 Something that you don't always see when you're looking at an early sidecar-equipped Harley-Davidson is the third footboard. As you know, 1914 was the first year of the rider footboard, and as sidecar travel became more and more popular, passengers wanted a comfortable place to rest their feet. They also wanted something to use as a brace when going fast. The Motor Company simply took one of the rubber-topped footboards (with Harley-Davidson written across it), and stuck it inside the front of the sidecar. Mounted perpendicularly to the bike (unlike the parallel-mounted rider footboards), there's plenty of room to position both feet on the rubber surface.

175 In 1926, The Motor Company introduced an option that didn't make the bikes ride any better, but made them a whole lot easier to park: the Jiffy Stand. Mounted on the left side of the frame, underneath the footboard, the spring-loaded Jiffy Stand allowed the rider to easily pull the stand forward with a foot and set the bike over on it instead of having to pull the bike up onto the rearstand every time. Little details such as this greatly furthered the ease and accessibility of motorcycles as daily transportation that required little effort to operate. Wonder why it was called the Jiffy Stand instead of a kickstand or sidestand? The H-D execs wanted to stress how fast and easy it was to operate the stand, and they thought that "jiffy" was the best word for it. To this day, all references to the kickstand/sidestand in H-D's service or parts and accessories materials refer to it as a Jiffy Stand.

THE POWERTRAIN

176 Harley-Davidson said good-bye to the last remnant of the motor bicycle era when it launched the 1916 3-speed models (twin and single) with a kickstarter on the right side in place of the pedals. It was no longer a significant workout to start the motorcycle; just step down on the kicker pedal and watch the motorcycle fire to life. Single-speed singles and twins did retain the bicycle pedals. The 1916 and later models lack the hole on the primary cover for the pedals. Simply for the practicality, some 1915 owners who

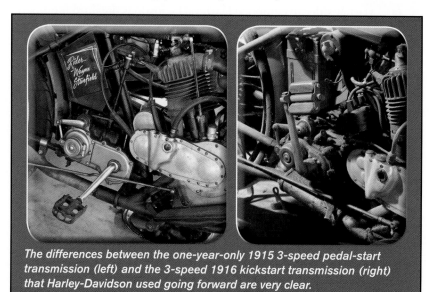

The differences between the one-year-only 1915 3-speed pedal-start transmission (left) and the 3-speed 1916 kickstart transmission (right) that Harley-Davidson used going forward are very clear.

ride their machines regularly have installed 1916 transmissions on their 1915s.

177 Until World War I, Harleys used German-made Bosch magnetos. As you'd expect, that became a slight problem after the war; The Motor Company switched to magnetos made by Dixie and other American manufacturers until the magneto became obsolete. In 1917, H-D gave its street V-twin the powerful four-lobe cam that it used in the eight-valve racers. That, along with timing and lift adjustments allowed the 17J to make 16 hp.

178 The popularity of sidecars continued to grow, and Harley-Davidson improved the hack ownership experience by recommending a 14-tooth countershaft sprocket with a higher gear ratio. Naturally, top speed decreased, but ridability at regular speed ranges improved. For the owner who also liked to ride solo, the 14-tooth sprocket worked fine. Both regular and sidecar gearing were available.

179 Indian introduced the 350-cc Prince model in 1925; Harley-Davidson responded quickly and powerfully with a pair of 350-cc singles for the consumer and for the racetrack. The 1926 Model A was the first sidevalve engine produced since H-D dropped the horizontally opposed W. At 344 cc (21 ci), it used a vertical cylinder like the older pocket-valve single, except that this one had a flat removable combustion chamber that housed the spark plug, similar to the W. It produced about 8 hp and was available with a magneto (AA) or a battery (AB).

180 As part of the response to the Indian Prince, Harley-Davidson also released an overhead valve (OHV) version of the Model A, dubbed the Model B, which marked the first time that an OHV Harley-Davidson was sold to the public. Many people mistakenly give the 1936 Knucklehead that glory. Designated as the BA (magneto) or BB (battery), the OHV single produced 12 hp; racers and sporting riders purchased most of them. Compared to the sidevalve, of which 4,000 were built, only 722 OHVs were produced.

181 The W Sport Twin, produced from 1919 to 1923, was Harley-Davidson's first attempt at selling a horizontally opposed twin. It pioneered engineering technology that wasn't seen for another decade at The Motor Company; it didn't release another Flathead twin until the 1929 D. The 36-ci 6-hp W uses a sidevalve, or Flathead, engine design that eliminates all moving parts from the cylinder head and rocker arms. Fewer parts make it more durable and run cooler. The construction of the engine differs from what we usually picture, which is the BMW design. The cylinders go front to back; that is, the front cylinder points toward the front wheel and the rear cylinder points toward the rear wheel. This kept the package narrow and well-balanced, but it did remove the cooling advantage associated with perpendicular opposed twins.

The intake and exhaust manifold on the model W Sport Twin looks more like something that you'd find on a GM small-block than on a Harley-Davidson! In addition to the completely awkward design, the hot exhaust pipes run alongside what should be a cool air intake tract.

182 Another first for Harley-Davidson is the Sport Twin's unit construction. This means that the transmission is actually inside the engine case, as it is on a modern Sportster. This efficient design wasn't seen again in a Harley twin until the 1952 K model. It was also the first to use an air cleaner to keep particles out of the carburetor. The 19W is the only H-D known to use an external flywheel (covered by a metal shroud) and the first to use a fully enclosed drive chain. The overall design eliminated several key areas known for oil seepage, making the W a very clean motorcycle to own and ride.

183 Harley-Davidson introduced its first 74-ci engine in the JD (battery) and FD (magneto) models for the 1921 lineup to compete with the power of the 4-cylinder models available from other manufacturers. The company actually looked into building a 4-cylinder version, but increasing the Big Twin's displacement made more sense. The new 74-ci V-twin sported a 3.42-inch bore with a 4-inch stroke to produce 18 hp. The 74-ci engine went on to be one of the most common for Big Twins until 1978.

184 Both the OHV and the sidevalve singles used newly designed removable heads developed by British engineer Harry Ricardo. Ricardo discovered that more turbulence in the combustion chamber allowed the air and fuel to mix better, thereby creating better combustion, which not only provided more power but better fuel economy and a cleaner engine. Ricardo achieved this greater turbulence by offsetting the cylinder head so that the head is within 1 mm away at top dead center (TDC) over part of the piston. This "squish band" shoots the air/fuel mixture into the larger combustion chamber at an intense speed, sending the mixture into a turbulent frenzy.

185 In 1929, The Motor Company introduced its zany four-muffler exhaust system on all twins. This particular exhaust system, which was used only in 1929, used a dual, side-exiting design that piggybacked one muffler on top of the other on either side. The entire system was quiet but heavy. In 1930, it decided to drop the left-side mufflers in favor of a pair of mufflers on the right. By 1931, a single, albeit larger, muffler was used, which was fed by both cylinders.

186 Harley-Davidson introduced the model JDH (74 ci) and JH (61 ci) in 1928 essentially as race-ready street bikes. The engine was a two-cam design based on what the H-D factory team campaigned to great success throughout the 1920s. They used F-head pocket-valve cylinders that housed Dow metal pistons, which were manufactured using magnesium alloy. With a price tag of $370, the JDH was the first Harley street bike capable of achieving 100 mph. The Two-Cam engines are immediately recognizable by the kidney-shaped cam cover that comes up in the back to cover the magneto. It is one of the most collectable Harley-Davidsons today; examples have sold for more than $100,000 at auction.

187 Even though the recirculating oil system was still nearly a decade away, The Motor Company realized that most riders didn't want to have to keep up with oiling their machines differently at different engine loads and throttle settings. The engineers came up with a way to automatically adjust oiling based on throttle position. They ran a cable to the oil pump, which then operates off the throttle linkage on the carburetor. More oil flows through the pump on the cam cover as the throttle is opened wider. An additional hand pump on the oil tank was still used for excessive uphill or sidecar loads. This system was in place until 1937, when all Flatheads were converted to recirculating oil.

188 Sure, Harleys are a great way to travel, but some times even the narrowest of motorcycles can't sneak through a traffic jam. So why don't you take to the air? In 1927, a do-it-yourself kit available through *Popular Mechanics* included an adapter that mounted to the primary sprocket shaft of a JD engine to which a builder then attached an airplane propeller and used that setup to power a homemade aircraft.

189 Another interesting propeller-driven variant is the ice glider kit available through the Mead Glider company. Unlike the aircraft propeller, the Mead kit ran a chain off the stock primary sprocket to turn the propeller, which was placed on the ice glider's chassis toward the top of the cylinder heads. The company advertised its kit to Harley-Davidson owners with the recommendation that they could build the ice glider easily. Then, during the winter, transfer their motorcycle engine into it.

190 When initially purchasing a motorcycle in the 1910s, it was important to mention whether or not it was for sidecar use. H-Ds meant for solo use arrived from the factory with a 15-tooth engine sprocket, which was well matched for the weight and acceleration versus top-speed needs. A sidecar rig with that gearing accelerated at a much slower rate while also putting too much pressure on the clutch, especially on hills. In addition, the added weight and running gear couldn't propel the machine to top speeds. Therefore, a 14-tooth engine sprocket was offered for sidecar customers so they could get the most out of the heavier machine.

191 In 1924, Harley-Davidson hired Ace's chief engineer, Everett DeLong, on a six-month contract to develop a 4-cylinder engine for The Motor Company. Ace had been successful with this type of engine for many years. Initially, he worked one of his inline-4 Ace designs into a JD chassis, but the production version would have required too much expensive tooling at the factory. His next prototype engine wouldn't have added much to the budget. He mounted two JD V-twins side by side, connected at the crankcase. The displacement of both engines would have to be reduced to end up with an 80-ci total displacement, but this design created no new cooling issues and required little factory tooling. In the end, Harley-Davidson vetoed the project, not wanting to diversify with risky models that might tarnish the brand.

192 Harley-Davidson solved a serious lubrication problem with the JD valvetrain in 1924 when it began fitting Alemite grease fittings into the heads. Using a standard grease gun, a bike's owner could easily lubricate all of the valvetrain bearings in the heads, greatly reducing noise and heat. In addition, the chassis included ten other Alemite grease fittings. New JDs were actually sold with a grease gun and a can of grease.

193 Harley-Davidson's first automatic oil pumps were built right into the cam cover on 1915–1919 H-Ds; they contained a sight glass so that the operator could ensure that oil was moving through the system. As bikes got faster and more complicated, it became unreasonable to ask the operator to continuously pump oil into the crankcase by hand. That's why these automatic systems evolved. However, the hand-pump was standard equipment until 1937, just in case the engine was under more stress than the oil pump could cover.

194 Today's big–cubic-inch Harleys and many heavily modified V-twins use compression releases mounted to the cylinder heads. They reduce compression when starting the engine for less strain on the starter motor. In 1916, when "step-starters" were introduced, they employed a similar, yet slightly more complex system for easy starts. A series of intricate linkages went from the kicker to the engine's exhaust valves that, upon kickstarting the bike, lifted the valves and reduced compression for less resistance.

195 Have you ever looked at an old H-D engine and wondered why all of the metal fuel and oil lines are coiled? The coils were used because the lines come from a solid point on the bike (such as the gas tank and oil tank) and go to a moving, vibrating part of the bike (the engine). If the metal lines went from Point A straight to Point B, they'd crack and break very quickly because of the stress. By putting a coil in the line, they can shake, rattle, and roll all they want without snapping because of the flex that is built in.

196 Although earlier Harley engines had the intake pocket valve mounted directly on top of the cylinder, later engines used a true Intake Over Exhaust (IOE) design by positioning both valves on the side of the cylinder, which creates a wider combustion chamber. Not only did the later valve design allow easier maintenance and adjustment on the intake valve, but it also allowed the engineers to use a shorter rocker arm, which was more dependable and easier to articulate.

197 In 1927, Harley-Davidson introduced its first "wasted spark" ignition system: A circuit breaker and a single ignition coil fired both spark plugs at the same time. In one cylinder, the air/fuel mixture was ignited, while the spark had no effect in the other cylinder. This system allowed the removal of the distributor and the second coil. In 1929, Flathead twins and IOE twins shared the same ignition spark coil.

198 In 1926, Harley-Davidson offered an exhaust cutout system that, for the first time, deflected gases away from the rider when it was open. The 1926 exhaust system uses a rear-facing deflector, which is positioned directly over the muffler's cutout exit to force exhaust gasses rearward. An otherwise identical exhaust system was actually used in 1925; when the cutout was open, a simple hole in the side of the muffler allowed hot exhaust gases to exit in every direction, including up toward the rider. Because 1925 and 1926 models are otherwise identical, taking a peek at the exhaust system is a good way to identify the year without getting down on your hands and knees to read the engine number.

199 The legendary Two-Cam street engines of 1928 and 1929 received a significant dose of detuning compared to the factory racers from which they were derived. However, some unique go-fast parts made it through to production. The most unique aspect of the Two-Cam compared to the standard single cams was the use of a direct valve gear system to operate the valves. Tappets, rather than roller arms, guided the cam lobes, which, in addition to stronger intake valvesprings, allowed the Two-Cam to rev higher and reach higher power numbers more reliably.

200 In 1924, The Motor Company introduced its line of aluminum-alloy-piston motorcycles with the E series. This series included the JE solo, JES sidecar, as well as the JDCA solo, and JDSCA sidecar. A Harley-Davidson advertisement in the October 1923 edition of *Popular Mechanics* gives insight into the practical use of aluminum-alloy pistons. The ad claims that aluminum-alloy pistons allow the rider to "hit up any speed and hold it, all day long if you want to, and the 1924 Harley-Davidson won't overheat." The ad also claims that the lightweight pistons "cut vibration in half" and are "far more durable."

PEOPLE AND POP CULTURE

201 Effie Hotchkiss and her mother, Avis, cemented their names into history in 1915 by becoming the first women to ride from coast to coast on a motorcycle. They traveled from their home izn Brooklyn, New York, to San Francisco, California, on a 1915 Harley-Davidson with a sidecar. The journey took two months to complete, and served as an inspiration to women motorcyclists then, as it still does today! Effie and Avis added to their legend by carrying a small bottle filled with water from the Atlantic Ocean. When they arrived at the Golden Gate Park beach, they emptied the bottle into the Pacific.

202 A 1926 Peashooter was featured on the September 5, 2013, episode of *Velocity*'s "What's In The Barn." Dale and Matt Walksler of Wheels Through Time museum uncovered one of these bikes in an old military surplus warehouse near the museum in North Carolina.

203 In 1918, Seattle dealer Harry Trainor gave Vaudeville star Trixie Friganza a ride in a 61-ci JD with sidecar. A famously portly woman, the press covered the ride around hilly Seattle, and portrayed the Harley-Davidson as a powerful and durable machine.

204 According to a 1929 Harley-Davidson advertisement, "Now comes the quiet motorcycle! Noise has gone out of fashion. The public has been demanding a more and more quiet-functioning mechanism." While that part about the public demands might be true today, "smooth, quiet, purring power" is not particularly fashionable today, even though it was apparently a hot selling feature in 1929.

205 Harley-Davidson ran an ad in 1920 featuring German-American dancer Gertrude Hoffman astride her model W Sport Twin. It's difficult not to love the early advertising material. The language and art has improved through the years, but the general concept has not. This particular ad states, "The Woman's Out-Door Companion. GERTRUDE HOFFMAN owns a motorcycle. It is the feature-refined, woman-kind Harley-Davidson." It goes on to say, "the Harley-Davidson responds to the guiding hand of a woman as did the kindest tempered steed of old."

206 Harley-Davidsons were competing everywhere by the 1920s, and one of the most exciting areas was in off-road exploration. On January 16, 1921, John Edwin Hogg completed the first successful motorcycle ride to the bottom of the Grand Canyon and back out again on a Harley-Davidson model W Sport Solo. The trip took him four days to complete and he claimed to have used only 2-1/2 gallons of fuel and 2 quarts of oil and "never touched a tool to the little Sport model." The Sport Solo itself was mostly stock. Hogg completed the Grand Canyon attempt after riding the machine from Los Angeles to Arizona.

207 What's the best fuel mileage you've ever pulled on an H-D? 50 mpg? 45? Those are certainly respectable numbers, but they hardly compare to the record that John F. Greenawalt set in 1913 aboard his H-D V-twin. In the Nomad Motorcycle Club economy test that year, Greenawalt massaged 19 miles out of his bike using only 23 ounces of gasoline, which worked out to 105 mpg! He set the world record for fuel economy, beating the previous year's record of 62.2 mpg.

208 Most automotive and motorcycle enthusiasts are familiar with actor Steve McQueen's car- and motorcycle-collecting passion, and may even be familiar with some of the stunning vehicles that once bore his name on the title. They tend to be very beautiful and very fast. And then there's his 1917 J with carrier that was used for transporting carrier pigeons during World War I. It's a cool machine, no doubt, but it certainly lacks that particular McQueen brand of sexiness that his other motorcycles exude.

209 What's the best way to get out and see the world? General Sales Manager Arthur Davidson and his wife, Clara, certainly had the right idea when they began traveling to the far reaches of the globe to promote the product and expand the dealer base. Arthur and Clara took a trip to the South Pacific in 1917 to recruit international dealers in Australia, American Samoa, New Zealand, and Tasmania. They made several international explorations throughout the 1910s and 1920s, all to increase the international reach of The Motor Company.

210 Long known as one of the best states for hunting, fishing, and general outdoor activities, Wisconsin has a way of breeding enthusiastic outdoorsmen. Bill Harley and Arthur Davidson were no exception. Remember, they originally wanted motorcycles to get to their favorite fishing spots faster. They accomplished their mission and were known to go fishing at Beaver Lake in nearby Waukesha, just outside Milwaukee, and as far away as Pine Lake, which is near Michigan's Upper Peninsula. Are either of those are your favorite fishing spots? Think of them when you ride your Harley there to catch a walleye!

211 The October 19, 1916, issue of *Motorcycle Illustrated* ran a blurb announcing that Danish Prince Axel was a motorcyclist. Even cooler than that, however, is that the report states that he purchased a 3-speed Harley-Davidson with an electric headlight on September 8 from The Motor Company's Copenhagen representative, C. Friss-Hansen & Co. Prince Axel previously rode an A.J.S. long-distance, but decided that a Harley-Davidson better suited his needs.

212 On July 11, 1919, Jack Fletcher rode his 1919 Sport Model to the top of Mount Baldy (also known as Mount San Antonio), the highest point in Los Angeles County, California. He completed the 10,080-foot climb in 3 hours 42 minutes, setting a world record for mountain climbing. The total route consisted of 7-1/2 miles of loose rock and crumbling granite, and some very steep grades. According to the June 16, 1919, issue of *MotorCycling and Bicycling* magazine, "The trip was made without experiencing any difficulty with the machine."

213 In 1919, "Hap" Scherer set the speed record for the New York City to Chicago run with a time of 31 hours 24 minutes on a Harley-Davidson Sport Model, 10 hours 56 minutes faster than the previous record. He averaged 32 mph on muddy, slippery roads from rain that also caused dense fog throughout the trip. Even still, Hap completed the 1,012-mile journey more than an hour ahead of schedule on a machine with a displacement of only 36 ci! Legend has it that Hap didn't eat a single bite of food throughout the entire trip. Like Jack Fletcher's trip, Hap had no difficulty with his machine either. In fact, the motorcycle's primary tool kit was sealed at the starting line, and, upon Hap's arrival in Chicago, the tool kit was still sealed. The only tools Hap was allowed to use were tire tools and a valve nut wrench (two, most likely) for adjusting the pushrods, which has to be done about every 200 miles.

214 The Sport Model, still very early in its production, was actually a failure on the showroom. "Hap" Scherer's record-setting run caused quite a bit of fanfare in the motorcycling world. Waiting for him at the finish line in Chicago was Harley-Davidson's advertising manager, Chicago dealer C. H. Lang, and the editor of *MotorCycling and Bicycling*. A "moving picture operator" was present to record the finish. Of course, Hap's wife was also there waiting for him.

215 What do you do if you want to take the whole family for a motorcycle ride but there's not enough room in the sidecar? Simple! Do what "Xen" Critchfield did and mount two sidecars, one on each side of his bike. Remember, many exported sidecar rigs had a left-side sidecar as opposed to the right-side fitment used in the United States. However, Xen took his double-sidecar rig to a much higher standard. He used flexible sidecars, from the Flxible Co. These undulating sidehacks didn't become famous until 1920 when they were first used for racing. By using flexibles, he could lean his Harley side to side and the sidecars leaned right along with it! In addition to the extra sporting nature, the flexibles were used primarily so that the motorcycle could keep both wheels on the ground at all times, even if the sidecar hit in the road.

216 Harley-Davidson wasn't just the racing motorcycle of choice in the United States; it excelled anywhere that motorcycle riders were going head to head against competitors or the clock. On December 26, 1919, H-D riders in Australia won two competition events and another set an endurance record. Claude Sainty took home the first-place trophy in the Senior Australian Tourist Trophy race in Goulborn, followed by Joe Mostyn who took first in the Junior class. That same day, Australian Fred Yott completed the Launceston-Hobart run in a sidecar in 3 hours 8 minutes, beating Erwin "Cannonball" Baker's record.

217 In an extremely rare occurrence in cinema history, a 1929 Harley-Davidson JDH Two-Cam appeared in Disney's 1991 film, *The Rocketeer*. Unfortunately, the beautiful green twin-headlight machine only has a couple of scenes when Cliff (actor Billy Campbell) rode it. Fun personal fact: my friend, Bob, who sold me my first Harley-Davidson, went on to produce the critically acclaimed 2013 film, *Copperhead*, starring Billy Campbell and another well-known cinema biker, Peter Fonda.

218 Motorcyclists of today might think that Howard Hughes' 1930 film, *Hell's Angels*, is about a motorcycle club, but they'd be wrong. It's actually about the fighter pilots of World War I, in particular, a pair of British brothers who enlist in the Royal Flying Corps. In the movie, the brothers ride a Harley-Davidson J with sidecar into town to let off some steam on the eve of their top-secret suicide mission. Not only was the use of the motorcycle historically correct as to what pilots used at the time, but it also allowed Hughes to show a different side of the main characters that only a Harley with a sidecar can do!

219 The Motorcycle & Allied Trades Association (M&ATA) was founded in 1916 as a vessel through which American motorcycle manufacturers could shape the perception of the sport of motorcycling. Before the M&ATA was transitioned into the American Motorcyclist Association (AMA) in 1924, one of its principal goals was to improve the professionalism of all dealers to make motorcycles more relatable to the public. Another goal was to promote civically responsible riding among the riding population. This includes maintaining a safe speed, being courteous, and maintaining use of quiet factory exhaust systems. The greatest fear that the OEMs had was that motorcycling would become a cult sport and would be banished in lawful society.

220 Leslie "Red" Parkhurst, Harley-Davidson's first factory racer, was quickly thrust into the national spotlight when he appeared in many ads for The Motor Company. He became friends with one of his biggest fans, iconic boxer Jack Dempsey, who held the World Heavyweight Championship title from 1919 to 1926. The two even got into a "fight" that was covered in the newspapers. Whether or not Dempsey was interested in Harley-Davidsons before he met Parkhurst is unknown, but he was photographed sitting on a single-cylinder Harley while training for a fight in Colorado. Later, The Motor Company used Jack Dempsey's name in a 1934 ad comparing his "fighting heart" to the 35-hp 74-ci V-twin available that year.

221 In May 1923, record-setting aviator Charles Lindbergh bought his first airplane, a Curtis JN-4 "Jenny," for $500 and, one week later, took his first solo flight in it. Guess what he rode to Southern Field, near Americus, Georgia? That's right, a Harley-Davidson. Unfortunately, it's believed that he traded that bike for part of the plane, in which he left the airfield.

222 Disabilities rarely stop a Harley rider from saddling up. In fact, history has shown that some of the toughest, most enthusiastic riders out there are disabled. One of the earliest examples of someone modifying an H-D to work for his specific needs is Alfred

Did you think that custom Harleys weren't available until the 1960s? Well, think again. Riders have been customizing these motorcycles since the very beginning for a variety of reasons. Alfred LeRoy was no different, and proved that anyone can ride a Harley-Davidson. (Photo Courtesy Harley-Davidson)

LeRoy, who lost both of his legs and half of his left arm when he was struck by a train at age 15. So, he built a Harley-Davidson with a left-side sidecar. The leather-padded sidecar was built to be comfortable for him, and he made a series of modifications to the motorcycle to allow him to operate it from there. He modified the handlebar to include a long tiller with a throttle on the end so he could steer and control speed. He affixed a speedometer to the sidecar and it's believed that the bike's brake was controlled by a lever located where the seat would otherwise be. The best part about his rig might just be the miniature sidecar that hung off the left side of his sidecar for his dog to ride in.

223 In episode 111 of *The Andy Griffith Show* (appropriately titled "Barney's Sidecar") Barney Fife buys a military surplus H-D sidecar rig. Even though the motorcycle was supposed to be from World War I, it's actually a 1927 JD painted in the familiar Olive Drab. Stuntman and actor George Dockstader owned the bike and modified it to fit in with the required theme. Dockstader did not actually serve as Barney's stunt double for the episode because of their different body sizes. Jerry Brutsche, another famous stunt double, did the riding scenes.

224 Easter Walters was an early 1920s silent film actress who rode her Harley-Davidson Model W all around Hollywood, and was a well-known sight. She performed all of her own stunts in her movies, which included 1919's *The Tiger's Trail* and 1920's *The Devil's Riddle.* Many today consider her early and very public use of a motorcycle to have had a pioneering effect for other women motorcyclists. Cris Sommer Simmons mentions Walters in her book, *The American Motorcycle Girls: 1900 to 1950.*

225 In 1928, legendary aviation stuntman and racer Charles W. "Speed" Holman bought a Harley-Davidson from his local Minneapolis, Minnesota, dealer, George Faulders. Speed won the 1927 National Air Races, and apparently wanted a machine that felt just as fast on the ground as what he was used to in the air. The bike itself is a 1928 single-cam JD, as evidenced by an image showing a front brake, single headlight, and straight cam cover. Speed gained fame in a variety of air races, and by doing a number of wing-walking and parachuting displays for spectators. Orville Wright signed his first pilot's license, and he later became the first commercial pilot for Northwest Airlines. Holman Field at the St. Paul Downtown Airport is named after him, as is Holman St. in St. Paul.

MILITARY, POLICE AND RACING

226 Harley-Davidson introduced its eight-valve racer in 1916 to compete with eight-valve Indians and Excelsiors. The potent engine originally used a 1915 11-K bottom end with redesigned cylinders and hemispherical heads with high-domed pistons. The biggest change is immediately visible on the outside in that instead of the standard pocket-valve design for which the F-heads are known, the eight-valve uses four overhead valves per cylinder. The same two pushrods per cylinder are used, and a linkage connects the rockers that operate two valves at the same time. The other defining feature of the engine is the dual exhaust pipes coming out of each cylinder head. It's believed that about 30 eight-valve racers were built and that less than 10 exist today.

227 Many people are familiar with the widespread use of Harley-Davidsons in World War I, but that was actually the second time that the military approached The Motor Company for a purpose-built motorcycle. The first official U.S. military order was in 1916 when General John "Blackjack" Pershing requested 12 units to join his modern, mechanized brigade in the fight against Mexican revolutionary Pancho Villa. The total number of motorcycles built for the expedition doubled to 24. The most notable of these motorcycles have to be those equipped with a sidecar gun carriage, which was developed by William S. Harley personally.

228 The United States officially entered WWI in 1917. During 1917 and 1918, the army took approximately 15,000 Harley-Davidson motorcycles to Europe, one-third of The Motor Company's total production for those two years. Early military versions were simply civilian model Js painted Olive Drab, which led to all motorcycles being delivered with the standard Olive paint until 1932. Later, H-D developed the FUS and LUS military-specific models, which were more effective in off-road, combat use thanks to their high, flat fenders. All military motorcycles from all brands used an Army-required gas headlamp instead of the standard electric lamps with which they were originally fitted. Military motorcycles were largely used as messengers, but many of them also saw front line action with sidecar-mounted machine guns or stretchers to ferry one or two wounded soldiers off the battlefield. 7,521 FUS models were built.

229 To provide support for the thousands of machines it built for use in World War I, Harley-Davidson opened the Quartermasters School to teach the repair and operation of its motorcycles to military mechanics. The first class was held in Milwaukee in July of 1917, lasted three weeks, and was attended by nine corporals from Fort Sam Houston in San Antonio, Texas.

230 One of the most famous photographs from World War I is of Corporal Ray Holtz of Chippewa Falls, Wisconsin, entering Germany on a Harley-Davidson as a line of awestruck soldiers on horseback turned their heads to look at him. Several days before the armistice treaty, Corporal Holtz and his captain were captured during a night mission in Belgium. Then, when his captors received word of the treaty, they and their motorcycle were released and sent on their way. They went back to the allied base on the Belgian border to check in. The following day, Corporal Holtz rode back into Germany on his H-D as the first American to occupy the territory.

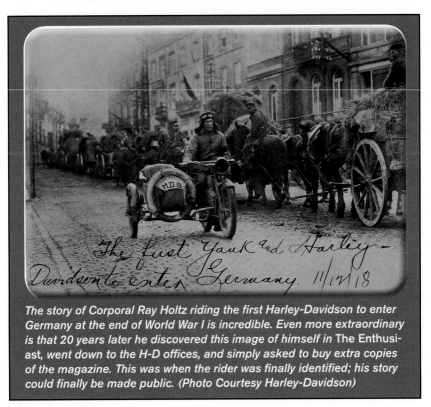

The story of Corporal Ray Holtz riding the first Harley-Davidson to enter Germany at the end of World War I is incredible. Even more extraordinary is that 20 years later he discovered this image of himself in The Enthusiast, went down to the H-D offices, and simply asked to buy extra copies of the magazine. This was when the rider was finally identified; his story could finally be made public. (Photo Courtesy Harley-Davidson)

231 The eight-valve racer had a 51-1/2-inch wheelbase and a seat mounted as tightly as possible to the gas tank and rear fender to drop the center of gravity. It used a shortened keystone frame that was open near a loop underneath the engine. The engine was

Harley-Davidson's keystone racing frame design allowed mounting of the engine as low as possible to improve handling and maneuverability. This 1924 JDCA racer shows how the keystone plates surrounded the engine case rather than cradling it from beneath. As you can see, the bike doesn't have a lot of ground clearance, but that wasn't important on the flat track.

mounted directly to the frame in the front with large brackets underneath that spanned the open distance. This made the engine a stressed member of the frame, which improved rigidity and saved weight. Low-slung handlebars let the rider lean forward over the small 1.43-gallon gas tank to reduce wind resistance and maintain more control of the bike at speed, which was important because eight-valves were capable of going well over 100 mph. The board-track race version had no brakes.

232 The practice of homologation in racing dates as far back as motorcycle racing itself and Federation of American Motorcyclists (FAM) rules stated that racing motorcycles must be made available to the public for sale to render them legal on the racetrack. Harley-Davidson complied, and it priced the eight-valve racer at $1,500, all but ensuring that no privateer challenged the factory's dominance. No records exist of any being sold and raced anywhere, although some have turned up through the years. Harley-Davidson had a very different philosophy to Indian, which priced its eight-valves similarly to its other twins and encouraged the public to own and race them.

233 The Motor Company built three eight-valve racers in 1916 and each used a different lubrication system. One used a manual oil pump, one used a mechanical oil pump, and the third used both. Obviously, the racing department still had some real world experimenting to do. The company's promotional materials advertise that a "buyer" of the $1,500 machine could have his choice of the three lubrication options.

234 To conserve weight, eight-valve racers had no starting system such as pedals or a kicker. To start one, it had to be towed by a car or another motorcycle and when it fired, the rider undid the rope and was on his own. Because boardtrack racers only needed one speed, "fast," they didn't have transmissions, either.

235 The AMA's smallest class was 350 cc in 1926, but even in that small-displacement division, Harley-Davidson and Indian competed ferociously and built machines that neither could have imagined just 10 years earlier. The Motor Company's big player in the little class was the S model OHV single, affectionately known as the *Peashooter*; its name came from the staccato popping exhaust note. Only about 25 were built in 1926. Because single-cylinder Harleys were extremely popular overseas, more than half were sent to Australia, New Zealand, and Europe to be raced.

236 Everything that could be eliminated from the factory racer was, including the brakes, clutch, transmission, and much of the frame. A telescopic fork was used; it was designed with the sliders mounted to the frame and the tubes mounted to the front wheel hub. This design resembles modern sport bikes more so than early Harleys. These alterations reduced weight from about 260 pounds in street trim to 215 as a racer. The racing Peashooter's engine received the usual works package and was reportedly able to hit 100 mph, 30 more than the showroom OHV could muster.

237 In 1925, Joe Petrali became the first man to finish a 100-mile race in less than 1 hour when he competed at the Altoona, Pennsylvania, National Championship. He achieved a time of 59 minutes 47-1/2 seconds with an average speed of 100.36 mph. Pretty good numbers for a guy who wasn't supposed to race that day, on a bike that wasn't his. When he first arrived in Altoona, it was discovered that his racebike had been accidentally shipped to Pittsburgh. His luck changed the next morning when he showed up to watch the race and learned that Harley-Davidson factory racer Ralph Hepburn had crashed in practice and injured his hand. Hepburn offered Petrali his ride in exchange for half of the prize money if he won; Petrali agreed. He was soon leading the race. Another racer, Eddie Brinck, went to the pits partway through the race to fix a small mechanical issue and reentered the racetrack running full out in an attempt to regain his lost laps. When he blew by Petrali, who was still in the lead, Petrali thought he had been passed, and pushed his motorcycle to catch up. Hepburn kept yelling from the sidelines for him to slow down and protect his equipment. Brinck managed to stay in front until the checkered flag fell, unbeknownst to Petrali, he was actually several laps behind. So, you could say that Joe Petrali's speed record was an accident. However, that board track record still stands, and it's likely that it will stand forever.

238 Many people think that the hot new Twin Cam is the first time that Harley-Davidson used two separate camshafts to power a high-performance valvetrain. Not so. In about 1917, engineering work began in the racing department on a two-cam race engine, which saw its first race in the 1920 season. The two-cam design reduced the reciprocating weight of the valvetrain, putting less stress on each of the parts, which was especially helpful considering that factory race engines used a total of eight overhead valves. These racebikes were able to rev higher, thereby achieving higher horsepower levels not available at lower RPM. The two-cam racing engine of the early 1920s became known as the "Banjo" engine because the shape of the cam cover resembled a banjo, unlike later two-cams, which had a distinctive kidney shape. A Banjo engine can also be identified by a small brass cover in front of the magneto gear on the cam cover and an oversized, black oil pump. In addition, Banjo engines used narrow 1914-and-earlier crankcases. Only two examples of this engine are known to exist; both are in their correct, as-last-raced chassis.

239 In 1925, during the Prohibition Era and the wave of organized crime that followed, Harley-Davidson produced a prototype crime-fighting motorcycle aimed squarely at taking on the bad guys. The machine used armor plating and bulletproof glass to protect the occupants. Fortunately for moonshiners and runners, the overall product was too heavy, and therefore too slow, to be used for its intended quick-strike purpose.

240 Milwaukee-based motorcycle builder Merkel closed its doors in 1916, and then Harley-Davidson's racing division hired Maldwyn Jones, Merkel's top racer and builder. Jones brought his personal Merkel chassis with him to the H-D team where it was implanted with an H-D engine. The Merkel frame and, especially, the front end, were superior on the racetrack; Harley-Davidson continued to use the Merkel design for years afterward. In 1922, Jones left to join the Excelsior team, where he raced for only one season before retiring.

241 Many branches of local government used Harley-Davidson motorcycles in the 1910s and early 1920s because of their dependability and cost-efficiency. One of the more curious uses of motorcycles is by the Buffalo, New York, Department of Health. It might not be the most economical option in a city that finds itself covered in at least 8 feet of snow throughout the winter, but it is known from a period photo that at least two of the machines (likely the department's entire fleet) were sidecar-equipped. The photo clearly shows both bikes with the words "DEPT. OF HEALTH Buffalo, N.Y." stenciled on the gas tanks instead of the usual Harley-Davidson script.

242 Did you know that fire departments used Harley-Davidsons? It was an efficient way for fire department officials to respond to a scene quickly and be able to get to multiple scenes efficiently. Of course, the Milwaukee Fire Department had a Harley by 1920. It probably wasn't painted red, but it did have a big "M.F.D." painted on the side.

243 Ralph Hepburn gave what some believe to be one of the best-ever racing displays on a motorcycle in the 1921 Dodge City 300, and it was easily the greatest win of his career. That July, he won the race on his Harley-Davidson eight-valve racer by 12 minutes! In the process of that victory he broke the 100-, 200-, and 300-mile world speed records. Hepburn signed with Indian the following year, but returned to The Motor Company in 1924.

244 On August 29, 1919, Ted Gilbert, aboard a Harley-Davidson W-model Sport Twin, became the first person to ride a motorcycle to the top of Rocky Butte, outside Portland, Oregon. The rugged, 11,000-foot-long trail to the top is covered heavily with downed trees, boulders, loose dirt, and brush. Gilbert completed the nearly 3-mile climb in 2 hours 20 minutes without the aid of tire chains or other special equipment. To commemorate the ride, a 4 x 6–foot sign was placed at the top noting that Ted Gilbert, aboard a Harley-Davidson Sport, proved that a motorcycle could indeed make it to the top.

245 Curly Fredericks ran the fastest lap ever on a boardtrack on August 21, 1926. He hit 120.3 mph at the 1-1/4-mile Rockingham, New Hampshire, track on a Harley-Davidson eight-valve racer. Because it doesn't appear that the extremely dangerous form of motorcycle racing will ever return, Fredericks' record is likely to be around forever.

246 Leslie "Red" Parkhurst made a name for himself not only racing against competitors, but also against time. In mid-February 1920, Red and fellow H-D racer Fred Ludlow took to the beaches of Daytona to attempt speed records with a Harley-Davidson eight-valve. At the end of the week, Red ended up with the most records, having hit a top speed of 103.39 mph, then covering 1-, 2-, and 5-mile stretches in record time. He also achieved a record speed of 84 mph with a sidecar rig shaped like a bullet. And Ludlow didn't leave empty-handed. He took a single-cylinder four-valve to a record average of 76 mph in the 5-mile run.

247 In 1913, Albert "Shrimp" Burns started racing motorcycles when he was 15 years old. In 1919, he had proven himself as a racer, and signed with the Harley-Davidson factory team. In his first racing event, he won the 5-mile solo race and then won the sidecar races. If only we all could be so successful on our first day of work! Or year, for that matter; Shrimp won several other short races that year as well as a 100-miler.

248 One of The Motor Company's greatest races occurred at the 100-mile championship at Ascot Park in Los Angeles on January 4, 1920. 25,000 spectators watched as the H-D factory riders took the top four spots. The winner, Otto Walker, even set a record for the fastest time on a 1-mile track with 77 minutes 42-3/5 seconds, which included two tire changes. Ralph Hepburn finished second, followed by Red Parkhurst and Fred Ludlow.

249 Even though most of Harley-Davidson's big racing successes occurred stateside, there are many examples of factory-prepped racing machines achieving greatness overseas. One of the most prestigious wins came when Englishman "Flying" Freddy Dixon won at Brooklands, in England, in October 1923 aboard a 1,000-cc two-cam eight-valve H-D racer. He earned a Gold Star award from the British Motor Cycle Racing Club, marking only the third time such an honor was awarded. The Gold Star was given because of his average speed of 100.1 mph, a significant record for that track; a speed that high had not previously been achieved in a race there.

250 The FH-series two-cam race engine replaced the Banjo engine in 1923; it powered factory racers until 1929. The new engine design used a kidney-shaped cam cover that curled up in the back; it is the more familiar of the two designs because of its use on the 1928 and 1929 JH and JDH street bikes. Unlike the Banjo engine, the later two-cam originally had its lifter blocks cast directly into the cam cover. However, later versions used lifter blocks bolted to the cam cover.

Pre-War Flatheads 1929–1941

THE MOTOR COMPANY

251 Like every other American manufacturer, Harley-Davidson was hit hard by the Great Depression, which began with the stock market crash on October 29, 1929, known as Black Tuesday. The Motor Company had been selling tens of thousands of motorcycles a year for a number of years. At the height of the depression in 1933, it built and sold only 3,700 motorcycles.

252 The Motor Company had to get creative to stay alive during these incredibly lean years, and a strange opportunity presented itself that provided enough cash to take the company through the next five years. Harley-Davidson signed a deal with the Japanese company Sankyo to license the blueprints and sell machinery, tools, and dies so that Sankyo could duplicate the H-D VL. The Japanese version of the VL was called the Rikuo, which is translated literally as "Continent King" although it's believed the Japanese meant it as "King of the Road."

253 The founders weren't happy with the deal, because it meant essentially giving up hope of selling motorcycles in Japan and the surrounding areas for years to come. But given the unfavorable yen to dollar rate at the time, it probably would not have been much business. However, thanks to this deal, The Motor Company survived The Great Depression, something many American companies unfortunately can't say. In addition, it gave the company some motivation to develop a new machine that would obsolete the VL.

254 The cheapest new Harley-Davidson motorcycle was the 1932 350-cc single, which retailed at $195. Base price of a 350-cc single in 1926: $210. By 1929, the economic effects of the Great Depression were felt in Europe and many countries increased import tariffs to support indigenous manufacturers. That all but sealed the fate of a single-cylinder Harley-Davidson. In fact, that was the last true single the company ever designed and built.

255 The Great Depression hit Harley-Davidson hard but the founders were determined to stay in business in spite of the hardships. Initially, many of Milwaukee's industry titans worked together to move labor staff around to the different companies as needed to save as many jobs as possible. Both management and labor worked at a significantly reduced pay. Eventually, things got so bad that massive layoffs were necessary all over the city.

256 With the factory racing program curtailed, and R&D spending at a minimum, The Motor Company used a special paint program to spruce up its motorcycles inexpensively and attract buyers during the Great Depression. A variety of art-deco paint schemes were offered each year. Perhaps the best known, and ironically, the most rare, is the 1933-only "Eagle's Head" tank decal. Five different color combinations were offered as standard compared to earlier and later years that saw fancy paint schemes as options.

Harley-Davidson built 3,703 total motorcycles in 1933, its lowest production year since 1910. Perhaps the attractive Eagle's Head paint scheme, one of my all-time favorites and offered for 1933 only, was responsible for a few of those sales.

257 Paint played a huge role in selling motorcycles and Harley-Davidson did just about everything it could to make its paint offerings exciting enough for someone to go out and buy a motorcycle. One such promotion occurred in 1934 when The Motor Company advertised a "Summer Color Special" on its V-twins. Copper Du Lux and Vermillion Red were available at no extra charge if you purchased a motorcycle that summer. As the announcement stated, the color copper "has taken the country by storm" and "to be sure of getting this new, outstanding color combination see your dealer and place your order immediately."

258 By 1931, the face of American motorcycling had changed dramatically. In the 1910s, more than 400 motorcycle manufacturers vied for the public's dollar. By the 1920s, only a handful of the largest remained to do battle on the racetrack and in the showroom. In September 1931, Excelsior and Henderson closed their doors for good. Both companies were owned by Schwinn, which believed that the worst of the Depression would last much longer than it did and closed the factories, even with orders still on the books, so that it could focus on its core bicycle business. Coming out of the Great Depression, only Harley-Davidson and Indian remained, battered but still standing.

259 The Servi-Car was produced for 41 years. It undoubtedly serves as one of the most practical Harley-Davidsons ever built, but it never hit the kind of commercial success that its owners reached. Over the course of its 41-year run, sales averaged about 450 per year; the biggest year was 1941 with 1,159 units sold.

260 Early in the Servi-Car's life, automotive dealerships and repair shops found that it was an incredible time-, money-, and energy-saving tool. By equipping the Servi-Car with a tow bar on the front end that could be latched to a car's rear bumper, a single employee could deliver a car to a customer and then return to work on the Servi-Car. An inefficient two-person job became a super-efficient one-person job. In addition, fueling and maintaining a Servi-Car was a lot easier and cheaper than maintaining a full-size automobile.

261 The Servi-Car became a great ally to any business because of its performance, but it also served as a great billboard for advertising. Its large box (with a flat rear) made an excellent canvas for company logos, addresses, and telephone numbers. The machine itself turned heads whether it was being towed by a car or ridden by an employee, which furthered its advertising potential. Harley-Davidson capitalized on this advertising potential by offering a pair of flat fender/wheel covers for $3.50. For this small investment, a company could make its Servi-Car a rolling billboard on three sides!

262 Short crossover periods have always existed at the end of one Big Twin engine's run and just before the dawn of the new engine, but it's never been as long as it was from 1936 to 1948. For a 12-year stretch, buyers could choose between two Big Twin engine types in essentially the same motorcycle. It may seem amazing now that anyone would want a Flathead instead of a Knucklehead. Wouldn't that be the same as someone now buying an Evo-powered Electra Glide instead of a Twin Cam-powered motorcycle? Not really. A better technological comparison would be to compare an Evolution engine to the V-Rod's 50-degree, overhead cam, liquid-cooled engine. And now maybe it's easier to understand why the big Flatty lasted as long as it did.

263 Congress passed the Hawley Act in 1930, which raised tariffs on almost all imported goods to the highest levels ever. The goal was to encourage consumers to buy American-made goods. It may have seemed a good idea on the surface, but, in turn, the countries affected raised their tariffs on American goods. Unfortunately, Harley-Davidson was one of the many U.S. companies that continued to see profits from its overseas sales, even as the economy at home crumbled. However, the tariff battle hit hard; 40 percent of The Motor Company's business was exports. Overall sales fell by 25 percent to 18,036 machines and it only got worse from there.

264 Like most U.S. companies in the early 1930s, Harley-Davidson had to think outside the box to maintain the amount of cash

The Davis Motor Mine cart used a 1926 single-cylinder Flathead and was originally put to work moving carts in a Northern California gold mine. This machine uses a Ford electric starter from a Model A and can pull ore out of an underground mine with nine different forward speeds and three reverse speeds. Harley-Davidson supported operations such as this when it introduced the stationary engine program in the early 1930s.

flow necessary to stay in business and, obviously, it succeeded. One such tactic was to do what it did best, which was build engines. Essential industries around the country needed stationary engines to power equipment such as cultivators and air compressors. H-D-branded single-cylinder engines, as well as V-twins, were built for these purposes from 1930 to 1933.

265 Legend has it that in the early days of The Motor Company, at least into the 1930s, unusable or busted parts were thrown into a scrap pile by the railroad tracks behind the factory. These parts could be anything from a cylinder with a broken fin to a fender with a ding. Any part deemed unworthy of being put on an H-D motorcycle was simply tossed into a pile where it waited until it was hauled off to the scrap yard. People would sneak onto the railroad property and rummage through the parts for their own motorcycle or bicycle projects. Just imagine how much cool stuff was tossed aside as scrap!

266 Think it's a great job being a Harley-Davidson test rider? It is, but that doesn't mean it's not a difficult task. When testing motorcycles, which was managed from Milwaukee in the 1930s, test riders showed up to work, punched in, and were given their assignment for the day. It was their job to put on 200 miles, or achieve a specific target, on the motorcycle they were assigned for that day. Testing was carried out year-round in Wisconsin, and winter-weather testing usually involved sidecars and at the very least, windshields and warm, heavy outerwear. One test rider, "Hal" Deckert, said he was once told to run a shaft-drive V-twin without ever adding oil to see how long it took to seize. It was a dangerous job, and often miserable.

267 Have you visited the Harley-Davidson headquarters on Juneau Avenue, or any of the factories or museums? The Motor Company has encouraged customer visits from the time that the first Chestnut Avenue factory opened its doors. When times got tough in the early 1930s, it encouraged visitors simply as a way for them to put miles on their motorcycles and enjoy the simple, inexpensive sport, and then buy the necessary accessories such as saddlebags and a windshield. In 1933, Harley-Davidson opened its first visitor's room at the Juneau Avenue factory to further encourage long-distance touring. The room contained photos of The Motor Company's history as well as a display of the latest and greatest accessories and new motorcycle models. Today, that visitors room exists as the Harley-Davidson Museum, although the lobby of the Juneau Avenue building still has a friendly receptionist and various brand-new models on display.

268 When the Juneau Avenue factory was buzzing at full speed in the late 1930s, the parts machines created 80 tons of waste each month in the form of metal splinters, shavings, and lots of dust. The waste was piled up outside until it could be hauled off the premises.

269 One of the many production aspects that made Harley-Davidson motorcycles seem so indestructible was the extremely high level of inspection of every single part placed on every motorcycle. Some parts were checked to one-millionth of an inch for clearance!

270 Just because an engine number on a vintage Harley-Davidson is higher or lower than another one, even of the exact same model, that doesn't necessarily mean that it was built before or after another engine. The way that production worked was that a batch of a single type of engine was rolled into the production facility and those engines were then installed in motorcycles, in no particular order. Frequently, one batch of engines sat in the parts room while other engines of the same variety were used instead. Sometimes, a single engine needed to be repaired, and it wound up with a much later batch of motorcycles. Just because you own RL 1304 and your friend tries to one-up you by buying RL 1303, it doesn't necessarily mean that his was built first. In fact, RL 1350 might actually have been built earlier than RL 1303 and RL 1304! However, all engine numbers were recorded after the motorcycle's build was completed. Although that specific information likely no longer exists, when new, The Motor Company could have told you the exact day and time your motorcycle was built.

271 The Motor Company gave out *numbers* to general engine families, not specific letters. So, every 45 in a given year was on the same number line whether it was an R, RL, RLD, or RLDR. There's no serial number 1001 for each of them. This is also the case with the introduction of dual-displacement engines of the VL and VLH and later E, EL, F, and FL engines. This methodology can sometimes be confusing when it comes to identifying rare vintage examples.

272 One of Harley-Davidson's more ominous moments came with the distribution of the June 1941 issue of *The Enthusiast*, which announced that The Motor Company would, at the request of the U.S. government, no longer be giving factory tours "for the duration of the present emergency." Pearl Harbor was attacked just a few months later on December 7.

273 Even after the Great Depression, when motorcycle orders began coming in again after the low of 1933, Harley-Davidson decided on a policy of not building a motorcycle until an actual order was received from a dealer. Not only was management being as fiscally tight as possible with warehoused parts and bikes, but the optional paint schemes from the early 1930s made it difficult to stock completed motorcycles that customers might actually order. Production was still so far below capacity that it didn't take long to make a bike from scratch after the order arrived.

274 Although many workers were laid off throughout the course of the Great Depression, the Harley-Davidson founders cut their own pay in half to keep as much cash in the company as possible. The employees who did remain on full-time took pay cuts of between 10 and 15 percent.

275 To usher in the new era of Harley-Davidson motorcycle with the Flathead engine, The Motor Company staged a nationwide open house event on March 1, 1929, which is prime motorcycle-buying season for most of the country. More than 400 dealers shared the one-day event; they welcomed potential customers and previous customers into their shops to see all the new models. More than 50,000 people across the country visited local dealerships to see the new Harleys for themselves.

THE CHASSIS

276 Harley-Davidson finally crafted a worthwhile answer to Indian's Scout and released its own small-displacement Flathead V-twin in 1929. It was dubbed the model D with regular compression and the DL for the high-compression versions. The D followed the design of the J models, except with a shorter frame that had a 57-1/2-inch wheelbase and a longer neck section. A new fork was also used on the 1929 D that became a defining feature of H-Ds for the next 20 years. The external springs on the I-beam fork this design identify the first of what is now called the springer front end. At $290, the D was much cheaper than a J.

277 When the new 45-ci R engine was launched in 1932, an updated frame was also introduced. Unlike the D's straight downtube, this new frame has a curved front downtube. All of the 45 R and W models used this frame, with only minor changes. The only big change was in 1941, when the 45 solo and Servi-Car frames received a tab for a third transmission mounting bolt.

278 The model V replaced the J in 1930; It was introduced to the public just two months before the Black Tuesday stock market crash on October 24, 1929. The V didn't look very different from the J. However, its frame was stronger, it had a lower seat height, and it used the new I-beam springer fork seen on the D models. A pair of 19-inch spoked wheels with bigger, 4.00-inch-wide tires gave the V additional ground clearance; 4.40-inch-wide tires were optional. The V weighed 100 pounds more than the J; it used larger brakes to slow and stop the extra bulk.

279 Harley-Davidson made some crucial updates to its sidecar for 1930, and these certainly helped sales of the practical add-on during the difficult economic times. The new sidecar used a connected drum brake to allow the added weight to slow much more safely. At the same time, the new sidecar used a wheel that was interchangeable with the other two wheels; owners could rotate tires for even wear and longer tire life.

280 For 1934, the front and rear fenders gained additional coverage and style. The front fender skirts received a rounder profile with a stylish curve in the back. The rear fender was overhauled completely, including much deeper fender skirts that ran all the way down to behind the transmission. The rear pivoting section was upgraded with an "Airflow" taillight that featured a built-in, body-color housing. Before the Airflow, the taillight mounted to a metal bracket that stuck off the fender.

281 The UX tested so well that Harley-Davidson introduced the UL in 1937 in 74- and 80-ci varieties. They featured all of the latest and greatest technology first released to the public in the form of the 1936 EL. The UL combined the proven, reliable performance of H-D's Flathead design with all of the chassis innovations of the new EL, including a recirculating oil system. The U was most popular as a sidecar rig and for commercial duty.

282 A commercial-grade vehicle that was efficient, stable, and multi-capable was needed to replace the old-fashioned sidecar box concept. In 1932, Harley-Davidson unveiled what became one of its longest running models ever, the Servi-Car. Servi-Cars have one wheel in the front and two wheels in the rear with a large cargo box between them. The Servi-Cars' rear wheels were set 42 inches apart, the same as most cars of the day, so that they could operate in the same road grooves. A solid-axle rear end connected the rear wheels. An internal drum brake, borrowed from the larger 74, was built into the rear end; the usual right-side brake pedal stopped both rear wheels. Even though the Servi-Car was the same as its solo counterpart in front, the direct-steering method and stable platform made it easy for anyone who knew how to operate a car to hop onto and use a Servi-Car.

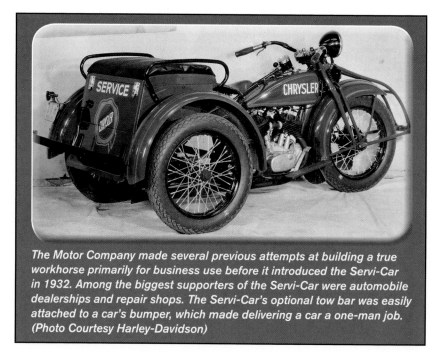

The Motor Company made several previous attempts at building a true workhorse primarily for business use before it introduced the Servi-Car in 1932. Among the biggest supporters of the Servi-Car were automobile dealerships and repair shops. The Servi-Car's optional tow bar was easily attached to a car's bumper, which made delivering a car a one-man job. (Photo Courtesy Harley-Davidson)

283 Back in 1932, the first Servi-Car box measured 29 inches wide, 23 inches long, and 12 inches high. The Tour-Pak on 2014-and-later Project Rushmore Harleys is almost the same size; it measures 27 inches wide, 21.6 inches long, and 13.7 inches high.

284 In 1931, in an effort to fulfill a need during the Great Depression, Harley-Davidson developed an efficient machine for road painting called the VCR (R for roadmarker). Using a VC sidecar platform as the base, the VCR replaced the sidecar with a platform that carried paint and an air compressor that powered the painting equipment. A small unit on the left side laid down the paint where the operator could monitor it; a boom extended off the sidecar frame to maintain the proper spacing.

285 Many Harley riders are couples that love to get out on the open road for time spent together with no distractions. Anybody who rides with a significant other knows and loves the feeling of a good arm-wrap. Harley-Davidson made it all possible in 1933 when Bill Harley and Frank Trispel invented the Buddy Seat. The Buddy Seat looks like an oversized one-person saddle, but the intent is that it can handle two people if the need arises. By today's luxurious two-up standards, the Buddy Seat was likely uncomfortable, but it allowed a couple to get close to each other while enjoying the motorcycle. Before the Buddy Seat, the passenger had to ride in a sidecar or on a separate seat mounted above the rear fender. Initially, the seat was sprung for one person; to adjust the suspension for two, a set of additional springs could be clipped on.

286 In 1937, all of the Flathead models received the same teardrop gas tanks with built-in speedometer and the dual-downtube frame that first appeared on the 1936 Knucklehead. This muscular, modern motorcycle look (the long, straight-frame backbone) has come to define the look of Harley-Davidson. Powertrain changes accompanied the new design and all of the Flatheads received new call letters. The RL became the WL, and the VL became the UL. Of course, the monster 80-ci version remained in the lineup and became the ULH.

287 Harley-Davidson's paint has long been one of the many notable "best in the business" aspects of its motorcycles. Around 1935, the factory implemented a painting booth system known as the water wash system. Instead of a standard building wall, the water wash system created a cascading flow of water, much like a waterfall. Water sat in a reservoir at the bottom of the wall, and then was pumped up and out a thin nozzle at the top. A fan sucked air toward the water, and any excess paint from the spray gun was blown into the wall of water where it was trapped. It was therefore unable to stick to the newly painted part.

288 There wasn't a whole lot of glitz and glam during the depression years, but people still tried to do what they could to enjoy luxuries on a budget. This is one of the reasons why factory custom paint offerings were so popular; they let you stand out from the crowd, for not a whole lot of extra money. Another popular option was the chrome-plated package. In 1933, it added $15 and made your art deco paint scheme stand out even more. The chrome-plated package included handlebars, chain guard, exhaust system, and a handful of other parts that made a utilitarian Flathead glisten in the sun.

289 Although the Flathead models remained nearly unchanged for the 1936 model year, Harley-Davidson unveiled an all-new sidecar. The earlier sidecars were styled to match the antiquated JD models, but the new sidecars were heavily modernized. The door was removed in favor of a simple step, and a windshield kept the occupant comfortable on the highway. Stainless steel trim was added and pinstripes ran around the side of the body. The pairing of the two was rather awkward. The new sidecar would have actually paired best with the 1936 EL Knucklehead, but that motorcycle wasn't originally meant to work with a sidecar.

290 Several versions of the Servi-Car were offered from the factory for different uses, even though the differences between them aren't always immediately noticeable. The model G was equipped with a small box and tow bar; the GA had a small box and no tow bar; the GD used a large box and no tow bar; and the GE was fitted with a large box, tow bar, and an air tank. In 1933, the GDT was added to the mix for shops that wanted both a large capacity box and a tow bar. In 1942, all Servi-Car boxes became the same size, which was between the original large and small boxes.

291 Until 1930, Harley-Davidson horns resembled the air horns on freight trains more closely than the small, flat electric horns found on the motorcycles today. In 1931, the big black horn underneath the headlight became a small, round, chrome horn that bolted to the front of the toolbox. This style of horn lasted in its front and center position on the fork until the springer fork went out of service in each respective family of Big Twins, WLs, and Servi-Cars. Today, that same style of horn is available as a parts and accessories item to give a vintage flair to your ride's left side.

Although most motorcyclists rarely use the horn, Harley-Davidson upgraded the electric horn and made it much easier and safer to do so. Before this, a rider had to compress a hand pump to make a noise. This required taking a hand off the handlebar, presumably just as something dangerous is happening. The electric horn requires merely pressing a button on the handlebar without even taking a hand off the grip.

292 When people really began to use their Harleys for a variety of business and pleasure purposes, they found that the factory suspension setup wasn't always well suited to the needs of the task at hand. To add adjustability to a springer front end, the engineers added a friction damper that consisted of plates on either side of the springs with a knob that could compress and release the springs. Consider it an early form of preload adjustment, whereby a rider could tune his bike's front suspension for different weight and/or sidecar use.

293 Along with the 1934 fender updates, Flatheads also received a new, rectangular toolbox. On the Big Twins, the new toolbox was positioned on the right side, between the upper and lower frame rails, just aft of the oil tank. On the 45 Flatties, it was mounted on the left side, opposite the drive chain. As with earlier models, it had a lock, and was large enough for tools and a few small spare parts. The same style of toolbox was used until World War II, after which a shapely, streamlined box replaced it.

294 In 1934, Harley-Davidson updated the hinges on its fenders to promote better structural rigidity and to support the additional weight of the new built-in taillight. The old system simply used three bolts on each fender, which mounted in the center. The hinge bracket was quite narrow and allowed flex when opening and closing. The new setup used mounting brackets that stretched over the entire inner width of the fender but only used two bolts on either side. The hinge was about twice as wide, although it looks cleaner and neater.

295 Harley-Davidson had been manufacturing its own sidecars for many years. However, when it introduced the 45-ci small twin in 1929, it decided to use an outside supplier for smaller, lightweight sidecars. The Motor Company contacted the Goulding Manufacturing Co. in Saginaw, Michigan, to design the chassis; the Abresch Body Co. in Milwaukee built the bodies. The chassis received "LS" model designation, which was short for "Litecar Sidecar."

296 Although they appear similar at first glance, there are a few notable differences between the springer front ends on 45s and Big Twins. The 45s use a smaller, 7/8-inch neck stem as opposed to the 1-1/8-inch neck stem on Big Twins. The front fender on the Big Twins is mounted to the sprung fork tube so that the fender rides with the front wheel and can be mounted closer to it. The fender on the 45s is mounted to the rear, solid fork tube so that the wheel bobs beneath it and there's a healthy gap between the two.

297 If thieves really want to steal your motorcycle, they'll be able to figure out a way, no matter how many locks you have on it. But every little bit of preventative security deters bike thieves just enough to make them rethink stealing your particular motorcycle. In 1930, Harley-Davidson took its first step toward security when it began adding steering head locks to the frame neck castings. Even though a robber could still lift the front of the bike and roll it away on the rear wheel, that's certainly a lot more complicated than just kicking up the Jiffy Stand and rolling it away.

298 For the ultimate storing and maintenance capabilities, Harley-Davidson offered a front stand that was available on almost every export model, and optional on domestic bikes. The front stand worked in the same way as the rear stand: it swung down from the front fender and held the wheel up off the ground so that a tire could be changed easily.

299 Most of the parts that were used on the earliest 1929 D models were carried over from the previous single-cylinder models. Because of the miscalculation in the 45's popularity, or its power, The Motor Company had to scramble to reengineer almost every part of the bike over the coming years. One such part that was far too weak for the 45's power and weight was the brakes. Harley-Davidson changed the brakes and wheels on the 45 six times from 1929 to 1935; the final renditions lasted until the 45's demise in 1952.

300 Imagine buying a new Harley-Davidson and not being able to ride it at low speeds with all of the lights on. Sounds crazy, right? But that's how it was in the early days of generators and battery-powered accessories. The 1929 DL, had the "third cylinder" upright generator that could only put out about 6 amps to recharge the battery. This was fine during the day when the ignition system didn't draw much, but two headlights, a taillight, and an instrument light required the full 6 amps. If you had a sidecar with running lights, they added another half an amp each. A 1929 company bulletin actually says that riding with all of the lights on at less than 20 mph, would put the system at 3 to 4 amps over the maximum discharge rate; the battery would be fully discharged in 4 to 5 hours.

THE POWERTRAIN

301 The 45-ci Flathead engine, introduced in 1929, is one of the simplest but most vital engines ever produced. It was used in motorcycles for 44 years in a relatively unchanged form and served as a low-cost workhorse for businesses during the Great Depression, fought in combat all over the world, and even ran to Victory Lane at Daytona. The first 45 was known as a D with regular compression and 15 hp. The DL high-compression, 18-1/2-hp version featured four cams, with each driving its own valve. In 1930, the super high-compression DLD was released, which used a larger carburetor and made 20 hp.

302 Unlike the F head that had the intake valve on the top, Flatheads have both intake and exhaust valves on the side; the head is essentially flat and without a single moving part. An upright generator in front and to the left of the forward cylinder distinguishes an early 45 very easily. In 1931, a super-high-compression version, the DLD, was introduced. The smaller V-twin's popularity led to the creation of the Sportster, a perpetually popular namesake among the Harley faithful.

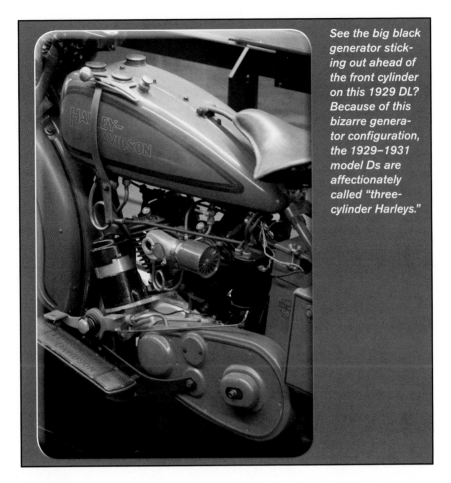

See the big black generator sticking out ahead of the front cylinder on this 1929 DL? Because of this bizarre generator configuration, the 1929–1931 model Ds are affectionately called "three-cylinder Harleys."

303 After just a few years of production, it became clear to H-D executives that the VL needed to be replaced with a more technologically advanced motorcycle with a more modern design. We now consider the Knucklehead engine to be an ingenious feat of engineering, with its OHV design and recirculating oil system. However, many customers in the mid-1930s weren't sold on the new technology, especially with some of the EL's early teething issues. Therefore, the VL was continued for an additional model year into 1936, to not alienate any potential buyers. The Motor Company was secretly working on a backup plan, just in case the EL turned out to be a dud. Using the EL's new chassis and components, engineers went to work developing an 80-ci Flathead engine that featured a recirculating oil system and was tucked neatly into the EL's chassis to work with the new 4-speed transmission. That motorcycle became known as the UX (X for experimental); and six were produced for testing. Of the six, three survive and all are on display at Wheels Through Time museum.

304 Just in case the modern styling and technology on the 1936 EL was too much, a buyer could still purchase a 1936 Big Twin Flathead with a single downtube frame and the old hand-operated manual oil pump. However, to keep up with the performance of the EL, The Motor Company created the VLH Flathead, an 80-ci high-compression version of the VL. Making 34 hp at 4,000 rpm, and available with a 3- or 4-speed transmission, the VLH marks the pinnacle of Harley-Davidson's early history.

305 Even with a new small-displacement V-twin appealing to budget-oriented riders, Harley-Davidson continued its single-cylinder program, which saw most of its success overseas. Along

Harley-Davidson produced the Thirty-Fifty single in both Flathead and overhead valve (OHV) varieties. While it was hardly the technological phenomenon that the 1936 EL was, you can see the OHV version here sporting dual cams. It would take The Motor Company another 75 years to build an OHV two-cam.

with the D and DL, it released the 30.50-ci model C, which quickly earned the nickname "Thirty-Fifty"; it was Milwaukee's biggest single to date. Making upward of 10 hp, the vertical Flathead single could propel a rider to 60 mph. The Thirty-Fifty was produced until 1934.

306 Like its smaller stablemate, the model D, the 74-ci V used a Flathead, or sidevalve, design with removable heads and four camshafts, one for each valve. The high-compression VL made 30 hp with a low 4-1/2:1 compression ratio, which was typical for Flatheads. The base V produced 28 hp. In 1930, Vs were available with a battery and 22-amp electrical system (V and VL) or with a magneto and generator (VM and VLM).

307 We now know that Harley-Davidson's Flatheads were some of the most dependable and easy-to-own vintage motorcycles. However, when the 1930 74-ci V was launched, it had teething issues all over the place. In fact, it was so bad that the company actually halted sales and production of the V for almost four months to fix the problems and send new parts to dealers. Customers were plagued with weaknesses in the clutch, flywheel, valvesprings, lubrication system, and pistons, in addition to poorly designed mufflers. Part of the overall fix was a set of larger flywheels, which meant the crankcase had to be larger, too. Not just that, but the frame was redesigned to fit the new, larger crankcase. 1,300 motorcycles had to be rebuilt, and the individual dealerships were stuck with the labor cost. Just what The Motor Company needed at the beginning of the Great Depression, right?

308 In 1932, The Motor Company unveiled a significantly updated 45-ci engine that changed the D model to the R model. The most obvious change is the mounting position of the generator; it's mounted horizontally in front of the front cylinder rather than vertically. New cylinders for better heat dissipation appeared on both the V and R models in 1932, as did an additional clutch plate and friction disc. The larger clutch meant that 1932 and later Flatheads also received a redesigned clutch cover. Larger flywheels and longer connecting rods improved horsepower in the RL and RLD to 19 and 22 hp, respectively, while compression remained the same from the DL and DLD. All models also received a new, more efficient oil pump in 1932.

309 High-performance enthusiasts, such as those who bought JDHs in 1928 and 1929 scoffed at the new Flatheads from day one. Flatheads were dependable touring machines that provided a comfortable ride at speed, but they lacked the response and sporting feel of the race-ready pocket-valve two-cam. These riders likely expected something more along the lines of the Knucklehead in 1930 rather than the same-old design that Indian had been using for years. They got their wish in 1934 with the VLD that, with a 5.0:1 compression ratio, produced 36 hp at 4,500 rpm. But the VLD wasn't just about the compression. It used new, aluminum alloy pistons along with a new head design, both of which helped with compression and heat dissipation. But air/fuel is also a key factor to power, and the engineers gave the VLH a special Y-shaped manifold to which a new brass Linkert carburetor was mounted. Moreover, by 1934, the exhaust problems were completely solved and machines were equipped with a single, high-flowing fishtail muffler.

310 Harley-Davidson introduced its first 4-speed transmission as an option in 1935. It became standard fare on the EL Knucklehead upon its debut in 1936 and came with all Flathead Big Twins for 1937 The 45s continued to use the 3-speed; sidecar machines with either Big Twin used a 3-speed plus reverse.

311 In 1937, as a cost-saving measure, Harley-Davidson lengthened the stroke on the 74-ci U models to match that of its 80-ci counterpart while simultaneously reducing the bore to match that of the 61-ci Knucklehead. This allowed the E and the U to use the same pistons, even though they were very different machines.

312 When the Servi-Car was introduced in 1932, it used the same 45-ci Flathead and 3-speed transmission that was found in the solo R models. Power was transferred from the transmission to the rear end by way of a single chain, which drove a differential powering both wheels. With the wider frame in the way, Servi-Car transmissions used an extended kickstarter, which placed the lever comfortably between the frame and fender when depressed. Early on, the Motor Company realized the Servi-Car's major downfall. It was nearly impossible to back up the heavy machine. A reverse gear was introduced to the 3-speed in 1933 and used through the end of Servi-Car production; it was also added to sidecar models.

313 As businesses and police departments discovered weak areas, Harley-Davidson beefed up the Servi-Car's components, seemingly every year. In 1937, a second drum brake was added on the rear end to double stopping power; the following year, the drive chain was enclosed, keeping the rider and rolling billboard clean. In 1939, the tow bar was strengthened and permanently mounted to the front end, instead of being attached and removed after each use. The Servi-Car also received a stronger axle housing in 1940 followed by a new frame and welded axle in 1941.

314 The Motor Company warmed over its Big Twin Flatheads in 1940 with standard aluminum heads on the 80, which were optional on the 74. The aluminum heads weighed 5 pounds less than the cast-iron heads and provided better heat dissipation. In addition, a quieter, more efficient "rocket-fin" muffler was added.

315 Harley-Davidson offered a reverse gear for the first time on VLs built after April 1931. The motorcycles had become so heavy that they were nearly impossible to push backward, especially with the popular addition of a sidecar. An entirely new transmission was designed to house the additional gear. The forward gears remained unchanged, except that neutral was relocated to between first and reverse, instead of its traditional location between first and second.

316 Remember the Ricardo-designed heads that The Motor Company used on its sidevalve single in the late 1920s? It continued that head design on the V-twin Flatheads as well, and used the

Ricardo name in marketing and promotional correspondence. In those days, burning oil was a part of running an engine, and fuel lacked consistent quality. Therefore, IOE cylinder heads and piston tops often had built-up carbon deposits that caused the piston and head to make contact. A nearly complete disassembly of the top end was required to clean both parts. By 1929, not much had changed in fuel and oil technology so one of the biggest advantages to a side-valve engine was the ease with which the cylinder heads could be removed and cleaned. The valves, the squish chamber, and piston are also all right there and can be cleaned easily in a matter of minutes. This made the Flatheads very easy to maintain.

317 Have you ever wondered what you would do if you ran out of gas and there was no gas station for miles? That happened to Bill Davidson Jr. and Bill Harley Jr. while trekking cross-country on their 1929 DL with sidecar. They walked up to a nearby farmhouse and, because no one was there, left some money, took a canister of something that smelled like gas, and filled up their Flathead with it. It turned out that the mystery fuel was a kerosene-like stove gas, and, with some popping and sputtering to contend with, they were able to run their Flathead to the nearest town to fill up with real automotive fuel. Please don't take this as a recommendation to fill your brand new CVO Breakout with kerosene if you run out of fuel. But if you are running an antique Flathead, you might just get away with it!

318 With the 1937 model year came the updated technology first seen on the OHV Knucklehead the previous year. All Flatheads were treated to the automatic recirculating oil system that didn't leak oil onto the primary (by design) and didn't require the rider to hand-pump oil into the crankcase when the engine was under heavy load. As part of these changes, the oil tank was moved from inside the gas tank (on Big Flatties only) to the familiar horseshoe tank that sits under the seat and wraps around the battery. For the 45s, the oil tank was moved to the right side of the gas tank, where a decal was placed beside the cap that read "OIL." The Big Twin Flatheads were also given the EL's 4-speed transmission; it replaced the 3-speed, which continued to be a hallmark of the 45 model line.

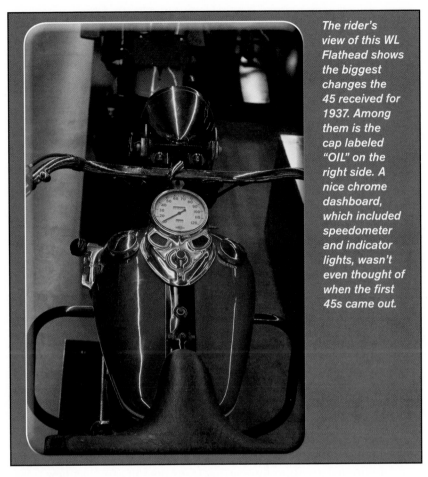

The rider's view of this WL Flathead shows the biggest changes the 45 received for 1937. Among them is the cap labeled "OIL" on the right side. A nice chrome dashboard, which included speedometer and indicator lights, wasn't even thought of when the first 45s came out.

319 One of the biggest failures in the Flathead engine line was piston wear. The piston skirts became so hot that they often seized inside the cylinder after a high-RPM run. Bill Harley and Ed Kieckbusch developed a new piston in 1939 that resisted heating; it was so different that they received a new patent for it. The new piston used a steel strut spread across the inside of the piston that expanded at a much lower rate than the rest of the aluminum piston. This strut greatly reduced expansion of the cylinder walls, which completely solved the problem of pistons seizing. With the newly designed pistons, Flatheads could be run with a significant amount of reliability. It's not quite clear if the change was made for the diminishing Flathead customer, or for the order of 90,000

WLA Flatheads that The Motor Company would be building for the military just a couple of years later. Reliability was of utmost importance for that particular order.

320 When Harley-Davidson changed the RL Flathead to the updated, recirculating-oil WL, it moved the ignition timer from underneath the right-side oil pump cover and made it a stand-alone unit that sat on top of the engine case. The round timer housing is topped with a chrome cover that sits upright above the cam cover. The WL's new automatic oil pump is visible on the finned cam cover, instead of hidden behind a cover, as it was on previous models.

321 The first D-model 45-ci Flatheads to use sidecars in 1929 used a huge 1:6.05 transmission gear ratio in high gear. The Motor Company must not have had enough faith in its durable little twin that first year, because that ratio was dropped to 1:5.45 for the 1930 models. The rear drive sprocket was also changed from a 40-tooth unit in 1929 to a 36-tooth sprocket in 1930.

322 Harley-Davidson used three different transmissions between 1929 and 1937. Not just different gears, but entirely different units. When The Motor Company realized that a reverse gear was needed for Servi-Car and sidecar models, it was impossible to fit an additional gear into the existing transmission case, so a new transmission was developed in 1933; it ran side-by-side with the original 1929 3-speed for two years. In 1935, H-D, disliking the redundancy of building two different transmission cases with identical mounting parts and almost identical internals, developed a new transmission that could be built with or without a reverse gear. The latest version was a copy of the reverse-gear tranny of 1933, except that a spacing collar could be swapped in instead of the reverse gear for solo models.

323 In the middle of 1933, Harley-Davidson changed carburetor makes from Schebler to Linkert and used them on 1934-and-later twins. The new Linkert carbs performed better and provided a longer service life. To promote the advantage of the new Linkert carburetors, H-D ran a special exchange offer in 1936. Anyone with an earlier Schebler carburetor could turn it in to their dealer and receive a brand-new Linkert for only $9.

324 You know that fuel consumption is denoted as "miles per gallon," but in the 1930s, that also described oil consumption. And, just like fuel use, the faster you rode your Flathead, the more oil you'd burn! Regarding the RL, specifically, traveling at around 38 mph on flat road, you should expect to get approximately 1,000 mpg. For oil, that is! That number dropped considerably as road speed increased. If you were traveling more than 55 mph, you'd likely average less than 400 mpg of oil. On modern Harleys that cruise comfortably at 80, that's comparable to completely refilling the oil tank at every gas stop!

325 In 1936, when Flatheads were only one year away from an entirely new recirculating oil engine, they received a somewhat strange engine update. Harley-Davidson gave the RL model new heads and cylinders. The new heads bolted on with eight head bolts instead of the previous seven, hence the new eight-stud cylinders. Also, the head fins were larger and reshaped into a "V" pattern for better cooling and airflow movement.

PEOPLE AND POP CULTURE

326 Clark Gable was a well-known motorcycle and automobile enthusiast. In 2007, his beautifully restored 1934 RL went up for auction and sold for $70,200 including premium, making it the most expensive street 45-ci Flathead ever sold at auction. The auction even included the original title with Gable's name. The motorcycle is not in a museum, but rather (as of this writing) on display at Kiehl's cosmetics shop on 13th Street and 3rd Avenue in New York City. Kiehl's displays a motorcycle in almost all of its shops; many are Harleys.

327 In the early 1930s, and with decades of hard work behind them, the company founders began to enjoy the fruits of their labors. However, they never forgot an early lesson that they learned from Margaret Davidson, which was to give back to the people and community, which had given them so much. In addition to the many charitable organizations to which the founders donated money, Arthur Davidson chose to buy a large plot of land outside Milwaukee and donate it to the Boy Scouts of America. To honor his generosity, the Boy Scouts named it Camp Arthur Davidson. The land remains a park today, as Arthur intended; it's now the site of the Franklin Woods Nature Center. In 1933, Arthur also donated another plot of land just north of Milwaukee to the Boy Scouts; it was sold five years later and became what is now Brown Deer Park.

328 After school let out for the summer in 1929, some of the founders' sons wanted a little more adventure than working at the factory would allow. Gordon Davidson, his brother Walter C. Davidson, and their cousin Allan Davidson decided that they wanted to see the country by motorcycle. At the time, Gordon was 17 but Walter and Allan were only 16. They received their fathers' blessings, but part of the deal that their fathers insisted on was that the trip had to include stopping at dealerships along the way. They were to show off the durability of the new 45-ci Flathead and as a way to introduce dealers to the next generation of the Harley-Davidson family. The route covered 13,000 miles and took the boys to California, Mexico, Canada, and back to Wisconsin. What a great way to test out the new DLs!

329 Allan, Gordon, and Walter C. lived a truly great adventure that summer, and enjoyed many crazy activities that can happen on a road trip. Each dealer tried to outdo the previous in terms of the activities planned for the boys. The dealer in Los Angeles arranged a ride in the (now famous) Goodyear blimp and they had an airplane ride in Seattle. The dealer in New Mexico showed the boys quite a time when he took them across the border to Mexico. That would have been the experience of a lifetime for a trio of teenagers from Milwaukee.

330 Bill Davidson and Bill J. Harley met up with the three in Denver, aboard a brand-new 1930 74 V equipped with a sidecar. While in Denver, the five H-D heirs met with Colorado's governor at the capitol, who gave them a note to be delivered to the Wisconsin governor, at the capitol building in Madison. So, not only were they promoting their brand and conducting business, but they also took part in strengthening political relationships between the states. Not bad for a summer's road trip!

331 Harley-Davidson held its 1935 dealer meeting at the Schroeder Hotel in Milwaukee, where it unveiled the new OHV Knucklehead motorcycle. According to Jean Davidson, in her book, *Growing Up Harley-Davidson*, the dealers loved the bike, and knew right away that The Motor Company was back in business after the long, slow years of the Great Depression. In fact, Jean says that one dealer, Bill "Cactus" Kennedy from Phoenix, Arizona, was so excited about the new model, that he pulled out his revolver in the middle of the dining hall and began shooting at the ceiling and the crystal chandelier while shouting, "Yippee!"

332 Vivian Bales traded her Harley-Davidson in for a new 1929 model D as soon as they became available and took off on a

Vivian Bales, otherwise known as "The Enthusiast Girl," gave people a different picture of exactly who a Harley-Davidson rider was. Not only did this 20-year-old "Georgia Peach" have an infectious smile, she was a real rider, which was more important. Harley-Davidson has a long history of supporting women riders, dating back even before Ms. Bales. (Photo Courtesy Harley-Davidson)

5,000-mile tour. She was featured on the cover of *The Enthusiast* after her trip and was given the nickname, "The Enthusiast Girl," by Harley-Davidson, which sent sweaters with this written in large letters across the front. Vivian left her hometown of Albany, Georgia, on June 1, 1929, and spent the next 78 days traveling to the Harley-Davidson factory in Milwaukee and then continuing on to Canada, New York, and Washington, D.C. before heading home. The Motor Company didn't formally sponsor the trip but it did arrange for hospitality for Vivian at dealerships along the way, including fuel, food, and accommodations. Vivian was only 20 years old at the time.

333 Upon her arrival in Washington, D.C., Vivian Bales' home state's senator, William J. Harris, introduced her to President Herbert Hoover. Her ride was a huge success for The Motor Company in terms of public relations. Arthur Davidson even referred to her as "the Georgia Peach."

334 In 1935, Earl and Dot Robinson set the transcontinental sidecar record when they rode from Los Angeles to New York City in 89 hours 58 minutes! That's less than four days. They completed the trip on a 1935 VL with a Goulding sidecar attached. What else would they use? Dot's father was Jim Goulding, creator of his namesake sidecar! Earl and Dot took turns driving and resting in the sidecar, although they both admitted that Dot did at least 60 percent of the driving, including one 12-hour stretch through a rainstorm. They claimed the secret to their mechanical success was that they filled the VL with nothing but Harley-Davidson oil!

335 Earl Robinson had some previous experience with transcontinental records; he set the record from New York City to Los Angeles on his 1935 RL the previous week. He did that trip in 77 hours 53 minutes, just over three days and, he did the entire run himself. To put both of these records in perspective, these were pre-Interstate, pre-quick-fuel rest area, and pre-GPS days on motorcycles with no rear suspension; Earl averaged nearly 1,000-mile days on his 45!

336 Although European motorcycles had been around just as long as the American brands, only a handful of machines were imported into the United States prior to World War II. And I do mean a handful. In 1931, 35 motorcycles were imported from Europe (23 from England and 12 from Germany), which was close to the 41 imported in 1920. By comparison, Harley-Davidson exported 37,000 motorcycles in 1920, and continued to export about 55 percent of its total production into 1931. Exports were one of the biggest saving graces at the onset of the Great Depression, although they were hardly enough to keep the company afloat, much less profitable. Interestingly, Harley-Davidson petitioned the U.S. government to lower tariff rates on imported motorcycles because their numbers were so miniscule and the company hoped that favorable tariffs in the United States might lead to favorable tariffs for its exports.

337 In the 1930s, Australia was one of the biggest importers of Harley-Davidsons, just as it is today. The road system and terrain are similar to the United States, and a durable, heavy-duty Harley-Davidson was, and still is, the motorcycle of choice Down Under. Initially, American bikes had only a 20-percent-higher tariff in Australia than their British counterparts, which the Aussies gladly paid. At the beginning of the global economic crisis of the early 1930s, Australia, as part of the British Empire, brought the tariff on British motorcycles down to zero, and bumped the tariff on American motorcycles to a full 20 percent. However, the Harleys continued to sell well. Then the Empire dropped the hammer, and jacked the tariffs up 50 percent on all motorcycles. The duties on British motorcycles remained at zero, while American bikes' duties were levied at 30 percent. This crushed Harley-Davidson's export business at the time it needed the sales the most.

338 The Milwaukee Electric Railway and Light Company's bus and streetcar system workers went on strike in 1934, virtually shutting down public transportation in Milwaukee. On the first day of the strike, Harley-Davidson's executives, including the founders, offered rides home to employees who had found themselves stranded with no public transportation.

339 Milwaukee Harley-Davidson dealer Bill Knuth came up with the concept for Knuth's Kollege in 1932 as a way to educate Harley riders about maintenance, repair, riding, and other general upkeep of their motorcycles. During the Great Depression, many motorcyclists skipped important maintenance procedures simply because money was so tight, but they often ended up with a far greater problem. Clubs and individual riders alike attended Knuth's Kollege, which was instructed by H-D employees "Hap" Jameson and John Nowak. It could hardly be considered a technical school like the factory's Service School, but it did provide owners with the information they needed to make better decisions regarding their motorcycles

340 Franklin Delano Roosevelt was sworn in as the 32nd President of the United States of America in 1933. And how did this effect Harley-Davidson? One of Roosevelt's first orders of business was repealing the Volstead Act to end prohibition. The first repeal, the Cullen-Harrison Act, went into effect in April 1933. It weaned Americans back onto alcohol by allowing up to a 3.2 percent alcohol content in beer and wine. Just like that, Milwaukee's local economy was kickstarted and its beer was sent all over the country. After struggling for such a long time, many Milwaukeeans had newfound jobs and money in their pockets, which they could spend on new Harley-Davidson motorcycles.

341 Many European countries followed Great Britain's high tariff lead in the 1930s to encourage sales of their own products. It was no longer profitable for Harley-Davidson's importers to continue to move motorcycles, and, by 1934, only Belgium and parts of Scandinavia were still importing H-Ds. Globally, Africa and several South American countries also continued to import Harleys, likely because they had no motorcycle industries to impact.

342 Who better to sell Harley-Davidsons than the people who ride them? The Motor Company had that very thought in 1931 when it initiated a marketing program that gave bronze, silver, and gold medals to regular customers who convinced friends, family, neighbors, *anybody*, to buy a 1931 Harley-Davidson. The person responsible for the most motorcycles sold received a sizeable cash prize.

343 Motor Officer Bill Curry of the Topeka, Kansas, police department is known as one of the fastest parking enforcers in the country, checking and marking cars from the seat of his Servi-Car. In 1942, he was even featured in Robert Ripley's "Believe-It-Or-Not" column after Curry claimed that he could check and mark between 16,000 and 18,000 parked cars a day, which works out to almost five million cars a year! A representative from Ripley's was sent to Topeka to fact check Curry's claim, and, after following him in a car at 20 mph while the motor officer chalked up cars, he was able to confirm the claim in only a few hours. The people of Topeka probably weren't Curry's biggest fans, but the rest of the country enjoyed listening to him on Robert Ripley's radio show and reading about him in the column.

344 Pan Am (World) Airways is a cultural icon of the 20th Century. It came to prominence when air travel was enjoyed with a cocktail, a beautiful stewardess, and a free travel bag. Pan Am also served as a postal carrier and it excelled at rush deliveries. The reason for such prompt delivery service had nothing to do with the latest and greatest aircraft, however, but with the fact that Pan Am employed WL Package Truck sidecar rigs to deliver rush packages straight from the tarmac to the recipients' front door. They were labeled with the appropriate blue globe (the "Blue Meatball") logo on the box.

345 Dick Dale, who many consider "The King of Surf Rock," also happened to ride a pretty mean Harley-Davidson around the streets of Southern California. The bike was a 1941 WL with a psychedelic paint job and ape hanger handlebars. The bike had no front fender, a homemade two-up seat, and a straight exhaust with a big fishtail on the back. This was no shop build, either, he did most of the work himself and he even machined the dog bone–style risers for the handlebars.

346 Believe it or not, but the sport of motorcycle polo was actually a popular pastime in the 1930s among more affluent motorcycle riders. Polo teams were made up of local motorcycle clubs that competed with clubs from different neighborhoods. One such club was the Three-Point Club based on Hollywood, California; it was known to attract local celebrities to events aboard their Harley-Davidsons.

347 Jack Nicholson proved that you don't need a Big Twin, or even one with overhead valves, to be cool when he starred as Bunny in the 1970 biker film *The Rebel Rousers*. He rode a hot little 45 bobber with massive trumpet exhaust pipes sticking up 4 or 5 feet over the back fender. *The Rebel Rousers* was actually filmed in 1967, but it wasn't released until after *Easy Rider* (with Nicholson) became a huge hit.

348 The 2011 film, *The Rum Diary,* starring Johnny Depp also starred a mid-1940s WL Flathead with an aftermarket sidecar. Unlike other actors throughout the years who played bikers on TV, Depp is actually a rider and rode the Harley around when it wasn't being used for filming. Hunter S. Thompson, whose name became synonymous with California's outlaw motorcycle culture, wrote the novel, *The Rum Diary*.

349 In the middle of The Great Depression, Harley-Davidson needed to sell some motorcycles badly. In 1932, the company discovered that when it comes to selling bikes, sex sells. With 1933 looking even worse than 1932, The Motor Company came out with one of the sexiest paint schemes ever applied to one of its motorcycles: the Eagle's Head gas tank decal. That wasn't enough, so The Motor Company turned to some female sex appeal and took a 1933 VL sidecar and a 1933 RL solo (both with Eagle graphics) to Milwaukee's Bradford Beach for a little photo shoot. A couple of models in bathing suits accompanied them and posed on the bikes. The shots included the well-known image of one of the women pulling off the shoulder straps of her bathing suit. The only image actually used by The Motor Company at the time was a shot of the two women, along with two men, having a picnic on the beach alongside their motorcycles. This image was on the cover of the July 1933 issue of *The Enthusiast*.

350 In 2014, author and female motorcycling ambassador Cris Sommer Simmons rode her 1934 Harley-Davidson VL on the Motorcycle Cannonball Endurance Run, but, unfortunately, mechanical problems caused her to finish early on day one and miss days two and three. After that, her bike ran perfectly for the next ten days, covering more than 3,000 miles across the country. The bike's previous owner would be proud, as her VL, nicknamed "Buddy," belonged to none other than legendary Hollywood stuntman Bud Ekins, from whom Cris bought it in 1993.

MILITARY, POLICE AND RACING

351 While Bill Davidson and Bill J. Harley were in Colorado, on their cross-country adventure, they visited the Pikes Peak Hill Climb races to show off the new 74 and sidecar to the spectators. No one had seen the new Big Twin Flathead yet; the 74 and the sidecar impressed everyone. Quite possibly caught up in being the center of attention at the event, as only teenage boys can be, they decided to give their stock 74 a run up the hill: sidecar, passenger, and all! Even though they weren't actually competing for anything, the fact the bike actually made it up is still pretty impressive.

352 After a successful 13,000-mile trip covering the best and worst that the West had to offer, Gordon, Bill, and Walter C. Davidson, along with Bill J. Harley decided to attempt the physically, mechanically, and emotionally challenging Jack Pine Enduro held near Lansing, Michigan. It was the most difficult test of man and machine at the time and easily on par with the Baja 1,000 and Paris-Dakar events of the modern era. That event convinced Gordon to give up his dreams of competitive racing, but Bill Davidson went on to win the event with 997 points of the possible 1,000. In another display of loyalty among the Harley-Davidson clan, Bill Davidson's watch, a necessary item to time progress in an endurance event,

The founders' sons followed in their fathers' footsteps when it came to taking part in The Harley-Davidson Motor Company. Here, Bill Davidson, Jr., is aboard a 1930 DL at that year's Jack Pine endurance challenge, which he won. (Photo Courtesy Harley-Davidson)

broke partway through the event; Bill J. Harley took the wristwatch off his own hand and gave it to him, all but ruining his own chances of winning the race

353 Milwaukee Harley-Davidson dealer Bill Knuth led a serious hillclimb race team out of his shop. He provided racers with a tuned machine and, in turn, they supported him with a percentage of the winnings. Bill Knuth was a friend of the Harley-Davidson founders, and enjoyed a special relationship with the factory as the company's most important hometown dealership. His name has become legendary in the antique motorcycle collector world because of one particular OHV 45 Flathead that he built. He took rare 21-ci OHV cylinders found on the Peashooter and mounted them to the 45's bottom end. The only other team with that engine was Harley-Davidson's own factory team, which has led some to suggest that there was some factory involvement with Bill Knuth's racing endeavors.

354 Bill Ottaway's racing department was eager to get its hands on the new 45. They knew immediately that the way to make the most power from this engine was to convert it to an overhead valvetrain. The DAH factory hillclimber, which debuted at Pittsburgh in July 1929, proved them right. It's believed that 25 examples were produced in the early 1930s for hillclimb use only. Joe Petrali and Herb Reiber rode machines that used double downtube frames and trailing link forks, although it's unknown how many of these were originally built.

355 In late 1935, Harley-Davidson built a handful of 80-ci VLDD Pursuit Specials. This stroked version of the potent VLD added prototype aluminum heads to its increased displacement to make one mean mount for a motor officer. It's known that the California Highway Patrol used some.

356 The AMA held the first Class C National Championship race on February 22, 1934 in Jacksonville, Florida. The winner of the first-ever Class C race, a 200-mile event, was Bremen Sykes of Savannah, Georgia, on a Harley-Davidson.

357 Without a formal racing program during the Great Depression, Harley-Davidson built and sold race bikes to privateers to keep the Bar & Shield logo visible on the tracks of America. In 1935, The Motor Company offered the RLDR for Class C competition. The RLDR had a 6:1 compression ratio that helped it achieve an estimated 25 hp.

358 In 1935, Joe Petrali, riding Harley-Davidson's Peashooter, took first place at all 13 AMA National Championship dirt track races that year. In the process, he broke four records, and was the first man in dirt track history to win all of the races in a single series aboard the same brand of motorcycle.

359 Police departments around the country loved the Servi-Car for the added versatility for parking enforcers. Because they could operate it safely at slow speeds, departments placed two riders on the machine; the officer in front drove and the officer in back used his chalk stick to mark car tires. It was a lot faster than walking and ticket writing was that much more efficient. And when they had to empty a full meter, the Servi-Car's trunk and heavy-duty suspension could handle a full load of coins.

360 Even though Harley-Davidson sold its VL design and tooling to the Sankyo Corporation of Japan as a way to bring in cash during the Great Depression, it took the Japanese company nearly five years to bring the first Rikuo to market in 1935. Therefore, many Japanese branches of government purchased VLs directly from Milwaukee to serve the Imperial army, navy, police, and post office in the meantime. The sidecar motorcycle became the prime security vehicle of the Imperial Guard, which surrounded the emperor when he was traveling. The Guard asked for 15 left-side and 15 right-side sidecars so they could form a protective shield around the emperor.

361 Not much information exists on Harley-Davidson's military exports to Japan before WWII. My friend "Panhead Jim" Mahaney, of RidingVintage.com, is an incredible source for H-D military and police history. He has uncovered photos taken by Harley-Davidson of a 1934 VL equipped for duty with the Imperial navy. It has a left-side-mounted sidecar, with machine gun mount, which is what the Imperial Navy requested, as well as a mounted machine gun on the rear fender rack.

362 Still without a formal racing division in 1938, Harley-Davidson introduced the WLDR high-performance 750-cc street-legal racer aimed at Class C flat track racing. Many of the amateur racers who participated in Class C actually rode their bikes to the racetrack then stripped off all the street parts and raced. Afterward, they'd put the lights and anything else back on and ride home. The WLDR made 27 hp with higher compression and larger valves than

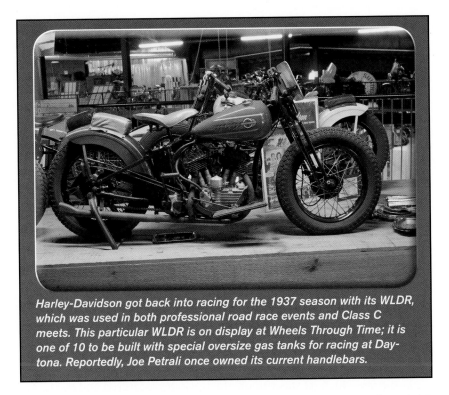

Harley-Davidson got back into racing for the 1937 season with its WLDR, which was used in both professional road race events and Class C meets. This particular WLDR is on display at Wheels Through Time; it is one of 10 to be built with special oversize gas tanks for racing at Daytona. Reportedly, Joe Petrali once owned its current handlebars.

the WL, but cost only $25 more. H-D upped the ante on the WLDR in 1939 when it included aluminum heads with larger intake ports. Horsepower on the 1939 is thought to somewhere in the mid-30s. Because AMA rules stipulated that motorcycles must be ridden to the track, the WR and its variants originally included a headlight, taillight, and front fender.

363 Class C racing grew more and more popular around the country and in 1941, Harley-Davidson released a pair of race-only machines based off the WLDR: the WR for flat track and the WRTT for road racing. The WLDR and its WR counterparts received a larger crankpin, stronger valve springs, more powerful cams, and a bigger carburetor. This new engine package produced 35 hp. Because they didn't require the same longevity of a street model, the race-only versions also received flat lifters instead of roller lifters, which certainly boosted track power even further. Class C rules had relaxed enough so that a racer could trailer his motorcycle to the event. Therefore, unlike the other WR racers, the WRTT was not fitted with a headlight or front fender

364 Unfortunately, because it was seen as a nonessential division at Harley-Davidson, the racing program was once again shut down, this time to support the massive war effort. The WLDR was discontinued in the summer of 1941, while WR and WRTT production was placed on hold.

365 Ever hear the saying, "you might be able to outrun a cop, but you can't outrun his radio?" The first known use of police Harley-Davidsons with radios was by the Cedar Rapids, Iowa, Police Department in 1932.

366 Ben Campanale became the first two-time back-to-back winner of the Daytona 200 when he won in 1938 and 1939, each time on a Harley-Davidson. He was a relative unknown in 1938, his first attempt at the 200, when he rode a street-legal WLDR with the lights removed. After a fierce battle with several of the top racers, during which he was run off the track, he recovered and then took home the checkered flag. In 1939, he rode a factory-prepped racer and won again.

367 As the story goes, after Lester Hillbish ran Ben Campanale off the track in 1938, he caught up and started kicking Hillbish's front tire until he slowed down and let Campanale pass. Hillbish protested to the AMA official Jim Davis, who had seen him clearly run Campanale off the track earlier in the race, but did not allow the protest. The following year, William Harley approached Campanale before the race and reportedly said, "if any shenanigans should happen during the race, you know what to do." And then he kicked the front tire of Campanale's bike.

368 Those who finished in the 1940 Daytona 200 might be better referred to as "survivors." Only 15 of the 77 starters even finished the race, but the winning trophy went to Babe Tancrede, who was riding a Harley-Davidson WLDR. This was a nice change

Motorcycle racing looked a lot different than it does today. The only thing Babe Tancrede wore for protection in the 1940 Daytona 200 was his team sweater, leather pants, and a half helmet. Those guys were tough, although I don't want to think about what happened to the 62 racers who didn't finish the race that year! (Photo Courtesy Harley-Davidson)

of pace for Tancrede; he had raced in the first Daytona 200 in 1937, but dropped out after 21 laps.

369 One of the rarest and most valuable motorcycles The Motor Company ever produced was the CAC racer in 1934. The vertical, single-cylinder racer had almost no suspension, except for a small amount of travel in the inverted, hydraulic fork. It was incredibly light in weight and was developed solely for use on short cinder tracks. The H-D race team went to California to test prototypes on real tracks against real competitor machines. Only 20 CAC racers were ever built, along with five spare engines. Unfortunately, most of the machines and engines were destroyed during races.

370 The rate at which Harley-Davidson broke records in the first few decades of motorcycling is unprecedented in modern times. On November 27, 1938, Sam Arena, riding a WLDR, won the 200-mile Pacific Coast Speedway Championship with a time of 2 hours 22 minutes 28 seconds. He crushed the track's previous record, not by seconds or milliseconds as today's records are set, but by a staggering 19 minutes 20 seconds! The H-D riders were nearly perfect in that race, occupying 9 of the top 10 finishing positions.

371 Harley-Davidson unleashed the DAH factory hillclimber in 1929; it used an OHV 45-ci engine. H-D's racing department built only 25 machines. Because hillclimbing was extremely rough on the motorcycles, only two are known to exist today. One of the two existing machines is the one that Joe Petrali used to win the 1932 National Hillclimb Championship. It used a lengthened, double-downtube frame with a super-strong front end that has the rear legs looping forward of the front legs. In addition to the DAH in the Harley-Davidson Museum, a version also lives outside and helps welcome visitors to the Harley-Davidson experience. Do you know what the outside DAH is made out of? Read on to find out.

372 After years of serious racing events that were solely for professional racers using alcohol and other high-performance fuel, the AMA finally approved Class C racing in 1933. These low-budget unofficial events had become popular for both riders and spectators. The events had about a nickel entrance fee for the racers and were usually free to watch. Most of the time, everyone enjoyed themselves more than if they were at an expensive professional race. The motorcycles raced in Class C had to be stock, except for the fenders and lights (which were easily damaged) and they didn't need a muffler. In addition, the rider had to own the bike, which had to run on regular pump gas. Nearly every form of racing was given a Class C division, which quickly grew to have one of the largest followings.

373 Although a group of Indian riders started the Sturgis motorcycle rally, an invitation was sent out far and wide for racers to come take a shot at the $750 purse. Only two Harley-Davidsons raced in a field of Indians, but H-D rider Johnny Spiegelhoff took the checkered flag. After this win at an Indian-dominated rally, Spiegelhoff earned the nickname "The Milwaukee Demon." He won the premier race at Sturgis several more times, but his biggest career win came at the 1947 Daytona 200. However, he had switched to riding Indians by this time.

374 The United States didn't officially enter World War II until after the attack on Pearl Harbor on December 7, 1941. However, long before that, many people were convinced that the war was coming. Although its first wartime contract was still several years away, The Motor Company had been discussing the military build-up with Pentagon officials and knew that a massive number of motorcycles would be needed for the war effort, when it finally happened. It had even produced a WLA prototype as early as 1937.

375 Although Harley-Davidsons were winning races right and left in Class C competition, it wasn't always on the latest and greatest 45 Flatheads or 61 OHVs from the showroom floor. Many riders were still competing successfully with the old IOE engines that hadn't been in production since 1929. This meant that there was no need to buy a brand-new motorcycle to win races. For the 1939 season, Harley-Davidson pressed the AMA to alter Class C rules to outlaw IOE engines from competition. The 1939 rules had used the word "side-valve" instead of "pocket-valve."

Chapter 4

Knucklehead Era 1936–1947

THE MOTOR COMPANY

376 Even though it was introduced as a 1936 model, the story of the EL Knucklehead begins as far back as 1931. It didn't take long for the executives to decide that a modern replacement for the VL was needed. Walter Davidson announced a new project to Harley-Davidson shareholders in November 1933. This new model even included plans for an autumn 1934 release. After a year of engineering redesigns and failures, members at the May 28, 1935, company board meeting decided to postpone discussion of a September or January launch until the next board meeting, while they first decided whether or not to build it at all! The outcome of that meeting is obvious; the EL, still in the development process, was unveiled at the November 1935 dealer show.

377 Doubts about the new model must have still loomed large because the EL was purposefully left out of 1936 model flyer. Harley's own magazine, *The Enthusiast*, even ran a feature in the January issue on all the new models for 1936 without mentioning the EL. Finally, in January 1936, dealers actually began receiving a few ELs. However, dealers were instructed to not add any hype to the launch and let customers develop their own first impressions.

378 In autumn 1941, with World War II already underway in Europe, Harley-Davidson informed its dealers that each dealer could only order one (yes, one) new motorcycle. In many cases, dealers never even received their order because of the government's wartime needs.

379 Company founder and President Walter Davidson died of exhaustion and a liver ailment in February 1942, before he could see his hardy motorcycles help lead the way to an Allied victory in Europe. He refused to allow anyone, including family, to visit him in his hospital bed, and even stationed a nurse outside his room to ensure his orders were followed. Then, right before he died, he called in his and the other founders' sons to inform them whom he decided should take over his duties as president. William

H. Davidson, age 37, earned that honor and remained as president until he resigned in 1973.

380 During the Great Depression, Harley-Davidson offered more color choices than it ever had with creative designs and decals. The complete opposite occurred during World War II. Anyone lucky enough to be approved to buy a motorcycle during the war years of 1943 and 1944 received a gray motorcycle only. Some silver motorcycles were sent out in 1944, but it was at the factory's discretion, not the customer's. Why was there no color limit in 1942? The Motor Company likely had a large enough supply of pre-war colors then to handle customer orders.

381 Even though the 61-ci E model Knucklehead was introduced as a 1936 model, the pre-production prototypes, such as those displayed at the 1935 dealer's meeting, had serial numbers starting with 35E. Rumor is that up to 12 such machines were given a "35E" prefix but just 3 are known to have actually existed. Because the company's initial goal was to launch the E as a 1936 model at the end of 1935, these machines might have been meant for dealer demonstrations. In addition, as you know from the UX, had they been used for experimental purposes only, they would have been called EX, which further cements their public status. But they still had major oil problems stemming from the open valvesprings and rockers. These problems included oil getting all over the rider and machine when ridden, so it was probably a wise decision to hold off the public introduction for a while.

382 Perhaps the "soft" launch of the EL went off a little too softly. In February, the company sent word to its dealers that it had the capacity to take more orders of the OHV 61 in late February 1936. The wording of the memo suggested that some customers might be under the impression that there was a long backlog for the new 61 and that dealers should contact their customers and let them know that orders could be filled immediately. In reality, unless they had visited a dealership in the past several months, there was a good chance most people didn't even know that a bold new Harley was available.

383 Harley-Davidson offered the wide color pallette offerings right up to the beginning of World War II, and this has become somewhat of an inconvenience for restorers, judges, and historians. In addition to the standard colors for these years, dealers were instructed to inform customers that many other colors, as well as custom combinations, could be ordered straight from the factory. Different colored panels, rims, lettering, and pinstripes could be ordered in just about any color a customer wanted. As The Motor Company learned during the Great Depression, a variety of colors is a cheap way of enticing customers. Some pretty crazy machines have appeared at bike shows all over the world, all with the very strong possibility that they're still wearing their original colors. Even so, most 1936s wear the classic Venetian Blue with Croydon Cream panels and rims that, along with the art-deco gas tank decal, capture the style of the era marvelously.

384 Strikes and organized labor unions were popping up all over the country in the 1930s. In March 1937, Harley-Davidson employees banded together to form their own union under the United Auto Workers.

385 Although Harley-Davidson continued to see huge profits from its massive government contract, World War II left the dealers in a bind. It wasn't just that people weren't buying motorcycles, because many probably wanted to, it's that there weren't any motorcycles to buy. In an effort to help guide its dealers through the war years, The Motor Company included a lot of advice in the dealer bulletins. The gist of the advice was, stop being a Harley-Davidson dealer, get a job within the war effort, invest in war bonds, and then use that money to reopen the dealership after the war. Dealers were also encouraged to pursue strong relationships with the local police departments by performing maintenance work and, later, by selling them motorcycles after the War Production Board approved such sales. Another suggestion was to try to buy motorcycles from "the boys going to war" and sell those in the dealer's showroom.

386 Raw materials became so scarce that in May 1942, Harley-Davidson began requiring dealers to send in broken or damaged pistons before receiving new pistons. The old pistons were melted down and used to make the replacements. Bottom line: during the war years, make sure you took good care of your Harley!

387 All civilian automobile production was halted on January 1, 1942. Harley-Davidson had produced only 906 74-ci Knucks and 784 61-ci Knucks for civilian use, making those lucky buyers the last regular civilians to purchase Knuckleheads until 1945.

388 By 1947, the last year of the Knucklehead, civilian bikes had just about returned to full production and also to their highly decorated state. However, the availability of raw materials still lagged and, because of this, 1947 Harleys saw a 20 percent price jump compared to 1946. The 74-ci Knuckleheads listed for $605 compared to $465 for a 1946 FL.

389 The late 1930s and 1940s were an interesting time in Harley-Davidson history; the company offered two different Big Twin models for a long period. The engines were different enough so as not to compete, but after World War II, most of the sales tide turned toward the company's OHV offerings. 1948 was the last model year for the big Flatty. Except for a couple overlapping years between engine designs (in the future), this was the last time that Harley-Davidson built two different Big Twin models at the same time.

390 The U.S. government's Marshall Plan was designed to help its war-torn allies in Europe jumpstart their economies by sending them raw materials and food. To further assist, the government greatly reduced tariffs on finished products imported into the United States. The Marshall Plan hurt Harley-Davidson doubly. The raw materials so desperately needed to build motorcycles were still unavailable, and British motorcycles became readily available at a lower cost. Perhaps the Marshall Plan helped Europe get back up and running, but it undoubtedly prevented many new Harley-Davidsons from running in the United States.

391 In 1947, Harley-Davidson bought a former wartime propeller plant on Capitol Drive in Wauwatosa, Wisconsin. Its initial purpose was as a machine shop that then shipped parts to the Juneau Avenue factory for final assembly. After a while, the Capitol Drive plant began manufacturing entire engines and transmissions, most recently those for Sportsters. By 2011, all engine manufacturing was moved to the Menomonee Falls plant on Pilgrim Road, where it is located today. Shortly thereafter, the factory and its 21 acres were sold and converted to a U-Haul facility.

The Motor Company's purchasing of the Capitol Drive plant in 1947 allowed it to produce large machined parts in bulk; then they were shipped to Juneau Avenue for final motorcycle assembly. Here you can see one of the company's massive metal presses is under construction. (Photo Courtesy Harley-Davidson)

392 Harley-Davidson introduced dealers to the new Capitol Drive plant during the annual dealers convention in Milwaukee. In typical fashion for the company, the introduction was hardly a simple bus ride, or even a motorcycle ride away. Dealers were loaded onto a train, at night, and taken to what was only referred to as a "secret destination." That secret destination turned out to be the old A.O. Smith propeller plant. The message was no secret at all; after the long, tough wartime years, Harley-Davidson was back and investing large sums of money into the business. Dealers should expect to be back on their feet very soon.

393 On May 12, 1943, Harley-Davidson received its first Army-Navy E award for exceptional performance in war materiel production. E awards were given to companies that went above and beyond in the production of goods for the Allied war effort. The presentation of the award took place at the Juneau Avenue facilities and every employee was given an emblem to wear as a badge of honor. The Motor Company went on to win three more E awards for its successful war effort.

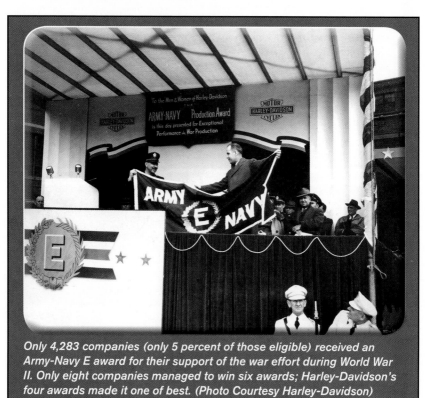

Only 4,283 companies (only 5 percent of those eligible) received an Army-Navy E award for their support of the war effort during World War II. Only eight companies managed to win six awards; Harley-Davidson's four awards made it one of best. (Photo Courtesy Harley-Davidson)

394 Looking back on the development of the Knucklehead engine, it's easy to think that it was an obvious choice and always destined to become the next Big Twin engine. At the time, that wasn't exactly the case. The engine was primed for a 1936 public launch, but even as late as mid-1935 talks were ongoing about abandoning the OHV engine. By early-1930s standards, it was extremely costly, and its development experienced setback after setback. Moreover, most motorcyclists had never ridden an OHV and weren't even familiar with the concept. Why go through the hassle and expense to build something that the public doesn't even know it wants?

395 Bill Harley passed away on September 18, 1943, at the age of 62. He was the engineer and draftsman who had invented, designed, and built so many of the parts that propelled Harley-Davidson to the position of world's best motorcycle. Since day one, he was the OHV Knucklehead's greatest champion, repeatedly saying that the OHV was The Motor Company's salvation to a bright future. He was right, and the Knucklehead turned out to be his final, and some might argue greatest, contribution to motorcycling.

396 The first public appearance of Harley-Davidson's all-new OHV twin was in the January 1936 issue of *The Enthusiast*. The photo taken in the back room at the recent dealer show in Milwaukee after the Knucklehead was unveiled. Although the namesake knuckled rocker box covers and right-side air cleaner cover are obvious today, it's doubtful that anyone at the time noticed them because the copy and image were printed so small.

397 After the introduction of the Knucklehead, and the 1937 chassis updates on the Flathead models, Harley-Davidson introduced even higher standards in the paint department. Colors and pinstripe options were numerous, and the products used in the prep and final protection steps also became extremely important to ensure a long-lasting finish. It's believed that prior to World War II, Harley-Davidson used 10,000 gallons of paint and associated products every single year!

398 An old story that is likely true based on first-person recollections is that Bill Davidson loaned money to employees in times of severe need simply as a friendly act. He'd even tell them not to worry about paying him back until they were back on their feet again. Often, upon giving Bill their first installment of a loan repayment, he'd tell them not to worry about the rest. Even with his seemingly casual attitude toward loaning money, he kept notes with names and amounts in his desk. After he died in 1937, his desk was gone through and all the notes were discovered. Bill Davidson had given thousands of dollars to his employees' families over the years to help support a sick child or to heat a house in the winter.

399 The yen-to-dollar exchange rate was so terrible in the 1930s that it wasn't even worthwhile to continue to export motorcycles to Japan. With the Sankyo company already in place producing 74-ci Flatheads, Harley-Davidson thought that it could sell Sankyo the design for the 61 OHV Knucklehead; it could be produced in Japan, sold under the Sankyo name, and H-D would not lose that entire market. The terms of the deal are unknown, but Sankyo opted not to purchase the rights to the new 61 OHV because of the many design problems, and all ties were cut between it and The Motor Company. Harley-Davidson continued to export motorcycles to Japan and the surrounding area, although far fewer than it would have liked.

400 Under the terms of the Marshall Plan, nearly 10,000 foreign (mostly British) motorcycles were imported into the United States in 1946. Many Harley-Davidson dealers and employees quickly switched to sell the British makes, which become very popular, very quickly, and provided yet another seemingly insurmountable hurdle for Harley-Davidson in the coming years.

THE CHASSIS

401 The 1936 EL Knucklehead, among its many firsts, used the now-familiar horseshoe oil tank underneath the seat, which was the closest location to the oil pump that the designers could use. Painted black to blend in with the frame, the one-gallon tank accomplished the secondary function of hiding the battery and wiring from view. There's as much of a backstory to this one seemingly simple part as there is to anything else on a 1936 Knucklehead, and it drives collectors and restorers crazy. Four different oil tank designs were used throughout the production run of only the 1936 EL. The first oil tank used is known to exist on prototype models and some of the very early machines. It is found only on this tank and is identified exclusively by a completely smooth top and a plugged hole on either side of the tank that is welded in place. The second oil tank, used in early examples, is essentially the same but without the welded plugs. The third tank has embossed indents for added strength on the top and, like the two before it, has its fittings welded in place. The final type of oil tank found on the 1936 Knuck has the embossed top except that the fittings are all swaged on instead of being welded. All 1936 tanks had a decal on the right side instructing owners to drain and flush the oil every 3,000 miles (or 5,000 km).

The legendary 1936 Knucklehead is the Harley-Davidson that all other models are based on. It was, and still is, the perfect motorcycle design and its lines can be seen in most brand-new Harleys today. In fact, The Motor Company suffered the financial consequences during the 1970s and early 1980s when it went away from this classic design until it came out with the Softail chassis. (Photo Courtesy Harley-Davidson)

402 Until the 1936 Knucklehead, Harleys were not factory equipped with speedometers, although most customers chose to order them from dealers. The only gauge was an ammeter, and the rudimentary dashboard had that and two keys. The 1936 E with a speedometer was also available with an optional resettable trip-meter. In 1937, the 100-mph speedo was replaced with a 120-mph speedo, which puts it among the many 1936-only parts that make that year so special.

403 To handle the additional power output of the OHV Knuck-lehead, a double-downtube frame was used for the first time, instead of the single cradle running underneath; all Harleys use this style today. This frame allowed for additional mounting points as well as more stability for the engine. The new frame also gave the Knucklehead one of the lowest seat heights yet, certainly the lowest for a Big Twin: 26 inches.

404 The first metal Harley-Davidson tank badge was used on 1940 models. The emblem, used until 1946, featured a teardrop design with "Harley-Davidson" written in red with two black speed lines above and below it. Previously, all designs were transferred right to the paint.

405 In 1937 only, all Harley-Davidson models had oil tanks painted the same color as the tank and fenders. It's difficult to say anything negative about the look of a 1937 Harley, but you can see why The Motor Company went back to black oil tanks for 1938; and why that theme for oil tank and battery covers continues to this day on some Softails and Sportsters. The design with a black tank is a little smoother, and more important, oil drips and leaks are hardly visible.

406 Even though Harley-Davidson kept the price of the 61-ci Knucklehead at $435 in 1939, it did make a number of visual updates to the bike. Until 1939, the Cat's Eye dash was only available in black but, in 1939, the dash was color-matched to the color on top of the gas tank. A new taillight adorned the rear fender, which saw the license plate bracket mounted above it; this practice continues on many H-D models today. The standard accessory package included a running light on the front fender, and this is seen on most 1939 and later Knucks.

407 The 1941 models saw 16-inch wheels finally came into play with beefy 5-inch tires; they provided style as well as a huge amount of comfort and on-road smoothness. 18s were optional, and chrome wheels were available for an additional $2.50 each. The 1941 Knuckleheads can be identified by the chrome strip down the side of the tank as well as by the new black-faced speedometer with large silver numbers. Because of the war effort, fewer than 2,500 74-ci Knucks were built that year.

408 Everybody knows about the popular fad in the 1950s that saw hot rodders hang fuzzy dice from their rearview mirrors. But did you know that you could order a new Knucklehead with a large black die as the shifter knob? It came with the Deluxe Solo Group option package or could be added to any motorcycle for 60 cents.

409 Harley-Davidson's first real dashboard console appeared on the 1936 Knucklehead and became a mainstay, in one way or another, atop Big Twin gas tanks to this day. Many Bar & Shield enthusiasts know of the "cat's eye" dashboard design, but the first design featured a larger analog amp and oil gauges that sort of resembled a human skull. Most people don't bother to look at the ammeter on their motorcycle, and most car drivers probably couldn't point to it if they tried. However, in the early days, an ammeter was an important instrument to a rider. With only a handful of electronics on the bike, a quick glance at the ammeter (which read –15 to 15) could indicate the operational status of the motorcycle to a rider. Now, a simple red light in the shape of an oil-can indicates oil pressure. However, late-1930s Harleys used a moving gauge that read "RUN" when oil pressure was above 4 psi and "OFF" when oil pressure went below 4 psi.

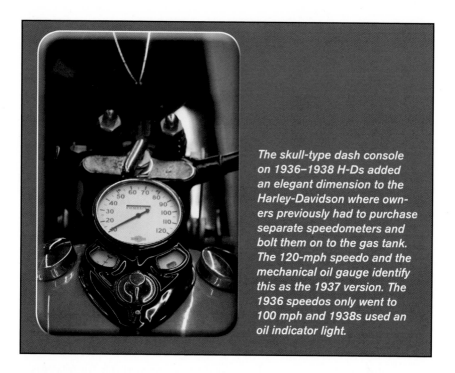

The skull-type dash console on 1936–1938 H-Ds added an elegant dimension to the Harley-Davidson where owners previously had to purchase separate speedometers and bolt them on to the gas tank. The 120-mph speedo and the mechanical oil gauge identify this as the 1937 version. The 1936 speedos only went to 100 mph and 1938s used an oil indicator light.

410 Along with the new dashboard in 1936 came a new key-lockable ignition system that used a single key instead of the two previously required. The center position is off. Turning the key to the left is essentially a park mode in which the front fender running light and taillight illuminate. One stop to the right engages the ignition system and allows the bike to run, but without any lights (convenient if there's a charging issue). Two clicks to the right is full on, arming the ignition system and lights.

411 Indian motorcycles are famous for being backward when it comes to clutching, shifting, and throttling, well, at least to Harley riders. But that's not to say that The Motor Company wouldn't give you left-handed equipment if you wanted it. Most didn't, but the southpaw package, as it was affectionately known, was picked up primarily by police departments. Motor officers wanted to be able to use their dominant hand while riding or chasing suspects; an officer can fire his gun while riding. Whether or not this is the primary reason can be debated among motor officers of today.

412 In 1938, Harley-Davidson continued its attempt to bring people to motorcycling who didn't want the mechanical responsibility associated with it. Believe it or not, some people were scared off by the ammeter and analog oil gauge because they didn't know what they were or what the warning signs meant. So the gauges were abandoned in favor of warning lights: green on the left and red on the right. If the battery voltage goes higher than the generator voltage, the green light lights up; if the oil pressure drops below 3 psi, the red light lights up. Just as on nonfaired H-Ds today, these functions are out of sight and out of mind until the little light pops on. Although purists complained about the lack of the necessary instruments, the change had two benefits: It saved the company a lot of money and reduced failure potential for both systems. Instead of the entire wiring circuit being run through the ammeter, now it only needed a single wire from a third terminal on the generator relay. And, where previously an oil line had to be wound up to the dash, now only a wire from a sensor switch on the oil pump was required. This update also gives the 1938 dash the distinction of being the only skull-type console with colored lenses for the lights. This was the third year in a row that a one-year-only dash console was used.

413 For 1939, Harley-Davidson introduced the newly styled "cat's eye" dash console, which was similar to the skull face, but used smaller, angled indicator lenses, which had a familiar feline appearance. It was a natural progression from the skull face console because the indicator lights no longer needed to be so large. The cat's eye design ran through 1946 on all models, including military WLAs, which saw a slightly modified version.

414 In 1939, Harley-Davidson used brown horsehide leather saddles instead of the traditional black cowhide saddles. Even though they're correct for 1939 only, it wasn't the last time that The Motor Company had to use horsehide. In 1942, the country's supply of cowhide leather went toward making boots for the soldiers, so seats were covered in horsehide yet again. The seats remained horsehide until 1947 when cowhide became available once more.

415 Up until 1940, gas tanks were completely separate containers that required the rider to fill up two tanks, and also operate two petcocks. This redundancy didn't fit well with The Motor Company's program of making its motorcycles easier to use. In 1940, it added a coiled fuel line between the tanks that allowed them to drain in unison. Unlike the one-piece tanks of today, when fueling a 1940 Knucklehead on its sidestand from the right-side fill cap, all the fuel rushes to the left tank and actually sits higher than the fill cap. If you removed the left fill cap at that point, gas flowed right out of it. As part of the gas tank update, a single instant reserve fuel valve on the left tank controlled fuel flow.

416 In 1940, the classic "half-moon" footboards were used for the first time, replacing the larger rectangular style. These D-shaped footboards have riveted rubber mats on top with "Harley-Davidson" written down the center. This design was used through 1965 before being changed back to a more rectangular design. That doesn't mean that the half-moons were gone forever, though. The retro Softail Slim uses the half-moon design and they're also available in the parts and accessories catalog for the other Softails.

417 Where is it written that the rarest Harley-Davidsons have to be the prettiest? The Motor Company only built 203 Knuckleheads in 1943 and, because almost all materiel went to the war effort, they were painted and coated with whatever could be rustled up. Just about everything, including many engine parts, was painted white and most of the body parts were painted gray. Nothing on the motorcycle was chromed except for the namesake bolts. A variety of other regularly chromed parts were also painted black. The rubber floorboard mats were replaced with a ribbed steel piece; both it and the floorboard were painted black. The rubber kickstarter pads were left off.

418 Ever go buy a new car and get lured in by a nice, low price only to find out that floormats, anti-rust coating, and other odds and ends made that low price not so low anymore? Well, that's kind of what it was like buying a Harley in the early days. For example, the sticker price on a 1936 EL Special Sport Solo, the most popular model by far, was $380. But you couldn't leave the dealership for that. New owners were required to choose an option package if they wanted their motorcycle equipped with things such as an engine guard, steering damper, and sidestand. The lowest price package was the Standard Solo Group for $14. The most expensive was the Deluxe Police Group for $80.50.

419 Before World War II, most of the world's supply of rubber materials came from a part of China that, unfortunately, Japan conquered early in the war. In 1940, B.F. Goodrich scientist Waldo Semon developed a cost-effective synthetic rubber and in 1942, the U.S. government put together a secret team of chemists to improve the product. Harley-Davidson's supply of rubber tires was depleted by 1944; motorcycles were equipped with S-3 synthetic rubber tires. In 1945 and 1946, synthetic tires on the 74-ci Knucklehead added a $4.08 surcharge to the machine that wasn't levied against 61-ci models.

420 The tombstone taillight made its first appearance in 1947, replacing the art-deco boattail taillight. It differed from the boattail in that it was flat and rectangular with a semi-circle top that resembled . . . a tombstone. These taillights were used on all models through 1954. If you want to see a tombstone today, you don't have to go any further than your local H-D dealership; it's standard equipment on the Softail Deluxe through (at least) the 2016 model. It adds a wonderful retro detail to the vintage-inspired motorcycle. Surprisingly, the Heritage Softail, uses the standard rectangular taillight even though the tombstone fit that model's genes perfectly.

421 Harley-Davidsons were available with an optional shock absorber beginning in 1945. Not in the rear or in the form of telescopic forks, but rather as a single hydraulic shock to dampen the spring-only front end. Hydraulic suspension was hardly a new concept in motorcycling in the 1940s, but the task for The Motor Company was how to add it in a way that didn't detract from the look and feel of its motorcycles. The optional shock absorber gave the front end much of the same action as a traditional hydraulic front end. The springs still handle the initial bump or pothole while the dampener is responsible for quickly bringing the springs back to neutral, otherwise they'd continue springing. All future models with springer front ends, such as the Springer Softail and Cross Bones, use a dampening shock absorber.

422 Harley-Davidson offered its now-iconic spotlights for the first time in 1938, as an accessory. The spotlights were mounted to a bar that ran across the forks, positioning them on either side of the headlight. Spotlights were accessory add-ons until the 1965 Electra Glide debuted them as standard equipment. Today, many Touring models, as well as the classically styled Heritage and Deluxe Softails, use spotlights as standard equipment.

423 When most Harley-Davidson experts think about delivery vehicles, the first models that come to mind are usually the long-lasting Servi-Car, the Fore-Car of the mid-1910s, or the sidecar-box Package Trucks that usually used an IOE engine or a 45-ci Flathead. Interestingly, service vehicles weren't limited to the more mundane, low-compression engines that we're used to seeing. Up to World War II, a business owner could order a model M Package Truck with his choice of Big Twin, any of which could move the truck's 500-pound carrying capacity. Those who desired the extra power usually opted for the dependable, low-maintenance 74-ci and 80-ci Flatheads. But at least one knucklehead ordered a 1941 FL equipped with a model M Package Truck. Not a bad way to consider a hot new 74-ci Knucklehead as a business deduction!

424 Harley-Davidson learned a valuable lesson in 1936 about how its customers used their motorcycles. Newsflash: it wasn't always exactly how the factory intended them to be used. The new EL had been designed as a fast sporting machine that could cover long distances at high speeds with one or two passengers. However, as soon as they took delivery, many riders began competing in hill climb events, welding sidecar mounts onto the frames, and basically pushing the machine to a much higher limit than test riders had ever even done! The frame was quickly discovered to be one of the EL's few weak points; it needed a major overhaul for 1937. Among the updates for 1937 were heavier tubing, forged sidecar lugs, and a fifth mounting bolt for the transmission. The new frame weighed 51 pounds, 6 more than the 1936 frame; it lasted in its basic design for many years. In fact, many 1936 EL owners actually scrapped their 1936 frames and replaced them with the newer, stronger 1937 frames, making real 1936 frames a true rarity today.

425 Today's riders know how important it is to have a functioning brake light while riding near other vehicles. Some aftermarket kits even modulate the brake light to provide additional warning to those behind the motorcycle. Brake lights weren't such a big deal back in 1936; in fact, they weren't even standard equipment on base-model Knuckleheads. To have a working brake light, the buyer needed to equip his (or her) bike with the Deluxe Solo Group or equivalent option package at the dealership. The first brake lights used a large metal housing that stuck out above the transmission and used a chain to actuate the light off the movement of the brake rod.

THE POWERTRAIN

426 One of the most important new engines, if not *the* most important, in Harley-Davidson's history is the 1936 Knucklehead. The 40-hp EL (61-ci) engine features two revolutionary firsts that completely changed the motorcycle game: a recirculating oil system and overhead valves. Previously, overhead valves were only seen on the high-performance race bikes of the 1920s. However, the exposed design of those bikes was rudimentary compared to the EL. An OHV setup increases airflow and allows higher compression, thereby providing significant power and throttle response gains over the previous Flathead and J engines.

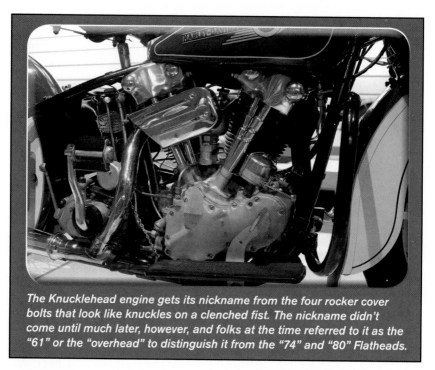

The Knucklehead engine gets its nickname from the four rocker cover bolts that look like knuckles on a clenched fist. The nickname didn't come until much later, however, and folks at the time referred to it as the "61" or the "overhead" to distinguish it from the "74" and "80" Flatheads.

427 Prior to the 1936 EL, Harley-Davidson motorcycles used a total-loss oiling system; the oil circulated through the engine before slowly dripping onto the primary chain. While riding, the rider had to pump oil into the engine using a hand pump on the gas tank's built-in oil tank to maintain the proper amount of lubricant. The oil tank level had to be checked at every fuel fill-up and filled as necessary. Recirculating oil means that after the oil goes through the engine, it is sent back to the tank for recirculation. This innovation made H-Ds easier for everyday use and more practical for a greater number of people.

428 Another major change to the EL from previous engines was the use of a single camshaft, a concept that Harley-Davidson retained until the Twin Cam was introduced in 1999. The single cam runs quieter and more efficiently than the four gear-driven cams on a Flathead. As we know now, it also decreases the RPM an engine can hit, but it didn't matter on the EL, for which power maxed out at 4,800 rpm.

429 Yep, it has a Hemi! Harley-Davidson realized that the key to getting the most power out of its OHV engines was through cylinder head design and a hemispherical combustion chamber helped in that regard. The new EL's valves approached the combustion chamber at 90-degree angles, which flowed more air in and more exhaust out than previous OHV designs that The Motor Company used.

430 In 1939, it wasn't just all about the looks; the 61's engine and transmission also received some improvements to make it that much better of a motorcycle. Splined pinion and oil pump gears added strength to the bottom end while a new intake manifold, pistons, and valvesprings added to the power capacity up top.

431 At an awkward time on the eve of World War II, Harley-Davidson unveiled a larger version of the Knucklehead engine in 1941, which it called the F (regular compression) and FL (high compression). The 61's stroke was increased to 3.50 inches while bore was upped to 3.43 inches, giving it a 74-ci displacement. Larger, heavier flywheels and larger-diameter crankpins were held in by a stronger crankcase on both E and F models. The new crankcases also got rid of the lubrication-equalizing baffles, which had been causing excessive crankcase pressure, robbing the engine of horsepower. Also helping to boost horsepower were larger intake ports, a redesigned intake manifold, and a larger Linkert carburetor. With a 7.1:1 compression ratio, the FL produced 48 hp at 5,000 rpm.

432 In 1939, both OHV and Flathead Big Twins received a new transmission that used a combination of sliding gear and constant-mesh components. For some reason, The Motor Company placed neutral between second and third gears instead of between first and second. Because there's nothing like accidentally putting the bike in neutral as you're trying to merge onto a highway, right? Not surprisingly, that transmission and shift pattern only lasted one year.

433 Here's something you'll probably never see again in internal combustion engines: primer cups. Early-1936 Knuckleheads, and only a handful of later Knucks, had a brass primer cup just to the inside of the spark plug on each cylinder head. When starting the motorcycle in cold weather, or after a long hibernation, the rider simply has to turn the cups to open a small tract to the cylinder head's intake port. Models with primer cups also used a right-side gas tank cap that had something like a squirt gun on the underside from which a small amount of gas could be sucked up into the tube and then squirted through the primer cups into the intake port. This initial charge of gas made starting the engine much easier, not to mention easier on the leg, too. Primer cups were gone with the 1938 model year.

434 You would think that with a new recirculating oil system, the Knucklehead engine would require oil changes every 3,000 miles and that's it. In reality, the early Knuckleheads went through about 1 quart of oil every 200 to 400 miles. Imagine having to add a quart of oil every time you stopped for gas on your Twin Cam! Even though those numbers seem miserable now, it was significantly better than the previous total-loss system, which didn't even have to run oil to overhead components.

435 With varying compression requirements among different types of riders, from motor officers to sidecars, to commuters to performance enthusiasts, stocking different heads and pistons for each scenario could easily get costly and confusing. So, for 1936 and 1937, E and EL Knuckleheads could further adjust their compression by using optional .05-inch-thick compression plates that raise the cylinder head off the cylinder, thus lowering the compression ratio. Adding a compression plate to an EL engine created a medium-high compression engine while adding a plate to an E created a low or medium-low compression engine. ES sidecar rigs and some low-speed police-duty machines used the latter setup. In 1938 and after, all engines used the same high-compression pistons and were only given compression plates to adjust compression ratios.

436 I remember being at the Wheels Through Time museum some time ago when Matt Walkser blew into the museum workshop aboard Buzz Kanter's new 1936 Knucklehead, which we had brought in for a "freshening up." Matt's grin went from one ear to the other as he stepped off the special motorcycle after a ride that only a lucky few ever get to enjoy. He exclaimed, "Man! It has real 1936 cams in there!" I thought he was full of it and just messing with me. I mean, there's no way you can tell the year of camshaft manufacture from a ride, right? As usual, Matt knew something I didn't, which was that 1936 Knucks used a uniquely hot "Lightning" cam straight from the factory. The factory gave 1936 cams a special lightening treatment (hence the nickname), which consisted of speed holes on the gear, in addition to the performance profile. The factory stopped using them in later years because of the tendency for backfires when starting, although sportier riders felt that was a fair tradeoff. Two other cams were used in 1936, one with slightly retarded timing compared to the initial Lightning cam, and one that had two sets of timing marks to adjust performance between solo and sidecar use.

The Lightning cam is the Holy Grail for a Harley hot rodder. Not only does it have a sportier grind than later cams, it has lightening holes, something that is usually reserved for race bikes. The Lightning cam (front) is surrounded by later Knucklehead cams.

437 For 1936, Harley-Davidson ditched the old sliding-gear transmission in favor of a stronger and smoother constant-mesh transmission. This 4-speed proved to be of such excellent design that it was used relatively unchanged all the way to 1964. Initially, the EL tranny had no significant support on the kicker side, which led to the case becoming dislodged or cracking off after many kicks. Several simple fixes occurred through the 1936 run, but it wasn't until 1937 that H-D cast a fifth transmission mount into the frame to support the force of a person heaving their body weight onto the kicker pedal.

438 The Motor Company increased the size of the Knucklehead's intake ports in 1940, which allowed even more air to flow through the hemi-head. The intake manifold was also made larger to accommodate more airflow; at the same time it was changed from a Y- to a T-design. Big power increases were made possible due to the new Linkert M-25 carburetor that had a 1/4-inch-larger venturi. The new carburetor increased power at the top end of the powerband, although at the expense of low-end torque. In 1941, it was scrapped in favor of the M-35 with a slightly smaller venturi.

439 Big ports may have been the battle cry of 1940, but big displacement was the battle cry of 1941. Harley-Davidson's first FL model was introduced as a 74-ci Knucklehead. A 1/8-inch-larger bore and a 15/32-inch-larger stroke along with new, matching cylinders, turned the 61 into a 74 that put out an additional 5 hp. To support the additional power and stroke, larger flywheels and a stronger clutch were used on both engines. Along with the larger flywheels came an updated engine case to accommodate them.

440 It took Harley-Davidson until 1947 to act on feedback from its customers regarding riders' left knees hitting the shifter when in fourth gear. Remember, the shift-gate pattern had first gear forward and fourth gear back (toward the rider). In addition to a larger, stylized shifter gate, The Motor Company reversed the shift pattern by putting first gear closer to the rider and fourth gear closer to the handlebars. This added room for the rider's leg in the

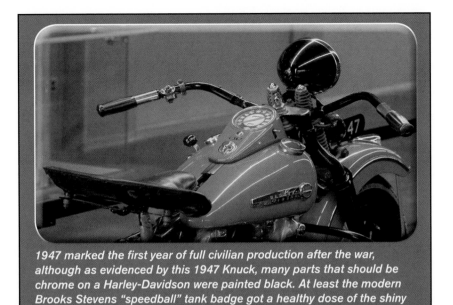

1947 marked the first year of full civilian production after the war, although as evidenced by this 1947 Knuck, many parts that should be chrome on a Harley-Davidson were painted black. At least the modern Brooks Stevens "speedball" tank badge got a healthy dose of the shiny stuff. You can barely see the tiny "GEN" and "OIL" indicator lenses on the painted dash console.

higher gears, which are used for most riding. The gearshift lever on the transmission was rotated 180 degrees to make this possible. The hand-shift lever received a slightly different bend to function with the new gate.

441 Initially, Harley-Davidson planned to build a single-cylinder version of the OHV Knucklehead, which it had been developing alongside the twin. Prototypes of this machine displaced 30.50 inches, the standard Milwaukee number, and it used all the same technology as the Knucklehead. Any ideas what a nickname for a half-Knucklehead single might be?

442 EL engine numbers start at 1,000. For some reason, engines numbered 1,200 to 1,300 were actually sold as the first Knucks; those with engine numbers 1,000 to 1,200 were sold and registered later. It's believed that the engines still had some issues, primarily in the oiling system, so The Motor Company wanted to bring this batch of engines up to the standard of the later batch before they were sold.

443 For a reason that nobody could figure out, the EL Knuckleheads coming out of Keith Ulicki's Kenosha, Wisconsin, dealership were noticeably faster than anyone else's. Kenosha is very close to Milwaukee, so "Uke" was invited to the factory to explain to a room-full of engineers, including Walter Davidson, exactly what he was doing. He pointed to the left crankcase that held the sprocket shaft bearing. He said that they forgot to drill an oil hole to lubricate this bearing, which would allow more horsepower to move down the driveline. The very next year, all the 1939 Knuckleheads had that little hole and they ran faster and more reliably throughout their entire production run. Uke's Harley-Davidson is still in business in Kenosha.

444 Many folks often wonder why Harley-Davidson's little twin, the 45 and later the K, didn't make the switch to an OHV design until the introduction of the Sportster in 1957. What's even more thought provoking is that H-D actually developed a seemingly perfect 45 OHV as early as 1939. Bill Harley's engineering department used existing parts to build the prototype 45 OHV, including a WR bottom end with racing components. Unfortunately, its new cylinders and heads didn't look like those from a Knucklehead, but they made the bike run like a Knuck. The valves on these new heads were completely enclosed and oil lines ran to them directly from the oil pump. It was, essentially, a perfected form of the Knucklehead.

445 Unlike some of The Motor Company's other prototype projects that never saw the light of day, the 45 OHV was given extensive real world testing alongside the new prototype 74 OHV. Test riders Art Kauper and Art Earlenbaugh left Milwaukee in the middle of a massive snowstorm aboard both new motorcycles and headed for Florida. Then, they rode on to Texas where they did the majority of the testing on the prototypes. Throughout the entire six-week test run, which ended up back in Milwaukee, the two put on more than 5,000 miles on each machine. The bikes were tested with and without sidecars and in all sorts of weather. The 45 OHV received a glowing report. The only real concern was that the transmission couldn't keep up with the additional power.

446 The 45 OHV project was scrapped, due to the expensive need for a redesigned transmission, and likely the lack of profit margin that was afforded the state-of-the-art, entry-level model. Not bringing the 45 OHV into production, at least after the war once all the WLAs were made, was possibly a huge mistake that could have held off the post-war invasion of fast, sexy, OHV British motorcycles. It took more than a decade following World War II for Harley-Davidson to correct this mistake with the immediately successful Sportster.

447 The clutch that Harley-Davidson developed in 1941 to handle the additional power output of the new 74-ci Knucklehead was used unchanged for 43 years. It was seriously overbuilt so that it could handle just about anything that anyone could ever think of doing with a Harley-Davidson. The new clutch used new, seven-plate friction discs (instead of the previous five plates) and hardened steel pins that created 65 percent more surface area than the previous clutch.

448 So many details make the 1936 Knucklehead a special and unique motorcycle, even compared to the ELs produced the following year. One obvious one-year-only styling exercise is the carburetor cover, so-called because no air filter element is actually inside the art-deco-style chrome cover. The impracticality of such a cover (compared to a real air filter) wasn't lost on the company because a round chrome cover and air filter was available as an accessory that year. Every year since 1936, Harleys have used real air filters to keep dust, water, and other undesirables out of the carburetor.

449 Many problems plagued the Knucklehead engine throughout its development and early production, specifically regarding oiling. One easily solved issue was that the rear cylinder and piston, because of the direction of the spinning flywheels, received much more oil than the front. The front piston was lubricated well enough, but the rear received too much. The Motor Company used some good old Milwaukee ingenuity to solve the problem: It ran an oil ring on the rear piston and skipped the ring on the front.

450 By 1939, the engineers had replaced the transmission throw-out bearing for the fourth time in four years. Nothing had worked to make the new 4-speed transmission as bulletproof as it should have been, for a Harley-Davidson. By 1939, they'd had enough. The new bearing was not only physically much larger, but it also used 25 ball bearings instead of the previous 10. In fact, this bearing was so strong that it was used in Big Twin transmissions for another 35 years.

PEOPLE AND POP CULTURE

451 Bill Cummings, the 1934 Indy 500 winner, posed for a Harley-Davidson advertisement on his personal machine, an all-white 1936 EL. Everything on his machine was white: frame, toolbox, oil tank, gas tank, fenders, and rims. This was an understandable style for him because race teams of the day traditionally wore all white.

452 Legendary Milwaukee industrial designer Brooks Stevens played a role in the history of The Motor Company when he designed the gas tank emblem for the 1947 Knucklehead, which was used through 1950. Brooks Stevens is known for such iconic designs as the "soft cross" Miller High Life logo, the Lawn Boy lawn mower, and even the Oscar Meyer Wienermobile. And for car enthusiasts, he also founded the Excalibur car company.

453 Ever hear of a guy called "Wrong Way" Corrigan? We all might have a buddy who has earned that nickname through the years, but Douglas Corrigan was definitely the first, and most likely the worst offender ever. In an attempt to fly a plane solo across the country from New York to California, he wound up in Dublin, Ireland. You'd think that the never-ending body of water beneath him might have been a giveaway. After his historic flight, Wrong Way took a trip to Milwaukee, and wanted to try riding a Harley-Davidson. Reportedly, he rode machine 38EL3325 to the airport, losing his police escort in the process. That Knucklehead ended up being purchased by, ironically, a Milwaukee motor officer.

454 I don't know who thought that wearing white while riding a motorcycle was a good idea, but that was certainly the growing fad in the late 1930s and continues to this day among the Motor Maids, one of the largest female riding organizations in the world. But in the 1930s, you'd likely be covered with dirt and oil after just a short ride! Apparently, this was the catalyst that inspired The Motor Company to fully enclose the OHV valvetrain in 1938, as evidenced by an ad touting the 1938s as having clean motors for those who wear "light-colored riding uniforms." Now, with paved roads everywhere and perfectly oil-tight Twin Cams, everyone wears black. It's all a part of the rebellious Harley-Davidson attitude!

455 Rationing of all sorts took effect after the attack on Pearl Harbor and the United States formally entered World War II. The good news for Harley-Davidson was that two of the most heavily rationed items, rubber and gasoline, required replacement less frequently on a motorcycle than a car. The amount of gasoline allowed for purchase was based on the sticker that an individual was given for his or her vehicle. "X" stickers, which were given to policemen, firemen, clergymen, defense officials, and congressmen, granted the vehicle an unlimited amount of gasoline. An "A" sticker was the lowest priority, entitling that vehicle to less than four gallons per week. This very quickly made the motorcycle an important mode of transportation because of its fuel efficiency and tire range. The federally imposed 35-mph speed limit must have put a damper on new FL Knucklehead owners.

456 Materials were in such short supply during the war that Harley-Davidson couldn't produce cans and bottles for products such as cleaners for removing grease and oil from motorcycles. Therefore, dealers purchased products in large containers and used recycled bottles to sell to customers. This may have been a nuisance to dealers and customers, but it was actually an economical and environmentally friendly method of selling products. Think about how many cans of cleaning solution and plastic quarts of oil motorcyclists use every year!

457 After VE-Day, many Americans believed that rationing would suddenly be over and that motorcycles and automobiles would be available immediately. At the very least, more of almost everything was available by the end of 1945 and into 1946. However, The Motor Company felt compelled to inform dealers that there would be "no special priority on motorcycles for veterans." Making a statement such as that in public today would be condemned, but it was different back then, when so many civilians also put their lives and dreams on hold to support the war effort in some way.

458 You probably wouldn't stereotype farmers as being targets for Harley-Davidson sales; they are some of the hardest-working Harley riders, perhaps, but hardly fall under the "wealthy" stereotype as Internet, technology, and financial workers of today might be. Following the destruction of much of Europe during the war, the United States agreed to send food and other supplies overseas to its allies. The Motor Company sent out a dealer bulletin suggesting that the sons of farmers were sharing in their family's significantly increased profits and were eager to spend it on a Harley-Davidson. And they often paid in cash for their new rides.

459 In 1940, Linda Dugeau and Dot Robinson formed the women-only Motor Maids riding club with 51 initial members. Both long-distance Harley riders, they set out on a three-year-long mission to find other women who loved motorcycling as much as they did. Dot went on to be president of the Motor Maids for more than 25 years and clocked more than 1.5 million miles on the 35 Harley-Davidson motorcycles she owned. Linda worked as a motorcycle courier in Los Angeles, where she could ride every day of the year. Today, almost every state and Canadian province has a chapter with membership totaling 1,200 women who are, per membership rules, required to legally own and ride their own motorcycle.

460 In 1947, Harley-Davidson MotorClothes began selling what many consider to be the ultimate black leather motorcycle jacket. An advertisement that year described it as "the jacket of your dreams." It was made of horsehide with the classic diagonal front zip, zipper cuffs, and snap-down collar. Have you priced a leather jacket at a Harley-Davidson dealer recently? If you were still in 1947, you could pick up this classic leather for $29.75 for men's and $24.90 for women's. The matching embossed leather belt was an extra $2.75 and a pair of slip-on horsehide gloves rang in at $3.75.

461 Attend the annual Sturgis motorcycle rally and you'll quickly figure out the motorcycle of choice for rally-goers: Harley-Davidson. But you might be surprised to learn that the Sturgis rally was actually started in 1938 by the local Indian dealer, Clarence "Pappy" Hoel who organized a small, nine-person race in the town of Sturgis. He purchased his Indian dealership in 1936 and formed a club, the Jackpine Gypsies, the same year. The Jackpine Gypsies own and operate the area's racetracks to this day! You might want to think twice before telling an Indian rider that he doesn't belong at Sturgis.

Although an Indian dealer founded the first Sturgis rally, Harley-Davidson riders loved the races and motorcycling camaraderie that took place in the Black Hills. The first-ever rally was even given the cover image of the May 1938 issue of The Enthusiast! *(Photo Courtesy Harley-Davidson)*

462 Ben Campanale was the first two-time Daytona 200 winner. After World War II (he wasn't drafted because of severe injuries suffered in a 1941 crash) he moved to California and opened a Harley-Davidson dealership in Pomona. One of his best customers was actor Clark Gable, and they often went to lunch at the restaurant across the street and ordered macaroni and cheese.

463 Don't drink it! With the wartime restrictions on steel, Harley-Davidson began supplying oil in see-through glass bottles beginning in 1943 and continuing until the steel restriction lifted.

464 The Motor Maids held its first national convention on May 27, 1944, in Columbus, Ohio. This has become an annual event where female and male motorcyclists make the two-wheel pilgrimage to wherever it's being held. Even those who aren't Motor Maids members make the trip to listen to speakers and participate in fun activities throughout the weekend. This is certainly one of the biggest events in the world for women riders.

465 The cover of the September 1944 *The Enthusiast* featured two military policemen resting on their H-D WLAs. Underneath the photo were the words, ". . . Somewhere in France." The two men are Private Ellis Allen of Durham, North Carolina, and Private Louis Wolf of Chicago. Harley-Davidson sent *The Enthusiast* to soldiers around the world, while riders back home must have enjoyed seeing their favorite motorcycle furthering the war effort.

466 Motorcyclists took to the streets of New York City for Motorcycle Day during the 1939 World's Fair. One of the many displays featured at the Fair was the effect of a stroboscope light on a Harley-Davidson wheel. More than 2,000 riders attended the Fair, and trophies were presented for achievements including the Best Uniformed Club and Longest Distance ridden to get there.

467 The very first EL purchased and ridden in Milwaukee belonged to Edmund Kelly, who worked in The Motor Company's inspection department and knew about the new model for some time. Unlike the more common blue and white trim for a 1936, Kelly ordered a red EL at Bill Knuth's dealership. Reportedly, even in the March ice and snow that covered Milwaukee's streets when he bought it, he'd still race VL Flatheads whenever he could.

468 Although many Indians, Hendersons, and other American motorcycles were registered in the state of Wisconsin in 1936, not a single foreign motorcycle was on record.

469 Joe Petrali retired from racing in 1938, but that doesn't mean he stopped doing great things. He went to work for legendary filmmaker and aviator Howard Hughes, helping to develop aircraft. Petrali's greatest moment had to have been when he served as one of the flight engineers for the famous flight of the Hughes H-4 Hercules (the *Spruce Goose*) on November 2, 1947. The first flight of the Hercules was short, but Petrali helped fly it. Interestingly, the Hercules is reported to have achieved a 135-mph airspeed, which is 1 mph slower than Petrali's 1936 EL land speed record at Daytona.

470 Wisconsin. You can't get a whole lot farther into the middle of the country, but that didn't stop the Milwaukee County Civilian Defense Council from forming the Civilian Motorcycle Dispatch Corps, which was responsible for quickly delivering messages across the state in case the war came to the shores of Lake Michigan. Of course, Harley-Davidsons were the mount of choice, and the riders were prepared to assist the war effort, just like the WLA riders overseas. Although it might seem somewhat unnecessary from today's viewpoint, there were constant worries of a German U-Boat entering Lake Michigan, and, as a major wartime supplier, Harley-Davidson would have been a prime target for a German bombing attack.

471 Celebrities of the early 1940s loved Knuckleheads! And why shouldn't they? There aren't a whole lot more stylish and fun ways to spend money than on a Harley-Davidson Big Twin. Plus, the celebs were just about the only ones who could manage an approval for a new motorcycle from the Wartime Production Board. Stars of the day including Ward Bond, Preston Foster, Clark Gable, Van Johnson, John Payne, Tyrone Power, Keenan Wynn, Robert Young, and leading lady Gene Tierney all rode and were photographed on Knuckleheads.

472 Most people are familiar with the modified silver Triumph that Fonzie (played by Henry Winkler) rode throughout most of the filming of *Happy Days*. But, did you know that he actually rode a 1947 Knucklehead chopper on screen in the first season? The Knuck was a much more fitting steed for the Fonz, considering his coolness and the fact that the show was based in Milwaukee. So, why the switch? Reportedly, Winkler had difficulty starting and riding the hopped-up Harley. In each riding scene, the bike had to be started for him and pointed in the right direction, and then other times, set assistants pushed him into the scene without the motorcycle running. After the first season, production of *Happy Days* moved from Milwaukee to a Los Angeles studio. The Knuck, and the only guy on staff who could kickstart it, stayed in Milwaukee. An interesting note is that the silver Triumph was built by Steve McQueen's friend and stunt double, Bud Ekins.

473 Fonzie's Knucklehead only appeared in the first season of *Happy Days* but that particular motorcycle had an illustrious career in film and television. Actor and stunt rider George Dockstader (originally from Wisconsin) owned it and used it in many of his movies. Among his many films were *The Wild One*, *Every Which Way But Loose*, and *Any Which Way You Can*, which all featured the 1947 Knuck in various trim, from outlaw chopper to a police bike.

474 One of the soccer world's biggest stars, David Beckham, is also one of Hollywood's "real riders," and is often seen cruising the streets of Los Angeles on his custom Knucklehead. Garage Company Customs built his bike and, although it looks as if it just rolled out of a barn after sitting for 70 years, it's completely new. It has a drum front brake and a disc in the rear but, unfortunately, it doesn't have a kickstart transmission.

475 Jay Leno featured his original, unrestored 1936 Knucklehead in an episode of his online show, *Jay Leno's Garage*. He tells the story of how he bought the bike after it had been sitting since 1952. He took it back to his shop, cleaned up the carburetor, changed the fluids, and was able to fire it up with two kicks! It then sat in his garage for nearly 30 years before he took it out and did a complete maintenance-only overhaul on it to make it safe for riding. As part of the 11-minute episode, he rides the 1936 Knuck on an interstate highway and some local roads while giving an informative lesson on what it's like to own and ride a Knucklehead.

MILITARY, POLICE AND RACING

476 In preparation for war, Harley-Davidson began production of almost 90,000 45-ci Flathead-powered motorcycles, 60,000 WLAs and 18,000 of the Canadian version, the WLC. The WLA, known as the Liberator for its effective use throughout the European theater, was produced through 1945; however, all were given 1942 engine stamps. These weren't simply olive drab WLs; the WLA was built to be the ultimate support machine of the era.

477 To make the engine more suitable for convoy work, Harley-Davidson engineers gave the WLA a lower compression ratio for durability and aluminum heads for better cooling. An improved oil pump and larger bearings increased the durability of the machine even further, as did a strengthened transmission and clutch. "Blackout" lighting was added to reduce the motorcycle's visibility from the air while still providing the rider enough light to see at night. A special oil-bath air cleaner cover was developed to allow the motorcycle to go through deeper water while also keeping out dust and other particulates from off-road use. To further increase ground clearance for off-road use, the new, tubular front fork was lengthened 2.375 inches. Skid plates, skirtless fenders, a heavy-duty rear rack, and a gun scabbard rounded out the combat-ready machine.

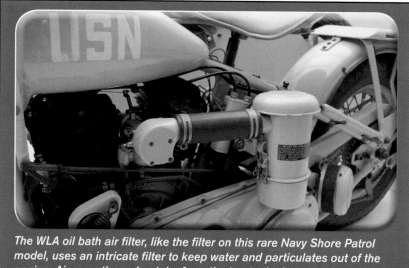

The WLA oil bath air filter, like the filter on this rare Navy Shore Patrol model, uses an intricate filter to keep water and particulates out of the engine. Air goes through a tube from the top to the bottom where it's released just above an oil bath, then it is pulled up through a filter element and then (finally) through the rubber hose to the carburetor. Water and particulates are caught in the oil bath at the bottom, which can be emptied and refilled quickly.

478 Two years before the United States formally entered World War II, Great Britain placed an order with Harley-Davidson for 5,000 motorcycles in autumn of 1939. Most British motorcycle manufacturers, located in England's West Midlands, had been heavily bombed, and couldn't fill enough orders. Harley-Davidson came to the rescue, even before President Roosevelt signed the Lend-Lease act into law in October of 1941. The Motor Company also sent 2,000 motorcycles to South Africa and an unknown number to the Soviet Union and China.

479 Today, new old stock (NOS) WLA parts are easily found via the Internet, at swap meets, and even at some Harley-Davidson dealers. In fact, it's still possible, and proved recently by Wheels Through Time curator Dale Walksler, that a person could build an entirely brand new motorcycle just from spare WLA parts! During the war, while The Motor Company was still producing WLAs and parts, Walter Davidson, ever the patriot and businessman of integrity, contacted the government procurement office and told them that their order was unnecessarily large, that they didn't need this many spares, and didn't have to spend so much money. The government told him it was okay, that that's the way things work. Flabbergasted, Arthur Davidson then traveled to Washington, D.C. to convince the procurement office to scale back its order, that it wouldn't need such an expensive order of parts. Again, the request was denied. So, WLA parts sit on warehouse shelves all over the world to this day!

480 After launching the new 61-ci OHV Knucklehead, and receiving great success and praise, Harley-Davidson wanted to prove that its new machine was the best. In 1937, Joe Petrali ran a Knucklehead at Daytona Beach to set a new speed record of 136.183 mph, beating the previous record set by Indian. His machine used a

Joe Petrali's 1936 EL streamliner ran more than 136 mph at Daytona Beach. As attractive as the purpose-built Knucklehead is, it actually ran faster without any of the fairings! That either says how good the new OHV engine was or how poor aerodynamic design was at the time. It is on permanent display at the Harley-Davidson Museum with the fairings fitted, as shown here. (Photo Courtesy Harley-Davidson)

small fairing and a narrow, shielded 1915 front end as well as a full-size cover on each side of the front wheel, which made the wheel look like a disc. Rearsets created from kickstarter pedals were bolted in front of a streamlined rear section that had cutouts for Petrali's legs. Downwardly bent handlebars and a resting pad on the gas tank allowed him to tuck in behind the front cowl. Engineers apparently hadn't quite figured out the right formula for aerodynamics. On his first run, the front end kept lifting off the sand and the rear section actually caught wind rather than dispersing it. For his second attempt, the wheel covers and entire tail section were removed and he achieved a record two-way average of 134.83 mph. Petrali knew his machine could do better; he took it for another run and beat his own record.

481 Speed is one thing, and consumers love it, but the Harley-Davidson motorcycle has always been more about endurance than speed. A test was needed to prove this side of the recirculating-oil OHV engine. Fred Ham, a motor officer, took his personal 1936 Knucklehead to Muroc Dry Lake in California to attempt a 24-hour record. He succeeded, completing 1,825 miles at an average pace of 76 mph.

482 The U.S. Signal Corps rode WLAs throughout the Panama Canal Zone during World War II as part of the effort to defend that vital waterway from the enemy. The Canal Zone was one of the most heavily-guarded areas during the war; disabling the canal would essentially cut off the U.S. navy from supporting ships in the Pacific or the Atlantic. The Signal Corps trained heavily, riding its WLAs through the thick forests and swamps of Panama. They regularly forded rivers that went up to the fenders and nearly all of the riding took place on primitive jungle trails.

483 One of the U.S. army's requirements for any military motorcycle submitted for testing was that it had to be capable of moving at 65 mph. Apparently, Harley-Davidson took that number literally. The data plate on WLAs and XAs stated "CAUTION" in big bold letters at the top, followed by "DO NOT EXCEED 65 M.P.H" right underneath. Surely adding to the confusion, both models were equipped with a 120-mph speedo.

484 The war in Europe loomed, and in 1938, Harley-Davidson began developing a variety of different motorcycles for the military. In 1939, prototypes using the 45-ci W engine and the 61-ci E engine were sent to the U.S. army for testing. The army decided on the 45, so The Motor Company sent a pair of completed WLAs to Fort Knox, Kentucky, for further testing. Shortly after the army received the prototype WLAs, Germany invaded Poland; many more WLAs would be needed.

485 Even though the WLA had tested admirably, the U.S. army repeatedly requested a BMW-style motorcycle with a boxer engine, full suspension, and foot-shift/hand-clutch 4-speed transmission. The Motor Company delivered the XA, a close copy of a reverse-engineered BMW. It used a 45-ci, horizontally opposed boxer engine; its 5.7:1 compression produced 23 hp at 4,600 rpm.

The XA engine resembles a BMW boxer engine, as it should; it was reverse-engineered from a captured BMW. It used an intricate powertrain that was not cost-effective for large-scale use. Notice the built-in oil bath filter in the center.

The numbers were similar to the 45, but the XA had a few upgrades over the WLA including an enclosed shaft-driven rear wheel, which was virtually maintenance-free and could stand up to much more abuse than an open chain. It also used a plunger-style rear suspension, similar to that of the Indian, in which a pair of upright shock absorbers was mounted to the frame at the top and the rear axle at the bottom. A 4-speed, foot-shift/hand-clutch transmission rounded out the technological package. At $870 each, it proved too costly, even for the U.S. army, which felt that the WLA was doing a fine job. Production halted after 1,000 XAs were made.

486 The first recorded race win by a Knucklehead occurred on February 2, 1936. Butch Quirk won a 350-mile endurance race in Portland, Oregon, aboard a 1936 EL with sidecar. In 1936, Knuckleheads raced in various types of competition although none from a factory program. AMA Class C racing rules were modified to find a place for the 61-ci OHV in the 80-ci Flathead class. Individuals tested their new machines in hill climbs, road races, and TT runs. A sidecar-equipped EL even took gold in a six-day endurance run in Germany that year. That win was recorded in *The Enthusiast*, much to the bewilderment of readers who had never heard of a 61-ci OHV model from Harley-Davidson.

487 Joe Petrali's record-setting 1936 Knucklehead was hardly stock in the engine department. It used a 3/4-inch shorter stroke with shorter cylinders and pushrods to match, likely to let the engine rev up a little faster. The engine used a pair of Linkert MR-2 racing carburetors, which fed air to the cylinder heads via their own cast-in manifolds on the left side. A magneto sat in place of a generator to save weight while a lightweight single-speed gearbox took the place of the standard 4-speed. No kickstarter was needed; to start the bike, it was pulled behind another vehicle, until Petrali dropped the clutch and fired the beast to life.

488 As usual, and deservedly so, police departments could order motorcycles that weren't necessarily available to civilians. In 1938, only the high-compression solo EL and the sidecar-rigged, medium-compression ES with sidecar gearing were available. However, most police motorcycles were medium-compression solos, which were required for low-speed operation; sidecar gearing was unnecessary. Police solos were marked 38E, making it a model not available to regular customers.

489 Although radar was invented in 1904, it was still many years before police departments used handheld units to track a vehicle's speed and motorists began using radar detectors to counter. Police models used a special speedo that used a second speed-hand that locked at top speed, just like the tachometer of a race car. A motor officer followed the perpetrator, maintaining the same speed, and when they both pulled over, he had evidence of how fast the speeder was going. A control arm on the left side of the dash console reset the hand lock.

490 In addition to the hand lock, police motorcycles had truly begun to look and act like the equipment in use today. In 1938, the California Highway Patrol set up their machines with the headlight on the right side of the fork and a flashing light on the left side. They were also equipped with a radio box on the left side where a saddlebag would otherwise be fitted. The standard toolbox was moved to the left side, underneath the radio box to make room for the siren, which was driven by a gear on the right side of the rear wheel. Lights, sirens, and full communication abilities made the Harley-Davidson motorcycle a highly effective police tool.

491 On June 5, 1938, Robert Tinoco won the 24-hour Bol d'Or race in France aboard his 1937 Knucklehead with sidecar. This marked the first time that race had ever been won by a motorcycle with a sidecar and Tinoco did it with an average speed of just over 52 mph!

492 Even though the WLA Flatheads were proving most effective as military motorcycles, Knucklehead-powered machines were requested for testing and use by both the U.S. and Canadian military. In 1942, Harley-Davidson built 45 ELCs for Canada and eight ELAs for the United States. They used many of the same parts as the 45 except for an XA front end and a sprung rear seat. The oil bath air filter system was mounted on the right side in front of the front cylinder instead of the left side of the rear cylinder because the sidecar for the ELC was designed for mounting on the left and enough clearance was needed for the kickstarter. A big toolbox was mounted to the front fender, as was a front stand that allowed the interchangeable wheels to be swapped in and out easily. These machines were built primarily for duty Stateside.

493 1943 brought good news to dealerships as the War Production Board began approving motorcycles for police use and guard duty at war production factories. The Motor Company worked with dealers to show them the best way to get their clients approved for wartime motorcycles. That year, 137 police departments purchased motorcycles, as did many war-related businesses, as an alternative to less efficient automobiles. The following year, 380 police departments were granted permission to purchase new H-Ds, including Milwaukee, which bought 21 machines.

494 Military surplus motorcycles entered the civilian market for the first time in 1944 with the sale of 15,000 WLAs and nearly the entire production run of XAs. WLAs sold for $450 while the XA cost $500. Many dealers jumped at the opportunity to buy bulk orders of cheap bikes that they could sell to a public that was desperate for new motorcycles. After the war, dealers continued to buy WLAs, paint and prep them for civilian use, and then sell them to customers. Among the largest groups buying WLAs were soldiers who had ridden them overseas and wanted one of their own after the war.

495 Harley-Davidson produced 670 military-spec UA Flatheads for the United States in 1939. They were more closely related to their civilian counterparts than the WLA was to the WL. The major design differences were olive drab or Navy gray paint, rifle holster on the front end, and a flattop luggage rack over the rear fender. In the engine, compression was lowered, as it was on the

WLA, to make the machine more effective at low-speed operation. Because many were equipped with a sidecar, sidecar gearing was standard. However, the United States wasn't the only recipient of the UA motorcycle. The South African Union Defense Forces used 1,156 sidecar-equipped (left-side) UAs that saw combat all over North and East Africa.

496 Harley-Davidson engines have been used in many different applications where you'd never expect to find Milwaukee iron. Although it never reached beyond the prototype state, H-D developed a twin-Knucklehead engine designed to power a light tank for the Canadian army. A fan-cooled version of the XA engine was produced for use as an auxiliary powerplant for American tanks. That particular XA variant was also commissioned for use in a small, lightweight vehicle from Willys that many called the "Jeeplet," for obvious reasons.

497 In 1940, Harley-Davidson built a Knucklehead-powered trike called the TA that looks more like something out of a Mad Max movie than the utilitarian military style of the WLA. With solid wheels and aggressive tires for off-road and combat duty overseas, the TA used a shaft final drive to power the rear wheels. The initial test mule was underpowered, so the 61-ci engine was bumped up to a 68-ci displacement by giving it a 3-7/16-inch bore and a 3-11/16-inch stroke. The following year, 1941, H-D released the FL Knucklehead engine with the same bore but a 4-inch stroke. 16 TAs were built in 1940 and 1941, but they were more expensive and less effective than the new Jeeps built by Ford and Willys, and so the project was scrapped.

498 Even though it was a race of semi-legal standing, the legend of the 1936 EL named *Soupy 61* is worth mentioning here. Harry Sebreny, an employee at The Motor Company, was one of the first owners of a Knucklehead, and relayed his story to Herbert Wagner in his incredible book, *Harley-Davidson 1930–1941: Revolutionary Motorcycles & Those Who Rode Them*. Being well-liked while working for H-D has its advantages, which include being called to the assembly line to watch your motorcycle being built as well as being given all the special trim that usually costs extra. In addition, all engines were dyno-tested before being placed in a frame, and the guys on the line gave Harry Sebreny one of the highest-rated engines they had ever tested. After taking delivery of his new 61, Bill Davidson Jr., found Harry and asked if he'd be willing to race it against a dealer from California who had shown up in a hot rod and didn't believe the 61 could possibly be that fast. Harry proved that it was when they raced on Highway 100 right after the road was built, before it was open to traffic. *Soupy 61* blew the California hot rod out of the water!

499 Although the 61s could run circles around the ancient Flat-heads of the same era, it's believed that no police departments bought Knuckleheads in that first year, not even in Milwaukee! The Milwaukee Police Department didn't buy a Knucklehead until 1938. Like many individuals at the time, police departments opted to stick with the tried and true Flathead, which provided quality service, especially with the 1937 updates. In 1939, EL police sales began to really ramp up and, by 1940, police-issue ELs were patrolling the streets all around the country.

500 The 500-mile Jack Pine enduro race. The toughest challenge any man and machine could take on, and if the route didn't break one or the other, the clock did. The 1938 event proved to be one of the most difficult ever and it was also the first time that the Knucklehead won, thanks to rider Ted Konecny of Saginaw, Michigan. In the June 1939 issue of *The Enthusiast*, Konecny's achievement was highlighted alongside Joe Petrali's record speed run and Fred Ham's Muroc stamina test. All three were used to advertise the incredible capability of the Harley-Davidson 61 OHV.

Chapter 5

Panhead Era
1948–1965

THE MOTOR COMPANY

501 In what may seem confusing at first, Harley-Davidson celebrated its 50th anniversary with its 1954 models. But wait, wasn't the company founded in 1903? Fortunately, this is one of the few inconsistencies that actually can be cleared up. In the early 1950s, The Motor Company considered 1904 its first year of manufacture because it believed that the first public motorcycle sale occurred in 1904 and all prior machines were prototypes. Later, a May 1916 issue of *Motor Cycle Illustrated* was discovered in which Walter Davidson was quoted, "We found in 1903 that there was a market for motorcycles. C. H. Lang, of Chicago, having heard of us in that year and buying one-third of our output." With a total output of three motorcycles in 1903, Walter's implication is that the company's first outside sale was of an original 1903 model, not a 1904 as previously thought.

502 With the celebration of its first half-century, Harley-Davidson released the first special anniversary models as 1954s. All models in the lineup received a 50th anniversary brass emblem mounted on the front fender. Anniversary Yellow was a one-year only color option and was available on EL/FLs, K models, and Servi-Cars.

Harley-Davidson riders love their history, and many do a double take when they discover that The Motor Company's 50th anniversary was celebrated with the 1954 models, which suggests that 1904 was the true first year of manufacture. Before you jump to conclusions, remember that the 1954 models were released in autumn of 1953! (Photo Courtesy Harley-Davidson)

503 Harley-Davidson's last American competitor, Indian Motocycle, went out of business in 1953, which left H-D as the only major manufacturer of American motorcycles (until the first Victory was sold in 1998). However, things were just starting to heat up in the early 1950s; an influx of technologically superior, less expensive foreign motorcycles had already begun to hit U.S. dealerships.

504 Helmets and Harley-Davidson riders don't always mix well, and this was especially true in the 1950s. That didn't stop The Motor Company from including its first hard-shell "safety helmet" in its 36-page 1958 accessory catalog. The half-helmet was available only in white for $23.50, and had many accessory options such as chin straps, ear covers, sizing pads, visors, and face shields, and more that likely wouldn't pass today's DOT and SNELL tests.

505 Harley-Davidson went public in 1965 with a $20 per share valuation so that founding family members who had little to do with The Motor Company could diversify their money. Shortly thereafter, Bangor Punta Corporation, based in Greenwich, Connecticut, began pursuing shareholders to buy their H-D stock. Bangor Punta was a conglomerate that owned companies producing a variety of products including sail and power yachts, Piper Aircraft, and Smith & Wesson firearms. It wanted Harley-Davidson as its flagship company. According to Jean Davidson, Bangor Punta representatives went to the homes of Harley and Davidson family members and tried to buy their stock on the spot with cash offers. Bangor Punta actually offered 50 percent over market price for the company.

506 At the age of 69, Arthur Davidson, the last surviving company founder, was killed along with his wife, Clara, and two others in a two-car accident. The December 3, 1950, collision occurred just 3 miles south of their dairy farm on Highway 59 in Waukesha, Wisconsin. At the time, Arthur was the company secretary and sales manager. He is buried in Forest Home Cemetery in Milwaukee along with his two brothers.

507 The early 1950s was a great period for the United States, economically, but it was an especially trying time for The Motor Company. For the first time in its history, it encountered motorcycle competition in terms of performance, price, and trendiness with which it could not compete. Indian Motocycle introduced its 80-ci Flathead Chief with hydraulic forks in 1950, and began importing British motorcycles and selling them in its dealerships. BSA, Norton, Matchless, Vincent, and others began appearing on roads all over the United States and were quickly recognized as the motorcycles of choice among new buyers. Triumph had two distribution facilities in the United States in 1950, one in Los Angeles and the other in Towson, Maryland; they combined to sell thousands of motorcycles each year. Harley-Davidson petitioned the U.S. Tariff Commission for relief from what it claimed was unfair foreign trade practices in June 1951. In 1952, the Tariff Commission denied the request.

508 In 1963, The Motor Company saw its worst single-year sales since 1940. Only 4,300 Panheads were sold out of a total of 9,873 motorcycles produced. Maybe it had something to do with Honda outselling all other motorcycle manufacturers combined. That, or maybe people just didn't feel like buying motorcycles while under the constant threat of a Soviet missile hitting their homes.

509 The once-great Indian Motocycle was in its death throes in the early 1950s, and Harley-Davidson management met to discuss the possibility of offering financial support or even buying it outright to keep the brand alive. The worry was that someone else could buy Indian and mount a charge against them. Realistically, it was difficult to own, operate, and race two competitive brands, so the decision was made not to purchase Indian.

510 In the early 1950s, the public perception of motorcycling's outlaw counter-culture lifestyle not only affected the brand's image, but also was difficult for the Davidson family to accept. They had worked hard to promote the American brand as a supporter of the military, police, and various other public service groups, and hated seeing the Bar & Shield portrayed negatively to the public. President William H. Davidson took a strong stance against anything that promoted the outlaw culture and working diligently to restore its image.

511 In 1960, Harley-Davidson launched its Topper scooter amid a competitive market that consisted of Cushman, Vespa, and soon, Honda. Toppers were used for a variety of purposes and could even be purchased with a sidecar! The Topper never caught on the way that the execs hoped it would. It's believed that fewer than 3,000 were produced between 1960 and 1965.

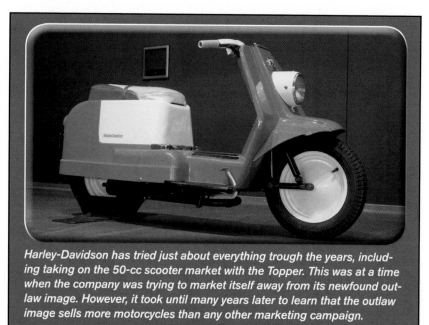

Harley-Davidson has tried just about everything trough the years, including taking on the 50-cc scooter market with the Topper. This was at a time when the company was trying to market itself away from its newfound outlaw image. However, it took until many years later to learn that the outlaw image sells more motorcycles than any other marketing campaign.

512 The Motor Company purchased a 49 percent interest in the Italian company Aermacchi, which produced small engines and performance aircraft. The company had previously developed an electric motorcycle prototype and had gained fame for building the fastest piston-engined seaplane ever. The new company was called Aermacchi Harley-Davidson and focused primarily on small-displacement, single-cylinder motorcycle engines. It was with

Aermacchi that H-D went on to produce the much-loved Sprint in larger displacements than the previous single-cylinders.

513 Harley-Davidson showed incredible foresight regarding the role fiberglass could play with its motorcycles, and purchased a 60-percent stake in the Tomahawk Boat Manufacturing Company in Tomahawk, Wisconsin. Being able to produce its own fiberglass components allowed the company to better implement those parts in the design process so that they didn't look like bolt-on aftermarket accessories. Fiberglass aided in the production and design of hard saddlebags, fairings, and fenders that live on both classic models as well as on new models today.

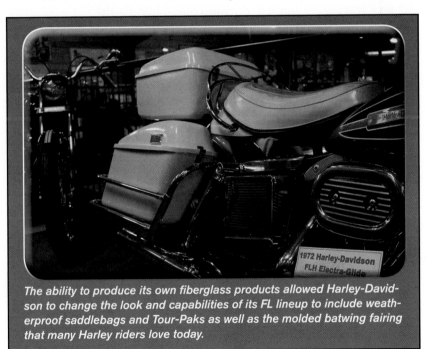

1972 Harley-Davidson FLH Electra-Glide

The ability to produce its own fiberglass products allowed Harley-Davidson to change the look and capabilities of its FL lineup to include weatherproof saddlebags and Tour-Paks as well as the molded batwing fairing that many Harley riders love today.

514 With the successful launch of the 1948 Panheads, Harley-Davidson set a peacetime sales record of 29,612 total machines sold that year, of which 12,924 were Panheads. Big Twin sales dropped tremendously throughout the 1950s and early 1960s, due, in large part, to foreign competition. The 1965 Panhead helped start the company on the road back to success by selling 6,930 machines, the most since 1951.

515 Early in the 1950s, it became clear that a Harley-Davidson owner wasn't finished with the simple purchase of a motorcycle. Many new owners chose from the variety of options packages, H-D parts and accessories, as well as aftermarket parts to outfit perfectly good, brand-new motorcycles. In 1950, Harley-Davidson made major additions to its parts and accessories catalog as well as its line of MotorClothes. The tradition of customizing a motorcycle after the initial purchase continues in earnest to this day.

516 What motorcycle do you consider to be the nemesis of the Harley-Davidson tourers? Many folks will immediately think of the plush, quiet, gadget-ridden Honda Gold Wing, which was first built in 1974 as a 1975 model. But, you might be surprised to know that Harley-Davidson, through its Aermacchi subsidiary, had actually been producing Gold Wing motorcycles since 1957. Called the Ala d'Oro (Italian for Gold Wing), the small-displacement, high-performance motorcycle eventually became known as the Sprint and Rapido in the United States. So, Harley-Davidson produced a Gold Wing (technically, at least) from the time it bought its first stake in Aermacchi in 1960 to the last Ala d'Oro built in 1972.

517 Currently, Milwaukee Golf Caddy makes racks to fit onto touring bikes in place of one of the saddlebags to allow a rider to tote his (or her) golf bag and clubs to the course in style. Apparently, H-Ds and golf have always gone together. In 1963, Harley-Davidson bought the Columbia Car Company and began producing golf carts. The first H-D golf cart used a 250-cc two-stroke and rode on three wheels; a tiller-style steering mechanism turned the single front wheel. Battery-powered golf carts were available soon after, as well as four-wheel machines with standard steering wheels. Interestingly, the golf carts were given the model designation of D, the first machine to use that letter since the early upright-generator 45 Flatheads. All production of golf carts ceased in 1980 and the division was sold to Columbia Par Car in 1981.

518 If you could work at Harley-Davidson, what department would you choose? Do you know about the secretive Department 43, the experimental branch? Department 43 consisted of some of the best mechanics and machining equipment The Motor Company had and it developed a small handful of one-off motorcycles, one at a time, in complete secrecy. This division is where things such as rubber-mounting technology, frame-mounted fairings, and light front ends on very heavy bikes were developed, sometimes 20 years before these innovations found their way onto production models.

519 The 1954 anniversary logo is the only one that doesn't feature some version of an eagle's wing. Every other anniversary logo from 1978 to 2013 features an eagle's wing, and that's likely a tradition that will continue for future logos.

520 As proven time and time again, The Motor Company's obsessive organization and storage of its past work has only helped it in the future. Even something as seemingly unnecessary as keeping an old 45 OHV prototype that took up valuable space was made worthwhile more than a decade later when engineers set out to build the first OHV Sportster. Where do you think they started? Right there in the company's archives; they dusted off that old prototype that had done so well on its 5,000-mile test run back in 1939. That old 45 OHV finally got its chance.

521 When Harley-Davidson introduced the Sportster, every dealer knew it was going to be an immediate hit, just like the 1936 EL. However, what customers wanted and what the factory offered weren't exactly the same. Consider California, one of the biggest motorcycling populations in the country. In the 1950s, off-road racing was the big craze. What young customers really wanted was a fast bike that could be raced off road, but also driven on the street for transportation. California dealerships got together and asked The Motor Company for such a version of the Sportster, which was approved, provided the dealerships took at least 60. Dealerships nationwide sold 239 XLCH models in 1958 and 1,059 in 1959, proving yet again that the dealers know their audience!

522 Because the California dealer–led version of the Sportster was called the XLCH, and because Harley-Davidson doesn't actually say what the letters mean, many enthusiasts argue to this day about whether the C stands for Competition or for California. Which one do you think it is?

523 Like to ride your Harley a lot? As much as we all do, actually hitting odometer milestones such as 50,000 or 100,000 is still a pretty special occurrence, and that kind of mileage was an even greater feat in the 1950s. To honor those who rode their motorcycles the way they were intended, The Motor Company instituted the Mileage Club in 1951, for which riders could earn pins and honorary membership cards to the club. Pins and membership cards were available at 50,000 and 100,000 miles; 25,000 miles got you only the card. The program began officially on January 1, 1951, and any mileage awards were based on miles ridden since that date. By 1955, only 73 riders had earned a 100,000-mile pin.

524 In 1960, The Motor Company announced the creation of Harley-Davidson International to gain a better grasp on the European markets without the overhead concerns of tariffs, varying regulations, and long-distance communication. The new subsidiary was based in Switzerland and handled all overseas marketing and sales of motorcycles and accessories. This strategy came about following the 1957 Treaty of Rome, which created the European Economic Community (EEC) to improve ease of trade between European countries. Of course, the only way for U.S. companies to benefit from this common market was to set up an overseas subsidiary.

525 Advertisements of the 1950s and 1960s were no doubt sensational, and Harley-Davidson ads were right up there with the best of them. One 1959 ad even went so far as to suggest, "SPORTSTERS give you jet-propulsion on or 'off the road.'" The ad featured an image of a Sportster with the words "JET-STREAM SPORTSTERS" underneath. That same ad also described the more powerful version of the FL Duo-Glide as the "Super-power FLH." Now that's a stretch!

THE CHASSIS

526 Interestingly, the release of the new Panhead engine didn't bring about any worthwhile changes in the design and chassis department. And that's part of what makes the 1948 Panhead so special; it's the only year that Panheads came with a springer fork. It also makes 1948 the last year Harley-Davidson produced a springer on Big Twins until its return in 1988. EL models sold for $635 and FLs sold for $650.

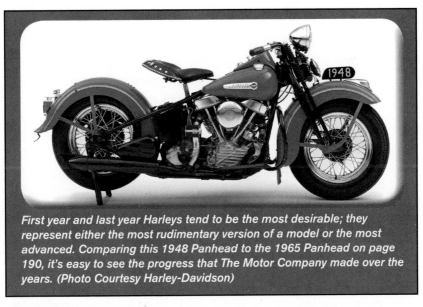

First year and last year Harleys tend to be the most desirable; they represent either the most rudimentary version of a model or the most advanced. Comparing this 1948 Panhead to the 1965 Panhead on page 190, it's easy to see the progress that The Motor Company made over the years. (Photo Courtesy Harley-Davidson)

527 The Hydra Glide model appeared in 1949, and with it the hydraulic, telescopic fork design still used on Harleys to this day. Although The Motor Company had developed its hydraulic fork a few years earlier, rumor has it that the company wanted to use up the existing supply of springers before introducing the hydraulic fork. Maybe it even went so far as to hold off bringing out the Hydra Glide an extra year following the introduction of the Panhead engine. The telescopic fork uses springs and oil inside the fork tubes that cushion impacts and provide a smoother ride than springs alone. The practice of using "Glide" in the names of Touring models continues today.

528 Harley-Davidson has always been interested in lightweight, small-displacement motorcycles that could help attract youthful and nontraditional buyers to the brand. Finally, the company was able to offer just such a motorcycle. The concept is actually from the German manufacturer DKW; the designs were given to Harley-Davidson as part of war reparations. Introduced in 1948 and known as the Hummer Model S-125, it weighed only 170 pounds dry, sported a 50-inch wheelbase, and could carry 1.75 gallons of fuel. At $325, it was half the price of a new Panhead. In 1951, the telescopic Tele-Glide front end replaced the girder front end.

529 With the recent influx of high-performance motorcycles coming from Great Britain, The Motor Company had to come up with a replacement for its aging Flathead-powered W models; something that could compete in both speed and handling. It succeeded with the 1952 Model K Sport and Sport Solo. The K uses a hydraulic front fork and, for the first time on a civilian H-D, a swingarm and twin hydraulic shocks on the rear. At 400 pounds, it was an excellent platform for future performance offerings.

530 For the new 1948 Panhead models, the company used a new frame. It was nicknamed the wishbone frame because the front downtubes spread downward in a V from a single starting point, like the wishbone in a bird. The wishbone frame was used until 1954. However, several slight changes were made during that period; the biggest was that 1948–1949 springer-equipped frames lacked flattened downtubes for horn block mounts.

531 Early 1948 Panheads were available with optional eagle fender tips on the front and rear. These metal tips feature an embossed eagle with its wings spread wide. Later 1948 models have simple, stylized metal tips, which were used until 1956.

532 1948–1952 Panheads use a newly designed Stewart-Warner speedometer with a bluish-gray center, a light green outer ring, and a red needle. The white numbers are written in their entirety, from 10 to 120, unlike later versions that didn't include zeroes. The odometer and tripmeter had black numbers, except for the tenths, which were red, on a white background. The Bar & Shield logo appeared at the bottom, making it the only time the logo appeared instead of the Harley-Davidson script during the Panhead era. Ten different speedometers were used throughout the 17-year run of Panheads; they are excellent for identification.

533 1948 was the last year that the springer front end came standard on all Big Twins, but it wasn't the last year that you could get a Panhead with a factory-equipped springer. Harley-Davidson introduced the P designation for the 1949 model year for motorcycles equipped with a springer. Springers could be ordered with solo models. However, most were used on sidecars and package trucks, per H-D recommendations that the Hydra Glide's front-end trail measurements were too steep for optimal stability in these variations. Bikes were designated as ELP, FP, etc. based on the original model. Occasionally, the P appears at the end of the engine case identification number, following the production number. Even though the springer was better suited to the task, it was still possible to buy a 1949 Panhead with a sidecar and Hydra Glide front end. In addition, ordering a springer on a 1949 meant that you actually received a 1948 frame, but it differed only in the horn block mount and flattened downtubes. The problem with the trail was solved for the 1950 model year with the introduction of the optional adjustable-trail Hydra Glide fork. It enabled an increase in trail for sidecar stability and a decrease in trail for solo sportiness.

534 Along with the Hydra Glide front end came a new, better front drum brake. Its size was increased from 7-1/4 to 8 inches, and it used an internal actuating lever instead of the older external style. A larger brake cable accompanied the updated brake system, which Harley used through 1965, the last year of the Panhead.

535 The 1954 Panheads saw the introduction of the whimsical and oh-so-1950s jubilee trumpet horn; these were last used on the 1964 models. The horn trumpet is mounted on the right side of the engine underneath the air cleaner and extends forward to the downtubes. It's connected to a horn body on the left side, which powers it; then it winds between the cylinders to meet the trumpet portion.

536 The venerable Big Twin's hardtail rear end was well behind the times by the mid-1950s. Harley-Davidson launched its flagship motorcycle into a new era with the introduction of the Duo-Glide in 1958. The biggest change for the Duo-Glide is the dual rear shock absorbers and articulating swingarm for a more comfortable and sporty ride.

537 In a departure from The Motor Company's usual tendency to make big changes one at a time, the 1958 Duo-Glide was also the first Big Twin to receive hydraulic brakes, which were referred to as "juice" brakes. A master cylinder was mounted alongside the right footboard and a new pedal forced the juice through a hydraulic line, new hub, and new backing plate with attached hydraulic cylinder. This style of brake was used, with only minor changes, until 1971.

538 Who doesn't love a classic Harley-Davidson with whitewall tires? Pesky purists, that's who. As good as whitewalls look with a hardtail frame, they were, unfortunately, not available until the 1958 Duo-Glide.

539 Although it was a relatively small change, the new "freight-train" headlight nacelle introduced on 1960 Panheads went a long way to modernize the look of the dual-suspension motorcycle. Take a look at a brand new Road King; obviously, the styling department was on to something in 1960. The new, one-piece headlight nacelle completely shrouds the headlight and upper forks and stretches the cockpit to give the rider somewhat of a "warp speed" feel.

540 Big Twins received a new console dash for 1962, which features The Motor Company's first use of the modern "idiot lights" with different colors to display the condition of the engine. We all know two of them by heart: green for neutral and red for low oil pressure, which, on a Harley, basically means no oil pressure. A blue light indicated generator status. Note the lack of an orange turn signal light; turn signals were not yet available. Handshift models didn't have the green neutral light because the location of the shifter indicated that the motorcycle was in neutral.

541 As modern as most of the Harley-Davidson fleet had become (footshifting, rear suspension, and numerous new engine components), the Flathead-powered Servi-Car remained one of the most vital machines. In 1959, 10 years after Big Twins received the telescopic front end, the three-wheeled workhorse finally received the Hydra Glide front end.

542 In the mid-1960s, the Servi-Car's metal box was replaced with a fiberglass box made at H-D's Tomahawk plant. The plant now produced other components, such as fairings and saddlebags, for the other models. Prior to Harley-Davidson producing its own fiberglass parts, the Chas Abresch Company in Milwaukee made metal Servi-Car boxes.

543 Harley-Davidson introduced the updated version of the K model in 1957 and gave it the name we all know and love: the

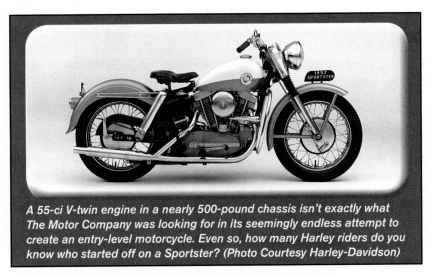

A 55-ci V-twin engine in a nearly 500-pound chassis isn't exactly what The Motor Company was looking for in its seemingly endless attempt to create an entry-level motorcycle. Even so, how many Harley riders do you know who started off on a Sportster? (Photo Courtesy Harley-Davidson)

XL Sportster. The 495-pound, dual-shock motorcycle was as much an exercise in styling as it was in performance, if not more so in its earliest rendition. Its 18-inch wheels, buckhorn handlebars, and a variety of two-tone paint schemes updated the appearance of the K model, but the real updates were in the engine.

544 After the first year's success of the Sportster, Harley-Davidson launched two additional versions in 1958: the XLH and XLCH. As known from previous models, the H represents a higher-performing engine (in this case via higher compression). Otherwise, the XLH differed little from the XL. On the other hand, the XLCH was a very different motorcycle. Intended mainly for competition, it came with no lights, dual straight pipes, a bobbed rear fender, 19-inch front wheel, and a smaller peanut tank. And it made a hell of a street machine when The Motor Company launched it as such in 1959.

545 The 1958 and 1959 XLCH each debuted a part that became an iconic Sportster detail, right up to the present. In 1958, to reduce weight and slim down the CH's width, designers borrowed the peanut-style gas tank from the Hummer. This gas tank has defined what a Sportster should look like. In addition, the 1948 Hummer led The Motor Company to create a model in its honor: the Forty-Eight, which debuted in 2010. The other iconic part is much smaller, but no less important in shaping the appearance of today's Sportster: the headlight visor. It debuted on the 1959 XLCH; it was an attempt to make the headlight appear as though it was an afterthought on an otherwise race-ready motorcycle.

546 Many folks are familiar with the modern Softail's suspension system: The shock absorbers reside hidden underneath the motorcycle's frame. That design for the Big Twin frame wasn't invented until the 1970s and not used by The Motor Company until 1984. However, Harley-Davidson actually released a Softail-style model 20 years earlier, in 1963, called the Scat. It's difficult to compare the 165-cc single-cylinder engine to the model bearing the 80-ci Evolution engine, but the hidden suspension system makes it

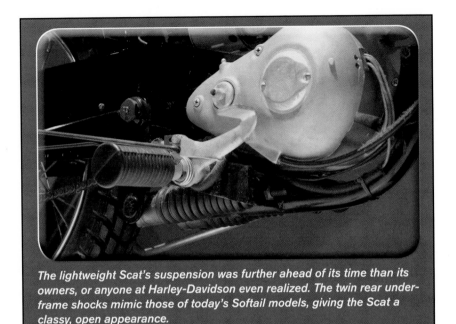

The lightweight Scat's suspension was further ahead of its time than its owners, or anyone at Harley-Davidson even realized. The twin rear underframe shocks mimic those of today's Softail models, giving the Scat a classy, open appearance.

easy to connect the dots. The Scat was primarily intended for dual-sport use, and it sported a large rear fender and lights. The street version was called the Pacer and a completely stripped, off-road racing version was called the Ranger. The Bobcat was a café racer version that was introduced a few years later. Interestingly, the Scat also used an upside-down hydraulic fork, a high-performance form of front suspension found today on only a handful of H-D models.

547 What do you do right before you dismount your parked bike? Drop the sidestand? That might be a difficult task if you purchased an XLH or XLCH Sportster before 1964, because sidestands were not yet standard equipment. That changed for the 1964 model year when Harley-Davidson included a new sidestand on all street motorcycle purchases, except, of course, the Servi-Car. Its official name was the Jiffy Stand.

548 Ah, the end of a magnificent era. Harley-Davidson released the Electra Glide for 1965 and it is truly the perfect culmination of the Panhead era. The major addition of the namesake electric start will be covered later, but the 1965 Electra Glide is a very different motorcycle than the Duo-Glide it replaced. The front fender trim stating Electra Glide, in script, easily identifies Electra Glides.

549 To make up for all the new standard goodies on the Electra Glide, the base price jumped $145 from the previous year to $1,530 for an FL. A black front engine guard, Jiffy Stand, and a new 5-gallon gas tank were among the standard features. Hand-shift models required using the old 3-3/4-gallon tanks, which had the indent on the left side for the hand-shifter.

550 To make room for the larger 12-volt battery and electric starter components, a new frame was introduced that eliminated the step-down section in front of the rear shocks. Because the battery was too big to fit in the traditional U section within the oil tank, a new, square oil tank, mounted on the right side of the bike, had to be used; the battery was mounted on the left side. Over the course of the Panhead's 18-year run, it gained almost 200 pounds, 75 of which came just from the Electra Glide's battery and starting system.

THE POWERTRAIN

551 An immediately recognizable favorite among Harley-Davidson enthusiasts to this day, The Motor Company released the Panhead engine in 1948. It's essentially a reengineered Knucklehead engine with the goal of resolving many of the complaints associated with the Knuck. On the Panhead, oil lines run inside the engine case to alleviate oil seepage, and an improved oil pump aided the system. Hydraulic lifters replaced the old mechanical lifters, reducing maintenance intervals because they automatically adjust for the gaps between lifter, pushrod, and valve. This also increased durability and decreased engine noise. Finally, aluminum heads were used for better heat dissipation and weight savings. On the surface, its smooth rocker covers resemble upside down cake pans, leading to its nickname. Two displacements were available for 1948: the 50-hp 61-ci EL and the 55-hp 74-ci FL.

552 Harley-Davidson ventured into the affordable lightweight market with its 1948 Model S-125 (Hummer). The 125-cc two-stroke engine is good for about 3 hp, which is actually enough to propel the 3-speed motorcycle to a 50-mph top speed. It's also the first Harley I've found that references using a factory foot-shift/ hand-clutch setup. In 1953, displacement was bumped to 165 cc, and the model designation followed suit.

553 The 45-ci W engine was completely redesigned for use in the 1952 K Model. It maintains the middleweight 750-cc displacement and sidevalve design, and that's about it. The K received larger cams, carburetor, and a higher 6.5:1 compression ratio that helped the aluminum, high-finned heads put out 30 hp. The biggest update, however, was the 4-speed unit transmission now located inside the engine case. A foot-shift/hand-clutch setup was used. However, the shifter is located on the right and the brake on the left, not to copy the British motorcycles, but to make an easier layout for flat track racing. Tests at the time found that a stock K ran about 16.8 seconds in the quarter-mile with a 53-mph trap speed. If you think that's

The Sportster's roots are obvious in the first 1952 K Model Harley-David-son. It was narrow, light, sporty, and matched with a torquey 45-degree V-twin that proved to be a recipe for success on the racetrack and in showrooms. The high-performance British invasion had begun; in 1952, The Motor Company fired back. (Photo Courtesy Harley-Davidson)

nothing special, you're right. The first K proved to be no faster than an FL Panhead of the same vintage. A new KK Model was introduced for 1953; it had hotter cams, head modifications, and cylinder porting for improved airflow. A faster-responding throttle was also added to the K and KK for 1953.

554 The Topper scooter is the only Harley-Davidson to ever use a rope pull-starter. The handle came out of the floor in front of the seat. Somehow, it didn't have quite the same effect as a kick-starter.

555 Harley-Davidson introduced the M-50 in 1965, and it was the smallest engine that the company ever put into a motorcycle. Motorcycle might be a strong word, however. The M-50 was a 50-cc two-stroke single-cylinder moped that produced 2-1/2 hp, could reach speeds of up to 40 mph, and claimed to achieve 180 mpg. Small displacement, yes; you decide if you want to call it a Harley-Davidson or not.

556 The engineers did everything but rest on their laurels when it came to the short-lived K Model. For 1954, it was given the designation of KH Sport and a displacement bump to 54 ci (883 cc) by using a longer, 4-9/16-inch stroke. Taller cylinders were used to accommodate the longer stroke, and the cylinders sported redesigned ports, larger intake valves, and even bigger cams than previous models. Now producing 38 hp, the 1954 KH could run the quarter-mile in 14.75 seconds. To handle the additional output, the clutch pack was enlarged from five discs to seven, with the primary cover made wider to clear it.

557 In case the new KH wasn't hot enough, The Motor Company offered the hand-built KHK Super Sport version, also in 1954. The KHK received additional porting and head machining to take full advantage of its high-lift cams, which differ little from those used in the KR racer. The stronger KR valvesprings also had to be used in the 40-hp engine.

558 For the 1948 model year, Panheads of both engine sizes came standard with the tried and true 4-speed transmission. However, buyers at the time could also choose a 3-speed transmission or a 3-speed with reverse at no additional cost. The plain 3-speed was only available in Big Twins for 1948, while the typical 4-speed and 3-plus-reverse continued.

559 With the introduction of the 1948 Panhead engine, Harley-Davidson became the first motorcycle to use hydraulic lifters. When running, the lifter assembly fills with oil and places pressure on an interior plunger that operates the pushrods. Oil is nearly incompressible, so it keeps the lifter in a solid state when in operation. As the cam turns and the lifter returns to its neutral state, a spring pushes the plunger down, allowing the assembly to fill with oil again. Because of this design, engineers no longer had to compromise for metal expansion between cold engine operation and warm engine operation. This nearly eliminated the required machining tolerances, which removed excess wear and tear on the moving parts. Owners no longer had to adjust clearances and only had to replace lifters when doing a high-mileage engine rebuild.

560 While the new hydraulic lifter system worked great for most customers, there were, as with any new technology, some teething issues. Most problems were caused by low oil pressure, even though Panheads were now fitted with a new oil pump with wider gears that provided 25 percent more flow. The problem was with the pump's governor, which was also used in Knuckleheads. It prevented over-oiling at low engine speeds. The fix was to replace the bypass valve governor with a valve-check spring like the one used on early Knuckleheads. Dealers were instructed to rebuild oil pumps not yet sold to the new specifications. The last 75 1948 Panheads built came from the factory with oil pumps already rebuilt.

561 Those new pan-shaped covers not only provided a modern, mid-century look to the flagship Big Twin, but they also housed numerous improvements. The Knucklehead uses separate covers for the intake and exhaust rockers, but the Panhead cover completely encloses the upper valvetrain and provides an improved oil seal. The 1948 covers are chrome-plated steel while the headers from other years are stainless steel or aluminum. In case you are ever quizzed on Panheads, the rocker box covers are attached with 12 screws, except for most 1955 models, which only have 6.

562 Throughout the 17-year run of the Panhead, Harley-Davidson used five different generators as well as an additional three optional two-way radio generators on all models in the lineup. Motorcycles from 1948 through early 1951 use the old model 32E, three-brush, six-volt generator in use since 1932. 1948 also had an optional 15-amp, two-brush, 32E2R generator for handling the additional amperage required for police two-way radios. A new, 20-amp generator, the model 48, debuted on 1951 models as a replacement for the 32E2R, before it was quickly replaced in favor of the model 51. Late-1952s received the model 52 generator, which is a three-brush six-volt system, just like the 32E, but with a greater amperage output. The 1958–1960 models use the model 58 generator, which is a two-brush six-volt design. The model 61 generator used until 1964 is the same as the 58 but with a new needle bearing end cover. The biggest generator update with which most people are familiar is the new model 65 12-volt generator, which debuted in 1965 along with electric start on Big Twins.

563 We all know chrome was popular in the 1950s, right? The Motor Company took the chrome age to a new level when it began using chrome-plated compression rings in 1951 engines. Before you laugh, the chrome compression rings reduced scuffing of the cylinder wall during initial engine break-in, which ensured a better seal for a longer period of time.

564 Finally, in 1952, foot-shift/hand-clutch was offered as a no-cost option on Big Twins and was assigned the ELF or FLF designation, depending on engine size. Hand-shift models were still offered to civilians; however, after only two years on the market, twice as many customers were purchasing foot-shifters than hand-shifters. To assist with clutch pull, the engineers added a spring-operated booster that mounted on the frame's left downtube (remember, a hand now pulled what a foot had previously pushed). Along with the foot-shift option came a new-left side gas tank that was completely smooth, without the usual indents for the shifter gate. Some later 1951s were available with the optional foot-shift/hand-clutch setup directly from the factory. The F was never stamped into the engine case, so there's no way to tell how the motorcycle was originally delivered from the factory.

565 How would you like to have Parko-Lubrized parts inside your motor? Harley-Davidson introduced parkerized engine valves in its 1952 motors and gave them that silly name, which people of the 1950s probably thought quite clever. Parkerized valves had the distinct property of being able to absorb oil, which protected the parts and their surfaces during engine break-in time.

566 The 61-ci E and EL engines were dropped from the Big Twin lineup for the 1953 model year. Fewer than 1,000 were sold in 1952 out of the total 6,700 Panheads sold.

567 Harley-Davidson introduced the FLH engine package in 1955 to compete with the high-performing British models that had helped reduce Big Twin sales to fewer than 5,000 units in 1954. The FLH Super Sport has a higher 8.0:1 compression ratio and polished intake tracts, which add up to about a 10 percent power boost over the standard FL. It accounted for 1,103 sales, or 20 percent of Panhead production, in its first year.

568 Anyone who's looked at the intake manifold on a pre-1955 Harley-Davidson might be shocked to discover that it's secured to the cylinder heads with plumbing nuts on either side. In the 1920s and 1930s, that might have been okay, but the 1950s? Chuck Yeager hit Mach 1 in 1947, men were in space by the end of 1963, and plumbing nuts were still used on a Harley engine? That changed with the 1955 models when it upgraded to the O-ring manifold, which provided a better, longer-lasting connection.

569 Until 1961, H-Ds used a single-fire, or wasted-spark, ignition system in which both spark plugs fired each time; of course, one spark was wasted. The 1961 Big Twins used a new, dual-point timer with a single-lobe cam instead of the previous single-point dual-lobe cam. New, rounded coils were used, two instead of one this time, and each powered its own spark plug.

570 In a somewhat strange move, the engineers reverted to the Panhead engine with external oil lines in 1963. Big Twins hadn't seen this since the 1947 Knucklehead. Anyone who's ever ridden or stood next to a Panhead after a ride knows how hot they run, and many believe this change was made to help cool the oil over the course of its circulation. Modified heads with oil line bosses and new cylinders without oil passages were used.

571 Even though the 1965 Electra Glide is often credited with being Harley-Davidson's first electric start motorcycle, that

The first-ever Electra Glide changed the way people looked at Harley-Davidsons and forever changed who could ride them. Kickstarting a 74-ci V-twin engine was a chore, especially if just the slightest thing was off. Electric start made the Harley-Davidson world available to anybody who wanted it. (Photo Courtesy Harley-Davidson)

honor actually belongs to the 1964 Servi-Car. But for our basic purposes, let's discuss the better-known Panhead version. Many folks at the time, as well as some vintage enthusiasts to this day, called it an "electric leg." The Electra Glide uses a noticeably bulked up engine with some important new parts. The largest new part is the 32-amp, 12-volt battery, which was stuffed into the new oil tank. The engine's new primary cover also enclosed the starter and solenoid, which sit just above the clutch on the left-hand side. To handle the torque of the starter drive on the clutch, the new inner and outer primary covers were beefed up so they were strong enough to maintain rigidity between the engine and transmission. Prior to this, they were connected only by the primary chain, which was not much of a connection at all. The kickstarter remained standard equipment and some owners even opted to remove the additional electric-start equipment.

572 As well as adding an electric starter to the 1965 Electra Glide, the electrical system was changed to 12-volt. Most cars and trucks, and some motorcycles, had already made the jump to the more powerful charging system, and after understanding the advantages, it's difficult to understand why H-D didn't do it sooner. Doubling the system's voltage meant that the generator has to work half as hard at any given draw. In addition, the generator's output is also increased because the wire that can be wrapped around the armature is lighter gauge, meaning that more wire can be used. Sportsters also received the new 12-volt system, and along with it came the need for 12-volt lightbulbs for both families of motorcycles.

573 As successful as Harley's Flathead K model was on the racetrack and with the performance it displayed on the street, an OHV replacement engine was needed to compete with the best Europe had to offer. The XL Sportster continued using the four-cam bottom end with unit transmission, but added a pair of OHV cast-iron heads to the package, which is why early Sportsters are called "Ironheads." The K model's 3.80-inch stroke was retained but bore was bumped up to 3 inches, giving the Sportster the familiar 883-cc displacement. By retaining the stroke, the XL engine was able to rev more quickly and, with a higher 9:1 compression ratio, it was able to achieve 40 hp at 5,500 rpm.

574 The heads on the new Sportster engine share the same "shovel" design as the Shovelhead Big Twin engine, which became available in 1966. Ironheads didn't have their better-known boxy head shape (with the notch in the center of the rocker cover) until 1971. It's an everyday term, but at the time, "Ironhead" was sort of an insult to Harley-Davidson because the engineers chose to use iron heads in the high-performance model instead of lightweight aluminum, which dissipates heat faster. H-D went for steadfastness instead of just fastness.

575 For every Sportster owner who loves revving up his or her quad-cam ripper, there's a nickel in the swear jar from H-D engineers who had to figure out how to successfully fit four cams into a small space and make them run quietly. That's not an actual fact; there are likely a lot more nickels than that. Obviously the one cam per pushrod design is a carryover from the 45 Flathead and KH, but why was that design never updated? No one at The Motor Company thought that the Sportster would be around long enough to be worth the effort and expense! Ironically, the Sportster is one of the longest continually produced vehicles in the United States, and certainly the least-changed. By the time it was obvious that the Sportster would last for quite a while longer (60 years as of this printing), it was too late to change the familiar and much-loved format.

PEOPLE AND POP CULTURE

576 In 1955, Elvis Presley, one of the most famous Bar & Shield enthusiasts of all time, purchased his first Harley-Davidson, a small 1956 ST 165. He outgrew it quickly and moved up to a Pepper Red 1956 Model KH from Memphis Harley-Davidson on January 14, 1956. Although he went on to own many motorcycles in his lifetime, that KH is arguably the best-known because of the amount

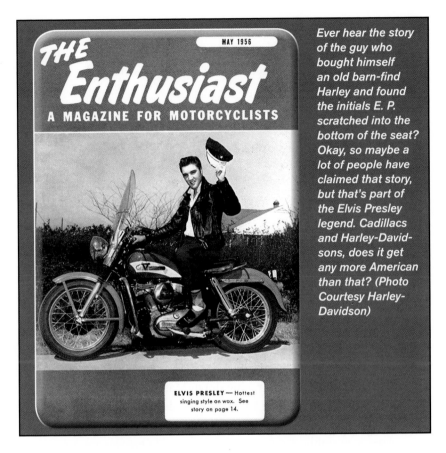

THE
Enthusiast

MAY 1956

A MAGAZINE FOR MOTORCYCLISTS

ELVIS PRESLEY — Hottest
singing style on wax. See
story on page 14.

Ever hear the story of the guy who bought himself an old barn-find Harley and found the initials E. P. scratched into the bottom of the seat? Okay, so maybe a lot of people have claimed that story, but that's part of the Elvis Presley legend. Cadillacs and Harley-Davidsons, does it get any more American than that? (Photo Courtesy Harley-Davidson)

of photography that shows Elvis riding it, including a cover shot on the May 1956 issue of *The Enthusiast*. One famous Alfred Wertheimer shot shows Elvis deep in thought with his head down and his arm on his hip. Actually, he had just run out of gas and was looking at the gas tank trying to figure out what to do. The Harley-Davidson Museum in Milwaukee now owns and displays his KH.

577 Marlon Brando and Lee Marvin star in the iconic 1953 film, *The Wild One*, which many consider to be the original outlaw biker film. The movie portrays a group of rough and rowdy bikers as they take over a small town and engage in acts of hooliganism that were considered shocking in the early 1950s. Both Harley-Davidsons and Triumphs were used in the filming, and the "meaner" of the two clubs wasn't riding the Triumphs. Americans' image of the typical

Harley rider changed with this negative view, which was only furthered by more outlaw films and many riders (of Harleys and other makes) wanting to perpetuate that image and stereotype.

578 Part of the aura of riding a Harley-Davidson prior to 1965 was that not everyone could do it. Even if you could handle the technical aspect of tuning and constant maintenance, you had to be physically able to kickstart the thing! It's no easy task, as anyone who's ever kicked a large-displacement, high-compression V-twin can tell you. It created a certain exclusivity and camaraderie among Harley riders that began to fade away with the Electra Glide's push-button starter and luxurious features. One of the more popular events in the antique motorcycle world today is the annual Motorcycle Kickstart Classic in which participants must start their motorcycles with the kickstarter only.

579 The Motor Company's image took a beating in the late 1940s after the nation read about an incident in Hollister, California, in 1947. A bunch of motorcyclists, many on H-Ds, terrorized the small town by drag racing down Main Street, riding their bikes into bars, and engaging in all sorts of debauchery. The exploits of motorcycle clubs became a new favorite topic for the press, and the American public ate it up. After *The Wild One* was released, there was no going back for Harley-Davidson's image.

580 Everyone loved Gordon Davidson, who was vice president of production at the time. In fact, he was so well liked that gifts from around the city and country constantly found their way to his front door. Usually it was Scotch and other fine liquor; sometimes it was edible delicacies such as lobster. Once, the Miami, Florida, dealer, Billy Temple, sent a pair of small alligators to the Davidson house. With few options for the young gators, Gordon donated them to the Milwaukee Zoo.

581 Marine, spy, *War Stories* host, and bestselling author, Oliver "Ollie" North is featured in what appears to be a Harley-Davidson marketing photo along with country-western singer Tammy

Wynette. They posed with a new 1965 Electra Glide on a baseball field with a game being played in the background. Does it get any more American that? Maybe. Among other hijinks, Ollie is known to have ridden his Harley-Davidson into class while he was teaching at the Marine Corps training school in Quantico, Virginia, in the early 1970s.

582 Harley-Davidson promoted its Topper scooter on the popular TV show *77 Sunset Strip* in an attempt to give the wholesome little machine a rebel image that might entice a Harley-oriented crowd. One of the show's characters, Ed "Kookie" Byrnes, was often seen with his Topper. But seriously, can anything be more badass than the Topper's advertised "Scoot-away" automatic transmission? A 1959 H-D ad featured a picture of Kookie aboard his Topper as well as a call to action for teenagers to hint to their parents that they wanted a Topper instead of borrowing the money for it themselves. Hmm, good idea!

583 Willie G. Davidson, grandson of founder William A. Davidson, began working for the family business in 1963. Prior to that, he attended the Art Center College of Design in Los Angeles and, unlike many of his family members, hadn't initially planned on working for The Motor Company. In a strange twist of fate, he took a job working for the legendary designer Brooks Stevens, also from Milwaukee.

584 What motorcyclist or baby boomer hasn't heard of the gonzo journalism of Hunter S. Thompson? One of Thompson's most famous exploits was riding with the Hell's Angels in Northern California to put together his 1967 book, *Hell's Angels*. He spent months riding with the club although, while the members rode faithfully on Harley-Davidsons, Thompson actually rode a BSA 650 throughout his tour. It's possible that he simply preferred a British vertical twin to the American V-twin, but it has been suggested that it was to distinguish himself as a nonmember.

585 That famous photo from the 1947 Hollister rally taken in front of Johnny's Bar of an overweight biker holding a beer bottle while astride a Harley-Davidson pretty much sums up the Hollister riots. Or does it? That photo, which appeared on the cover of *Life* magazine, seemingly turned the country against H-D–riding hooligans. It was actually staged by a *Life* photographer; the two men in the photo weren't even there for the rally or members of any of the clubs involved. It sure made for a good story though!

586 Many of the major Milwaukee brands support each other as best they can. In the late 1950s, Major League Baseball's Milwaukee Braves (now the Milwaukee Brewers) used a three-wheeled Topper scooter to bring pitchers from the dugout to the mound.

587 Cities across the country took part in the 15th Annual Safe Driving Day on December 15, 1954. President Dwight D. Eisenhower's President's Action Committee for Traffic Safety led the initiative; it was meant as a public promotion for awareness while driving and riding in an effort to reduce traffic accidents. Milwaukee participated in its own special way with a parade of police sidecars with lights and sirens going followed by a police car broadcasting information about the day. Because it was mid-December, the motor officers equipped their bikes with canvas shields across the front to stymie the chill.

588 The Milwaukee Press Club is one of the city's prized organizations and has been for many years. It has hosted presidents, foreign dignitaries, and various celebrities. In 1959, the Press Club invited Carroll Resweber and William H. Davidson, as distinguished Wisconsinites, to speak at its annual banquet for Wisconsin athletes.

589 Harley-Davidson has had a long affiliation with the Boy Scouts, another all-American tradition. On November 9, 1958, the Boy Scouts held a benefit scramble in Maryland in which racers competed to raise money for the organization's summer camp fund. Even though the real winner was the Boy Scouts organization, Harley-Davidson racers filled the podium in the second-class race.

590 Remember Arthur Davidson's old friend Walter Dunlap, the young advertising executive who agreed to publish

Harley-Davidson's first catalog on spec? That was obviously a risk that paid major dividends, and the Klau Van Pietersom Dunlap advertising agency honored Harley-Davidson's 50 years in business by hosting a celebratory dinner on September 3, 1953. Frank V. Birch, president of the agency, is quoted as saying, "The internationally famous name of Harley-Davidson is a tribute to the vision, ability, and progressiveness that have characterized this company since it was founded 50 years ago. Klau Van Pietersom Dunlap, Inc., is proud to have been associated with the advertising and merchandising of the Harley-Davidson products for almost as many years. We are particularly proud of this, as it is a record with few equals in annals of advertising."

591 Most people equate the motorcycle-riding Elvis Presley with his wholesome Model KH or one of his dresser Panheads. However, few, including some in Elvis' family, even knew that he also had a pretty mean, extended-fork chopper. This was hardly the kind of motorcycle you'd expect to see Elvis ride, maybe that's why he only put about 500 miles on it before stashing it away under a collection of old bicycles. It was a typical 1970s-style chopper; it used a single-downtube frame, King and Queen seat, and had a 4-inch-over front end. It had a skinny front tire with no fender (it did have a brake) as well as a red and black scallop paint job. That bike was found after his death and was used in the Elvis on Tour show.

592 The 1969 film *Easy Rider* actually got its start in 1967 with a beer- and marijuana-infused 4 am phone call from Peter Fonda to Dennis Hopper. That's probably not even the interesting part. Their concept for the movie was the modern western: two men exploring the country on two memorable steeds. Fonda knew that the motorcycles were as important as anything else, so he went to the Los Angeles Police Department auction and purchased four used and abused Panheads: a 1950, two 1951s, and a 1952. He paid only $500 each for them.

593 Ralph Nader's *Unsafe At Any Speed* was published in 1965 and ripped into the nation's automakers, which he claimed were making and selling unsafe vehicles. Ralph Nader went on to help create the Environmental Protection Agency (EPA) and get the Clean Air Act passed. Perhaps one of the positives that came out of *Unsafe At Any Speed* (for motorcyclists) was the revelation that, in 1965, $320 million of federal money went toward "highway beautification" while only $500,000 went toward highway safety measures. As much as we all like to ride on pretty highways, being on an unsafe road on two wheels is a much bigger problem than it is if you are on four.

594 *Unsafe At Any Speed* inspired a whole era of super-safe, yet utterly ridiculous automobiles and technology that make you want to drive blindfolded so you don't have to see anything. That ridiculousness hit the motorcycle world a few years later when the National Highway Traffic Safety Administration decided to build what it deemed to be a perfectly safe motorcycle. The AMA found this most hideous of contraptions in 1979. The machine used a low-slung frame with a rear-mounted engine and a roll cage going across the top. A pair of several-foot-long outriggers was mounted to either side and used little wheels to stabilize the "machine" when it leaned over too far. The machine failed its first and only road test, in the sense that it was completely unridable and very dangerous.

595 Following the Hollister incident of 1947, the Gypsy Tour returned to Hollister in 1948 to continue the rally's racing tradition. You probably haven't heard about it because it wasn't really the "yellow journalism" media slam-a-thon that the previous year supposedly was. A much smaller crowd of 2,000 motorcyclists showed up to watch the races, which continued annually until the early 1960s. Shocker alert: not a single biker was arrested or cited in any way by law enforcement during the 1948 event.

596 Chrome-wrapped exotic cars and motorcycles might be all the rage today, but in the 1950s and 1960s that shiny goodness was generally reserved for trim components. In 1958, an unnamed gentleman from Venezuela was way ahead of the game, however, when he ordered his Harley-Davidson Duo-Glide chromed completely from fender to fender. The gas tank, engine, forks, shocks, wheels, exhaust, oil tank, frame, and, well, everything, was chrome plated, making it one of the shiniest motorcycles of all time. He ordered the bike through Tramontin Harley-Davidson in Clifton, New Jersey. It took five months for the dealership to complete the motorcycle and cost a reported $3,500, nearly three times the price of a stock, base-model Duo-Glide at the time.

597 Ever hear of the Panhead switcheroo? One of the best examples is in the 2007 film *Wild Hogs*. The four riding buddies stop at a roadside bar run by a one-percenter club and see a 1948 Panhead sitting outside. William H. Macy's character comments on the bike to its supposed owner, who then offers to trade it for Macy's Sportster. He jumps on the deal only to learn that the deal wasn't for the complete 1948 outside, but for a basket case frame with a Panhead engine in it out back in the junkyard. You'll have to watch the movie to see how it ends, but a Panhead engine, transmission, frame, and front end would still have been worth more than his used Sportster 1200 Custom, which had been wrecked at least once.

598 One of the most famous images of Jimi Hendrix was taken of him sitting aboard a 1964 Panhead chopper shortly before he died in 1970. Ed Thrasher shot it on the back lot of Warner Brothers film studios. It wasn't used in broad context until it became the cover image of the 1997 album *South Saturn Delta*, which featured songs that Hendrix had recorded but not released.

599 One of the coolest movie bikes ever, in part because it resembles *Captain America* from *Easy Rider*, is the Panhead chopper that Nicolas Cage rides in 2007's *Ghost Rider*. Cage's character, Johnny Blaze, is a motorcycle stunt rider and the movie is full of great motorcycle scenes. The motorcycle theme doesn't end there, nor does the *Easy Rider* theme; Peter Fonda plays a key role in the movie. Another well-known movie biker who plays an important role is actor Sam Elliott.

600 Prior to filming *Easy Rider*, both Jack Nicholson and Peter Fonda starred in classic 1960s "bikesploitation" movies that feature Panheads galore. Peter Fonda starred in 1966's *The Wild Angels* and Jack Nicholson took the lead spot in 1967's *Hells Angels on Wheels*. Both films revolve around the Hells Angels motorcycle club and the cool custom choppers that they rode in the 1960s. Unlike *Easy Rider,* which portrayed a free-spirited motorcycle journey, the earlier films focus on the ticket-selling violent side of the outlaw motorcycle world.

MILITARY, POLICE AND RACING

601 1948 was one of Harley-Davidson's most successful racing seasons of all time. The company's riders won 19 of 23 races including an absolute domination of Daytona, which saw 7 Harleys finish in the top 10, even though Floyd Emde on an Indian took the checkered flag.

602 The story of AMA Hall of Famer Larry Headrick is one of the greatest underdog stories, but one that remains relatively unknown. In his first and only AMA Grand National season, Headrick rode his Tom Sifton-prepared WR-750 racer to three major wins and the national championship. He won his first race at the Bay Meadows Mile in San Mateo, California; no one expected him to be a contender in the star-studded field there. Still considered a long shot, Headrick went to the Springfield Mile in Illinois and outlasted the greatest racers of the time in the 25-mile race, earning the win, and the 1950 National Championship. He is the first West Coast rider to win at Springfield. He followed up that win a week later with another win at the Milwaukee Mile, which netted him the three most prestigious races of the year. Many still consider his 1950 season to be one of the greatest in history. Unfortunately, Headrick returned to California to care for his ill wife instead of competing in the last mile-long track on the schedule in Langhorne, Pennsylvania. A few months after that, his left leg was shattered when a car struck him while he was riding his motorcycle on the street; he gave up racing for good.

603 Larry Headrick's remarkable season was only a small percentage of The Motor Company's overall success on the racetrack in

1950. By the end of the year, riders on Harley-Davidson motorcycles won 18 of 24 national championships and set six new racing records.

604 Harley-Davidson took its new, full-suspension, unit-powertrain K model and developed the race-only KR for 1953. Paul Goldsmith proved the KR's capability right out of the gate by taking the company's first win at Daytona since 1940. The KR was fitted with a rigid rear end for flat track use, and it picked up 5 AMA Class C national events in its first year followed by 13 of 18 races in 1954. One of the most successful road-racing motorcycles ever, the KR took 11 more Daytona victories (including a seven-year consecutive stretch), its last coming in 1969, 13 years after production of the street version ceased. In a further show of the KR's adaptability and prowess, it won the first Daytona 200 to take place at the speedway in 1961. All previous races were run on the sandy beach track.

605 It wasn't until 1957 that the U.S. Army came back to Harley-Davidson looking for a motorcycle. Unlike the combat-ready WLA of World War II, the Army needed a fast, reliable, and efficient machine for patrolling bases. Production of the XLA began in 1957, the first year of the OHV XL. These bikes sported the standard Olive Drab paint with engine guards, luggage rack, and solo seat. Early XLAs received an oil bath air cleaner, skid plate, and deep-water breathers, all of which were found to be unnecessary and removed as production went on. The biggest difference between the civilian and military version is the XLA's destroked engine, which displaces 750 cc. Only 418 XLAs were produced in 1957, with the next biggest run being in 1964 with about 100. The easiest way to tell the difference is that the 1964s have a full headlight nacelle whereas the 1957s use a bucket. XLAs of various years have popped up, but no number documentation is available. The most recent one I know of has a 1973 engine-case number.

606 One of the least-known models that Harley-Davidson produced is the XLB; it had an incredibly specific function as a police and military model for the Southeast Asian and possibly South American market. All of the XLBs that I've been able to locate are from the mid-1960s. Apparently, these bikes use 1957 cams with low-compression pistons and were used primarily for escort duty and parades. No information exists from H-D, leading some to speculate CIA involvement in that part of the world. Who doesn't love a good conspiracy theory?

607 After H-D discontinued its low-compression, mild-cam E engines after 1952, it launched the FLE Traffic Combination to suit the needs of police departments and other commercial duties. The 1953 and 1954 FLEs used the old 61's cam and the M-61 Linkert carburetor to make it easier for low-speed operation. In 1955, the FLE was upgraded with the standard Linkert M-74B carburetor, although it retained the E engine's camshaft. Traffic Combination models were offered with regular, police, or sidecar gearing and in foot- or hand-shift versions.

608 The XLCH might have only lasted a year in competition form before The Motor Company gave in and produced a street version, but that wasn't the case with the XLR. It actually takes on a similar appearance to the first stripped-down XLCH, but the V-twin engine is an entirely new animal built solely for winning races. It used higher-flowing heads, lighter crankshaft, sportier cams, with new pistons and valves. The other major difference was that the magneto was mounted in front of the front cylinder instead of underneath the oil tank, as it was on an XLCH. The XLR pulled about 80 hp, nearly twice that of a stock XL, and weighed in at only 300 pounds, 200 less than a stock XL. Riders used the XLR for all sorts of racing including TT scrambles, drag racing, and road racing. Only about 500 were produced over the course of 10 years, so it is not only a fast bike, but also a rare one.

609 Even though the Harley-Davidson/Aermacchi Sprint was a formidable racer, it certainly didn't have the displacement to keep up with the high-performance Sportsters. Unless, of course, you wrap a streamliner body around it. That's just what Harley-Davidson did in 1965 with what it claimed was a stock-engine 250-cc Sprint CR running pump gas. Ohioan George Roeder piloted the

It may not look like a Harley-Davidson (some might argue that it's not), but the name on the side of this stream-liner is all that mattered when it took the Class A and Class C land speed records at Bonneville in 1965! (Photo Courtesy Harley-Davidson)

factory streamliner to an average of 177.225 mph and obliterated the land speed records for Class A and Class C at Bonneville. That's a lot of speed for an 18-hp 247-cc four-stroke!

610 In 1956, Leroy Winters rode his Model 165 Hummer to victory at the famously treacherous Jack Pine Enduro. It was the first time a lightweight, small-displacement motorcycle won the event, which was always dominated by heavyweight twins. Winters modified his stripped-down Hummer with a twin-shock, swingarm rear suspension and an off-road-ready fuel tank. The small motorcycle might make sense by today's off-road standards, but before Winters' victory, 23 of the previous 29 Jack Pine Enduros were won by Harley-Davidson Big Twins with wide tires and lots of power.

611 Everyone loves a winner, right? If that's the case, Harley-Davidson fans everywhere must have really loved Texan Carroll Resweber of the H-D factory team who won four AMA Grand National Championships in a row from 1958 to 1961. Ironically, although he raced in the Daytona 200 in each of those years, his best finish was fourth place in 1958. A fatal, four-rider crash in 1962 ended his run for five in a row; he was never able to race again. That doesn't mean he left the world of Harley-Davidson, however; he went on to work at the company until he retired in 1992.

612 Before the famed KR racer was introduced, Harley-Davidson experimented with some of the components that helped make it such an effective winning machine. A 1947 photo of Leo Anthony at the Milwaukee Mile (within the Wisconsin State Fair Park) shows him astride a WR-powered machine with double downtubes, left-side foot shifter and a handlebar-mounted clutch lever.

613 Babe Tancrede, winner of the 1940 Daytona 200, retired from racing in 1952. Although he was only 46, it was old for a racer, even back then. He stated publically that he had difficulty adapting to the new foot-shift, hand-clutch machines (such as the KR) that were the standard in 1952. However, he did go on to make a living with motorcycles as a motor officer. Police models were the last to give up the old hand-shift, and that wasn't until the early 1970s.

614 Factory rider Ralph White took the checkered flag for Harley-Davidson at the 1963 Daytona 200. But it wasn't an easy victory. White had been riding all week with a broken wrist in a bulky leather brace, and he appeared to only make things worse when he crashed on lap 24 of the main event. He battled his way back to the lead after several all-stars experienced mechanical difficulties. Only 18 of the 65 starters finished that race, with White leading the pack by a solid lap and a half. As a side note, the 1963 Daytona 200 was the first time bikes were allowed to run fairings at that racetrack.

615 On June 17, 1956, Harley-Davidson factory rider Brad Andres won the Laconia 100-mile National Road Race Championship for the third year in a row. For his 1956 win, he demolished the course record, which he held, by 6 minutes 31 seconds. In the time trials, Andres and fellow H-D rider Joe Leonard were the only riders to lap the track in less than 60 seconds with a 59.16 and 59.25, respectively. Harley-Davidson motorcycles won all eight events at Laconia that year.

616 What do you do in Michigan in the middle of the winter when you need to get your Harley fix? Simple, go ice racing! In the Michigan State Ice Race Championships that took place on Fenton Lake outside Flint, Michigan, on February 12, 1961,

Harley-Davidson motorcycles won every single class. Bart Markel, one of the better-known participants, won both the lightweight solo class and the heavyweight solo class.

617 What better place to set a speed record on a Harley-Davidson than right in Milwaukee. On August 27, 1949, factory rider Jimmy Chann completed a 15-mile race in 11 minutes 18 seconds for the win and the AMA speed record. That's averaging more than 79 mph for the entire race!

618 In 1958 Grand National racing competition, Harley-Davidson factory riders set three new records and took an incredible eight victories. Joe Leonard set the Daytona 200 beach/road course record by completing the race in 1 hour 59 minutes 11.3 seconds, giving him an average speed of just over 100 mph! Leonard went on to set the 50-mile record at the Springfield Mile that year with a time of 34 minutes 33 seconds. 1958's last record came from Carroll Resweber, who finished the 20-mile race at the 1-mile Du Quoin, Illinois, track in 14 minutes 5.12 seconds.

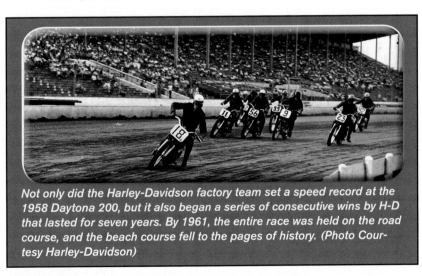

Not only did the Harley-Davidson factory team set a speed record at the 1958 Daytona 200, but it also began a series of consecutive wins by H-D that lasted for seven years. By 1961, the entire race was held on the road course, and the beach course fell to the pages of history. (Photo Courtesy Harley-Davidson)

619 Earl Robinson, who had previously set the solo and sidecar transcontinental records, continued racing for many years after those 1935 runs. In January 1953, he participated in and won a reliability run contest held in Detroit. The entire 58.4-mile course was covered with ice and ran through the woods and across marshes. He used a Harley-Davidson Model 165 in the event and achieved 976 points out of the possible 1,000. Those conditions certainly proved the lightweight 165 as a contender!

620 Don Hawley, a Harley-Davidson factory rider, won the first motorcycle TT race held at the famous Ascot Park in Los Angeles on December 20, 1960. Of course, the challenging TT course featured right and left turns, but the biggest obstacle was a 10-foot-high jump that launched competitors into the air. The race was 15 laps long, which meant that Hawley, second place finisher Joe Leonard, and all the other competitors had to make that jump 15 times on motorcycles with still-rudimentary suspension systems. Today's motocross guys don't know how easy they have it.

621 Harley-Davidson factory rider Bart Markel, who went on to hold the record for most Grand National wins, won his first race in 1960 at the Peoria TT on August 28th. He ended up third overall that season, but stormed back to have a record-breaking career. His best season was in 1962 when he won six races, the most wins by a single rider since Joe Leonard won eight races in 1954. Naturally, Markel took the Grand National Championship title that year, his first of three.

622 In 1949, Class C had become the predominant division of motorcycle racing; Class A was suspended a decade earlier due to lack of interest. Without a top-flight racing division, the AMA had a meeting to discuss rules that would keep Class C racing fun, fair, and accessible to the amateurs for whom it was originally intended. Two rules came out of that meeting to ensure these goals. The first was a homologation requirement that manufacturers must produce and sell at least 25 examples of the motorcycle being raced. Then, to ensure that companies didn't just produce 25 high-end exotics, the AMA instituted a claiming clause. It said that a race motorcycle might be purchased no more than 30 minutes after a race for $1,000. Nobody would ever put more than that into a machine only to win, and then have the motorcycle claimed by someone else! Certainly, factories wouldn't risk putting all that research and development into a motorcycle only to have it fall into the hands of a competitor for a measly $1,000.

623 Tom Sifton owned a Harley-Davidson dealership in San Jose, California. He was one of the best race tuners in the world and today his name is synonymous with Harley-Davidson performance. Throughout the 1930s, 1940s, and 1950s, many of the biggest names in racing raced for him and they found themselves on the podium more than any other team, including Harley-Davidson's own factory team. The Motor Company finally got tired of seeing a dealer's team winning instead of its own, so it requested that Sifton turn over his engine designs to the R&D department. But Sifton loved winning, and he loved beating the big-money factory team just as much, therefore, he declined to hand over his tuning secrets. As is often the case, he finally gave in after some years and accepted a commission to build cams for the factory race team.

624 Sullivan County, New York, instituted a program that involved uniformed women riding Panheads in the Courtesy Copettes Corps. These ladies pulled drivers over and, instead of issuing a ticket, discussed proper safe-driving etiquette, and explained the specific laws of the county. So let me get this straight, you can drive fast, talk to a pretty girl on a Panhead, and then get let off without a ticket? Too bad Sullivan County doesn't still have the Copettes!

625 Along with the introduction of the first Safety Helmet in the Harley-Davidson accessories catalog came versions for motor officers and racers. The Police Special helmet had a built-in visor, detachable ear covers, and a special badge on the front; it cost $26. The Competition helmet was approved by the AMA for Class C racing and came down farther to protect the ears and back of the head, like 3/4-style helmets today. A detachable snap visor was included with the helmet, which was advertised as being "worn by America's top racing stars." It cost a whopping $32.50.

Chapter 6

Shovelhead Era
1966–1984

THE MOTOR COMPANY

626 Harley-Davidson's popular history is that AMF (American Machine and Foundry) saved the company from certain bankruptcy, but it wasn't the only suitable buyer. After a failed attempt to buy the company privately, Bangor Punta purchased more than 16 percent of H-D stock and attempted a public takeover. Bangor Punta needed 33 percent of Harley-Davidson in order to prevent a merger with AMF, but could not acquire that much stock. AMF raised its offer, followed by Bangor Punta offering nearly triple the public value of the company. Harley-Davidson executives preferred AMF, and they somehow convinced shareholders to vote for an offer that was 20 percent less than Bangor Punta's offer!

627 As part of the move to the York factory, AMF told Harley-Davidson workers that no jobs would be lost. And then the layoffs came, which led the workers to form the Harley Workers Action Group (HAWG), which refused to work overtime and, in some cases, committed acts of sabotage against the factory. Harley workers staged a walkout when AMF refused to renegotiate their union contract. The workers were so angry that they actually turned down a federally mediated deal after two months of striking. With no new models produced in nearly four months, AMF gave in to worker demands. This strike has come to be known as the 100-Day Strike.

628 Led by Willie G.'s styling innovations, Harley-Davidson's FX line of motorcycles became a major hit among the motorcycling public. In 1981, a decade after the first boattail Super Glide hit showroom floors, FX sales more than doubled that of the larger FL with 22,708 FX models sold that year versus 8,796 FLs.

629 In 1973, all motorcycle assembly operations moved to the new, modern, 400,000-square-foot plant in York, Pennsylvania. The additional space allowed for improved production capacity and opened the Milwaukee and Tomahawk, Wisconsin, plants up for specialized work. The Capitol drive plant in Milwaukee took over production of the heart of the Harley-Davidson: the engine.

630 The Motor Company begins offering one of its most-loved institutions, the factory tour, with the opening of the York assembly plant. To promote the family aspect of the company's relationship with consumers, factory tours were, and always have been, free. Eventually, as the popularity of the factory tours grew, the Vaughn L. Beals Tour Center opened at the York plant to host visitors more effectively. The Beals Center features manufacturing exhibits, current production motorcycles for visitors to sit on, and a gift shop. It also features the Kids Corner, designed for visitors under the age of 12 to enjoy the magic of Harley-Davidson. Today, 50,000 people tour the York assembly plant every year!

631 Headed for bankruptcy, Harley-Davidson was purchased by AMF in 1969 after several years of financial troubles. AMF's plan for success was to increase production by building bikes faster and more cost-effectively. Speeding up the assembly line left little time for H-D's usual careful assembly, and quality suffered. Even though several strikes occurred under the AMF banner, some of the coolest and most-loved motorcycles today were built during those years. At the very least, few people would question the fact that the AMF merger saved The Motor Company from bankruptcy and possible closure.

632 In stark contrast to its primary, warm-weather motorcycle business, Harley-Davidson began producing snowmobiles in 1971. Its parent company, AMF, had been building snowmobiles, dubbed the Ski-Daddler and the Sno-Clipper, since 1965, but they never gained a real following. After its 1969 takeover of H-D, AMF decided to redesign a snowmobile using the Harley-Davidson name and its reputation of quality and performance. The snowmobiles used 398- and 440-cc Aermacchi two-stroke, parallel-twin engines and were produced in Oak Creek, Missouri, along with H-D's golf carts. Just about as quickly as it got into the snow business, The Motor Company got out of it in 1975. While they don't fetch particularly high prices, Harley-Davidson snowmobiles have become quite a rare collector's item and a fun toy or conversation piece for enthusiasts living in northern climates.

633 Most enthusiasts are familiar with Willie G. Davidson and his children, Bill and Karen, who all hold positions at the company in addition to making public appearances and interacting with motorcycle owners. But one of the most asked questions is, what happened to the Harley family? Founder Bill Harley's son, William J. Harley served as engineering vice president until his death in 1971 while his other son, John, served at H-D until his death in 1976. John was the last of the Harley family to work at The Motor Company.

634 AMF decided that the Aermacchi business had become too much of a drain on the Harley-Davidson brand, so it was sold to Cagiva in 1978. It wasn't The Motor Company's last run-in with the Italian brand, which went on to include Ducati and Husqvarna as part of its portfolio.

635 H-Ds are available with all sorts of different security options today from the proximity key fob included with most new models to the latest and greatest CVO (custom vehicle operations) electronically controlled luggage-compartment locks. A range of alarms is available from the parts and accessories catalog. They can beep loudly from a car, send a vibration to a key fob in your pocket, and then use global positioning to track your motorcycle after it's been stolen. Most of these were not yet created in 1974 even though crime in the country was on a serious rise, especially in urban centers such as New York City. To combat motorcycle theft, H-D offered an optional alarm system; it was actually a black box integrated into the bike's license plate. The device used mercury to sense movement and was armed and disarmed with a key. Its use ceased in 1976, likely due to false alarms when the temperature changed by more than a few degrees.

636 To curb the easy theft and registration of its motorcycles, in 1970 Harley-Davidson began using a matching VIN on the left engine case and the frame. Although the numbers match, the official number is the one on the frame, meaning that you can drop in a replacement engine with different numbers, but a new frame requires a new VIN. From 1970 to 1980, H-D VINs are interpreted this way: The first two numbers are the model code, the next five digits are the production number (starting at 10001), and the last two digits are the year code beginning with H for 1970s and J for 1980. The model codes are extremely specific, right down to the model, engine, and original use. Custom builders today love pre-1970 engines because they can use any frame they want and still easily register the bike. Former *American Iron Magazine* Editor Chris Maida once told me how he used to have a Sportster chopper and a Sportster bobber and simply transferred the registered Iron-head engine into whichever bike he felt like riding.

637 Have you ever owned a 1979 Harley-Davidson and thought it was stolen because of the mismatched VINs on the engine and frame? It was actually just a really bad idea on the part of The Motor Company. Motorcycles produced from January 9 to February 7 used a 10-digit number on the engine case that was different from the 9-digit VIN on the frame. The rumor is that the company stopped this practice after law enforcement officials warned that it made the bikes look stolen. The VINs affected by this (frame, remember?) are 43000H9 through 48199H9.

638 The VIN system changed nationwide in 1981 to a new 17-character standard for motorcycles and automobiles by mandate of the National Highway Traffic Safety Administration (NHTSA). Any Harley-Davidson manufactured for sale within the United States starts with 1HD. An abbreviated version of the VIN is found on the left engine case.

639 After the gas crises of the 1970s and the new regulations coming from the EPA, Harley-Davidson knew it wouldn't be long before emissions requirements caught up with it. The new Evolution engine was already under development by the early 1980s, with about one quarter of all engineering man-hours being spent on emissions in 1982.

640 "The Eagle Soars Alone" became the battle cry of 1981 when 13 senior executives bought the Harley-Davidson Motor Company from AMF. Led by Vaughn L. Beals and Willie G. Davidson, the members of the group paid a reported $1 million of their own money and $70 million worth of debt for the company. Unfortunately, more than a change in management was needed to save the ailing company. When a recession hit the country in 1982, the company was forced to cut motorcycle production in half and the workforce by 40 percent. At any point after that, lenders could have foreclosed on the company, but thanks to Tom Gelb's implementation of the MAN system (see fact 643), enough cash was saved to keep the banks away, at least for the time being.

Can you pick out Willie G. Davidson from this group of executives? He's the one not wearing a tie. This is the group of 13 who put everything on the line to rescue The Motor Company from the clutches of AMF and get it back to building the best motorcycles on the planet. (Photo Courtesy Harley-Davidson)

641 To commemorate the buyback, two-dozen executives, accompanied by their families and the press, embarked on a ceremonial ride from the York factory in Pennsylvania to the Juneau Ave. headquarters in Milwaukee. While at York, documents were officially signed that marked the ownership change, followed by the ceremonial pulling of the first motorcycle completed on the assembly line under the new ownership. The ride back to Milwaukee, led by Vaughn Beals and Willie G., also raised funds for the Muscular Dystrophy Association. Upon arrival in Milwaukee, Beals became the new chairman and CEO while Willie G. finally had the chance to continue his family's legacy. "I was practically crying today," Willie G. said. "I watched my dad and how the company grew, and after the AMF takeover I didn't think I would ever have a chance to be an owner."

642 With quality control and production efficiency in terrible shape during AMF's ownership, the new executives visited Honda's Marysville plant in Ohio. They discovered a clean facility with an uncluttered assembly line. This differed greatly from H-D's assembly line, which was littered with spare parts and paperwork on each motorcycle. In addition, only 5 percent of Honda motorcycles failed final quality inspection while more than 50 percent of Harleys failed the same test. At the same time, Honda's productivity was 30 percent greater.

643 To match Honda's super-efficient production capabilities, the York plant introduced the Materials As Needed (MAN)

The Materials As Needed system revolutionized the way Harley-Davidson built motorcycles. It was able to keep up with modern demand while also improving the quality level. Moreover, the cost of running the factory was lowered considerably. (Photo Courtesy Harley-Davidson)

system, which allows the purchase of parts and raw materials as they're actually needed on the assembly line. The implementation of the MAN system freed working capital by reducing parts inventory. It reduced clutter in the factory and allowed managers to keep better tabs on parts. It also placed more responsibility on those handling the products to constantly check for high quality.

644 In addition to the MAN system, Harley-Davidson initiated a program that empowered employees of all levels with the knowledge and know-how to take action to assure quality manufacturing. With less inventory at any given time, thanks to MAN, employees could more easily find and resolve quality issues with parts or production. The practice of line workers contributing to management's decision-making process was developed because they had a more intimate knowledge of the production process and could help management guide it in a better direction.

645 As part of Harley-Davidson's rebuilding process, it needed a break from the onslaught of inexpensive, better-performing Japanese motorcycles on sales floors across the country. In 1983, the company successfully petitioned the International Trade Commission and President Ronald Reagan for tariff relief on the grounds that Japanese manufacturers intended to harm or threaten domestic motorcycle producers. The five-year tariff, which was granted on April 1, 1983, placed a 45 percent import tax on all Japanese motorcycles of 700 cc and larger.

646 To let everyone know that Harley-Davidson was back in business and had gone back to its roots of building classy cruisers, The Motor Company built 1,001 Heritage Edition FLHs for the 1981 model year. It was the first motorcycle off the assembly line following AMF's departure from Milwaukee and featured the classic two-tone paint scheme of orange and green that had been on many pre-Knucklehead Harleys. It used a black leather sprung seat, black leather saddlebags, and a special 80 Heritage Edition derby cover to further distinguish it as a retro model. The dash console featured a special gold-colored insert along with an engraved plaque stating,

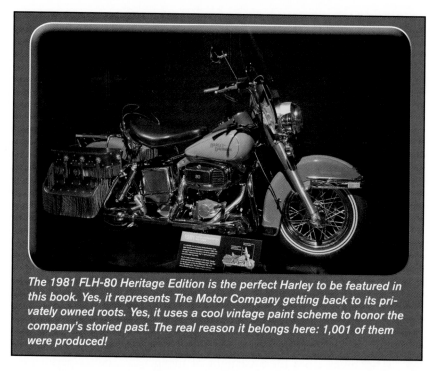

The 1981 FLH-80 Heritage Edition is the perfect Harley to be featured in this book. Yes, it represents The Motor Company getting back to its privately owned roots. Yes, it uses a cool vintage paint scheme to honor the company's storied past. The real reason it belongs here: 1,001 of them were produced!

"This 80 Heritage Edition built for" with the new owner's name engraved underneath. What a cool motorcycle to have if you're the original owner, otherwise you have a motorcycle with someone else's name engraved right on the top where you see it every time you ride. Naturally, many of these were ground down over the years and that makes an original plaque with a name an extreme rarity.

647 Just several years after the bankruptcy scare and AMF buyout, Harley-Davidson had its biggest sales year ever; 75,403 total machines sold in 1975. It wasn't a one-year fluke, either; 70,903 were sold in 1973, 68,210 in 1974, and 61,375 in 1976. The manufacturing process and style was never intended to put out this many machines in a single year and workers couldn't keep up with the usual quality control checks and fixes. Quickly, The Motor Company lost its hard-earned reputation of durability and quality, and sales (and prices) began to drop, reaching just 41,606 by 1981, the last full year of AMF ownership.

648 In the mid-1970s, Aermacchi motorcycles began to back up at H-D dealers because of poor sales. An Italian labor law stated that although a company could cut production, it could not lay off employees. AMF thought that, if it had to pay the workforce, it might as well be building motorcycles. The Aermacchis piled up in warehouses in Brazil, Italy, and the United States, except they hadn't been prepped for storage. Naturally, they were rusty by the time they were discovered and couldn't even be sold.

649 Harley-Davidson initiated one of its most thoroughly enjoyed institutions with the new Harley Owners Group (H.O.G.) in 1983. Designed as an alternative to the traditional motorcycle club, H.O.G. allows local H-D owners to get together for factory- and dealer-sponsored rides and events. It also provides another avenue for The Motor Company to promote its products and lifestyle. A one-year H.O.G. membership accompanies every new motorcycle purchase as a great way to welcome those new to the brand into the Harley-Davidson family.

650 The Shovelhead era is considered one of the greatest transition periods in The Motor Company's history. In 1966, only four Big Twin models were in the main V-twin lineup, which were differentiated only by compression, and sidecar or police use. By the time the last Shovelhead-powered Big Twin rolled off the assembly line in 1983–1984, 16 different FLs, FXs, and FXRs were available for purchase.

THE CHASSIS

651 The 5-gallon H-D Fat Bob gas tank. Ever wonder where that name came from? In the years following World War II, the idea behind customizing motorcycles was to chop 'em down to make 'em light and fast. Most folks did away with the front fender, but the rear fender was often cut down or, as they said at the time, "bobbed." That's the origin of the bobber style. The bikes were slim and trim all around, except for the two fat gas tanks on either side of the frame's backbone. That's what turned these early customs into fat bobs. Today's Fat Bob motorcycle pays homage to these early machines with 16-inch wheels, bobtail rear fender, and big fat 5-gallon gas tanks with a dash console in the center.

652 The Willie G.–designed FX Super Glide was released in 1971 to mixed enthusiasm. It was, essentially, the first true "cruiser" motorcycle ever built and riders loved the lightweight, maneuverable chassis loaded with a Big Twin. It used the smaller XL front end for stripped-down looks and quick steering instead of the bulky FL front end. All 1971s received white paint with red and blue accents. Ironically, the least favorite part at the time is the part that makes the 1971 Super Glide such a collectible today: the one-year-only, two-person boattail seat. Many purchasers removed the seat and replaced it with a more traditional seat and fender, much to the mortification of purists today.

The 1971 Super Glide goes on the short list of motorcycles that changed Harley-Davidson. Most buyers of the day couldn't get over that boattail seat and replaced it with something more traditional. Only one other Harley came with a seat like that, do you know what it is?

653 The FXS Low Rider was first released to the public at Daytona Bike Week 1977. This sportier package featured drag-style handlebars, dual disc brakes, and a performance-inspired paint scheme. Shorter rear shocks and a 1-inch-longer front end furthered its cool cruiser personality. The rider sits lower for a more confident and low cruiser-like rider feel. Raised-white-letter tires gave the FXS an American muscle appearance and the 2-into-1 exhaust system produced a mean bark. Over the years, Harley-Davidson took the Low Rider out of production for a year or two, and then relaunched it with a new design.

654 Toward the end of the Shovelhead's run, Harley-Davidson introduced the FLHS Electra Glide Sport. The name probably sounds sportier than the bike actually was, but the FLHS was an interesting departure from the rest of the FL line in that it had no saddlebags, windshield, or fairing. The FLHS also used a handful of FX parts including the tall handlebars, forward controls, and staggered exhaust. It was just a big, no-frills cruiser for the rider who wanted more comfort, range, and aesthetics than an FX but without all the accessories associated with a touring bike. With the chrome shocks and fender struts, as well as the smooth rear fender used at the time, it was a pretty attractive package.

655 FX owners loved the lean, yet muscular look and feel of the late 1970s Super Glides. However, the distance between fill-ups was less than desirable, so Harley-Davidson released the FXEF Fat Bob with a 3-1/2-gallon two-piece gas tank and an FL-style instrument panel mounted in the center. H-D advertisements claimed more than 150 miles of cruising ability for the Fat Bob. Cast or spoked wheels were available as was the 74- or 80-ci Shovelhead engine. For 1979, buckhorn bars became the standard on the Super Glide and the Fat Bob.

656 Willie G. designed the 1977 XLCR Sportster Café Racer as a dirt track-inspired take on the traditional British café racer featuring a sporty riding position and barebones dynamic. A complete departure from any other road-going motorcycle that

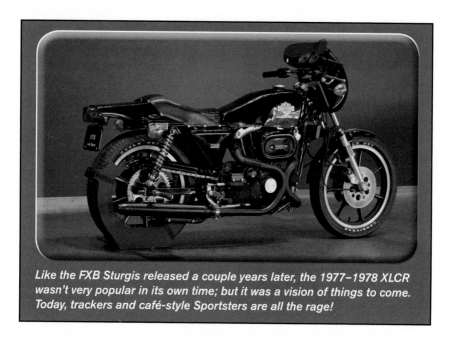

Like the FXB Sturgis released a couple years later, the 1977–1978 XLCR wasn't very popular in its own time; but it was a vision of things to come. Today, trackers and café-style Sportsters are all the rage!

Harley-Davidson had ever created, the CR ended up functioning better as a styling experiment than as a high-performance road machine. It featured a completely blacked-out persona from head to tail including black (the only available paint option) on its XR-750-inspired fiberglass fender/seat and coffin-shaped gas tank. Low-rise bars were hidden behind a small fairing while the whole package rode on black cast aluminum wheels with dual disc brakes up front. The CR failed to live up to its aggressive styling; its brakes, speed, and handling were subpar to the Japanese competition. Produced only in 1977 and 1978, the XLCR turned out to be a dud in the showroom and many dealers simply stashed unsold units in the storage room to collect dust. It's known today as one of the more collectable and fashionable Harleys produced in the 1970s.

657 Harley-Davidson's first frame-mounted full-size fairing appears on the 1980 FLT Tour Glide. The unique "shark nose" fairing features dual headlights and convenient glove boxes. It also considerably lightens the front end's weight and aerodynamics, which improved the performance of the motorcycle and significantly reduced rider fatigue. 1980 is the accepted year of full FLT production; however, 19 FLTs were built as 1979 models, most likely for testing and dealer demonstrations.

658 What's the baddest bike at your local Harley dealer? A few responses are appropriate, no doubt, but the majority of enthusiasts would likely pick the flame-riddled, long-fork, slammed-shock Dyna Wide Glide. The first, and baddest, of the bad Wide Glides appeared in 1980 and perpetuated what it meant to be a factory-custom chopper. Its narrow 21-inch front wheel and skinny fender sit between a pair of lengthened fork tubes that sit farther apart than on other FXs. A separate passenger pillion backs up to a sissy bar while the rider seat butts up to a 5-gallon Fat Bob gas tank that, yes, you could have covered in orange and yellow flames.

659 The Ultra Classic and the Limited are the modern incarnation of today's full-dress Electra Glides. The model was introduced in 1983 as the FLHT; these letters are still used for these models today. Until the arrival of the FLHT, Touring riders had to choose either the rubber-mounted engine with 5-speed transmission of the FLT (and its frame-mounted shark-nose fairing) or the solid-mounted engine with 4-speed transmission of the FLH with classic Harley styling. The FLHT brought the best of both machines together to offer riders the ultimate in Harley-Davidson style and performance. Like the Tour Glide, the Electra Glide also had a highly optioned counterpart, the Electra Glide Classic, which, in both FLTC and FLHTC forms, had a larger Tour-Pak, different paint, and additional chrome.

660 One of the most hated motorcycles when it was first introduced is now one of The Motor Company's most revered models. The high-performance FXR/FXRS Super Glide II was launched in 1982 and initial comments were that it looked "too Japanese" and "not like a Harley-Davidson." A well-designed, large-tube, square-backboned frame and suspension package allowed it to handle as well as an imported sportbike, while the rubber-mounted 80-ci Shovelhead and 5-speed transmission made the 620-pound cruiser faster than any other production Big Twin to that point. The frame's characteristic triangular section underneath the seat is seen in the design of most of today's frames. The once-maligned FXR is now one of the most popular styles among custom builders and performance enthusiasts.

661 Harley-Davidsons have used Japanese-made suspension components since 1973 when Super Glides and Sportsters began using Kayaba forks. In 1977, Showa forks replaced the Kayaba forks, and the company continues to use Showa front and rear suspensions today.

662 The entire 1979 Sportster line was treated to the updated, modernized, straight-tube frame that first debuted in the 1977 XLCR. A triangular section was added under the seat to house the covered oil tank on the right side, and the covered battery on the left, a staple Sportster design element that continues to this day. The frame, which was used only until 1981, differs from the XLCR frame only in the rear; the XLCR had extra tubing to support the seat and fender. The stiffer frame offered a vast improvement in terms of handling, but the Harley faithful weren't happy with it. They complained that the straight-tube frame and sidecovers looked too foreign.

663 Sportsters received a full disc brake setup for 1979. With the removal of the kickstarter, a new master cylinder was easily engineered and located against the transmission drive sprocket cover. This lightened the rear wheel for better acceleration and suspension control as well as the obvious improvement in braking performance. The location of the master cylinder remained the same until the introduction of rubber mounts in 2004.

664 The H-D execs took what they learned from the sales failure of the XLCR and in 1979 introduced the nearly opposite Sportster XLS, as well as a host of improvements to the Sportster line. The XLCR sought to challenge other performance motorcycles of the day, but the XLS channeled the attitude of the more traditional FX Low Rider. A two-tone paint scheme, a sissy bar with stash pouch, drag bars, a fat 16-inch rear wheel and tire, longer raked forks, and a low seat height created, essentially, a mini Low Rider.

665 Harley-Davidson's ad agency, tasked with marketing the XLS, wanted to separate it even further from other Sportsters by giving it a name. The results of a public contest led to the 1980 model being named the Roadster. It received some extra trim and, most notably, the Super Glide's 3.3-gallon fuel tank instead of the typical 2-1/4-gallon Sportster tank.

666 Women had always been an important part of Harley-Davidson's history, but The Motor Company hadn't built a bike with them in mind since the 1920 model W. That changed with the introduction of the 1980 XLH Hugger. It was essentially a variation of the successful XLS Roadster. The Hugger had shorter shocks and a thinner seat making it easier to flatfoot the ground. In addition to the obvious safety factor of being able to comfortably touch the ground, a lower center of gravity improves rider confidence throughout all aspects of riding. Unlike some Harleys today, which are particularly marketed to the fairer sex, the Hugger's intentions were never made clear officially for fear that women wouldn't want a "girl's bike."

667 Harley-Davidson broke down another barrier in 1983 with the introduction of the bare bones XLX Sportster with a $3,995 price tag. It had a solo seat, a single front brake disk, and very little chrome, all of which allowed pricing several hundred dollars less than other Sportsters. The price tag and the legendary Sportster name drove first-time motorcycle buyers into the showroom where they were introduced to larger, better-equipped models that could be their next purchase. Many XLX buyers added accessories later on that made the XLX more of a capable, attractive motorcycle.

668 Anyone who's ever attended a motorcycle swap meet is certainly familiar with the massive air cleaner that Harleys began using in 1979. Small, easy-flowing air cleaners are great for looks and power, but a lot of noise is associated with them. New noise regulations meant that Harley-Davidson had to increase the size of the air cleaner to the point that it covered almost the whole engine on Big Twins and Sportsters. Shorter riders even complained that they could barely get their right leg around the unit. A plate on the air cleaner displays the bike's engine displacement as "80," "1200," or "1000." As with the siamesed exhaust systems, these air cleaners usually found a place on the shelf or in the trash right away when replaced with a high-performance S&S Cycle teardrop.

669 Unlike the Panhead, which was launched initially in 1948 as a lightweight sport model with a big OHV engine, the 1966 FL Shovelhead was just as big and heavy as the 790-pound behemoth from a year earlier. But the brand-new engine's power output was only marginally improved, which made the early FL Shovels slower than every FL Panhead except the 1965 Electra Glide. The engineers spent all this time developing a new engine with the same displacement that was used in bikes weighing 200 pounds less!

670 For 1966, Harley-Davidson moved the fuel control lever from the top of the gas tank to the familiar left-side petcock that remained until the introduction of fuel injection in the mid-1990s and 2000s. The convenient steel line that connected both gas tank halves was replaced with a rubber line that didn't flow fuel nearly as quickly, and required the rider to fill tanks separately yet again. A sleek new emblem with long, white triangles and "Harley-Davidson" written in the middle adorned both sides of the gas tank; it was used until 1971. This made it the last non-AMF Harley-Davidson emblem until 1982. Although 1971 used the same emblem, a small, separate AMF emblem was underneath.

671 In 1968, Harleys moved a little further away from their style-oriented roots with the addition of a new dash console that eliminated the three separate, round, indicator lights. Now, a utilitarian rectangular strip of lights and lenses in the center accomplishes the task. The look of indicator lights has improved through the years thanks to LED technology. However, the designers must have done something right with the barrel-lock key switch in 1968 because it's almost exactly the same today, but with the added position of running the motorcycle without lights. Later, a choke knob was added to the dash console, which allowed for incredibly simple operation; you no longer had to reach behind the air cleaner to access the carburetor. The entire dash remained relatively unchanged into the Evolution years.

672 You probably don't have to walk far to take a look at a Harley-Davidson batwing fairing. This classic windbreaker is fitted to most of the bikes that The Motor Company sells today, including the global-best-selling Street Glide. Unlike the modern Street Glide, the first batwing fairing appeared in 1969 as a simple, white, fiberglass panel shaped with minimal aerodynamics. Unlike the electronically loaded fairings of today with speakers, navigation, and radios, the first fairing was little more than a glorified windshield that also provided hand protection. The full touring package also included white fiberglass saddlebags and a white fiberglass Tour-Pak mounted to the rear fender rack. And just like that, Harley-Davidson's place as the ultimate touring motorcycle was established.

673 Big drum brakes might have been all the rage in the 1930s and 1940s when Big Twins weighed less than 600 pounds. But for the 800-plus-pound behemoths of 1972 that had the ability to easily haul two people and lots of gear, drum brakes were quite simply, ineffective. In 1972, Harley-Davidson began using a hydraulic disc brake on the front of FLs. Early calipers were bulky and stretched out over the top of the disc and in front of the fork, very much unlike the compact little pucks hidden in the back of the fork today. Because of their rounded shape, these early brakes are called "banana brakes." A hydraulic rear disc brake, also a banana, joined the FL line for 1973, while the FX series received the front banana brake that same year.

674 Passengers today who travel on the back of a motorcycle have many of the modern comforts and conveniences found in some luxury automobiles. The motorcycles of Harley-Davidson's Touring line are designed with passengers in mind, but this wasn't always the case. In fact, FLs only began using a sculpted two-person seat in 1977. Before that, riders and passengers shared a "buddy seat," which was just an elongated rider seat with heavier springs that sat the rider and passenger very, very close together. The 1977 "Dual-Bucket" seat was longer than the buddy seat and had two distinct sitting areas as well as grab handles for the passenger. Likely an attempt to dampen the bike's vibration, the Dual-Bucket seat was still mounted on the pogo in-frame mount. In 1979, H-D finally started mounting the seats on FL models directly to the frame, as it does today, instead of the pogo frame mount. Suspension and vibration-containment technology certainly had a role in the new mounting style, but an added benefit for riders was a lower seat height for easier flatfooting and a lower center of gravity. However, sprung seats were still available as a factory option.

675 The big 75th anniversary was celebrated in 1978 and featured a Midnight Black with gold stripe paint scheme on the Sportster and the FLH-1200. A gold stripe on the FL's front fender reads "Harley-Davidson's 75th Anniversary 1200-cc Electra Glide." The cast-aluminum alloy wheels were painted gold on both the Sportster and the Electra Glide. No anniversary edition FX was produced, which is curious because the FX was one of the best-selling platforms of the late 1970s; nearly 20,000 units were sold in 1978 alone. Maybe the logic was to introduce buyers to the other V-twin families to boost sales there.

THE POWERTRAIN

676 Harley-Davidson unveiled its new Shovelhead engine with the 1966 Big Twin models; this engine saw more major redesigns in its 14-year lifespan than any other. The lower end of the 1966–1969 Shovelhead, along with its generator, closely resembles that of the Panhead. These early Shovels are called Flatsides because of the flat cam cover that also covers the generator. The major improvement was in the heads and valvetrain, which received more efficient rocker arms, smoother-flowing intake manifold, and Power Pac aluminum heads that produced about 10 percent more power. Displacement remained at 74 ci.

677 The Shovelhead engine was given its first big update in 1970 with the addition of a modern alternator charging system, which is still used. In addition to vastly improved charging ability, the biggest change was to the shape of the engine crankcase to fit the alternator between the left case and the engine sprocket. The right case received a cone in the cam cover to house the ignition system's breaker points. Use of the cone-style lower end continued throughout the Evolution years. The kickstarter was removed on FLs, but reappeared a year later on the new FX models.

678 Even as Harley-Davidson battled the Japanese manufacturers on the streets, racetracks, and sales floors, 1974 saw the replacement of the Bendix carburetor with a Keihin, which Honda had been using successfully for a few years. The Keihin had fewer adjustment options than previous carbs that H-D used, making the motorcycle that much easier to use.

679 When Harley-Davidson launched the XLCR in 1977, it had one of the most aggressive looks of any Harley-Davidson ever. Everything about it screamed "fast" and "fun." It might have been attractive and fun, but unfortunately, it wasn't fast. Its lighter weight, compared to contemporary Sportsters, wasn't enough to make the 1,000-cc quad-cammer do its job. The CR only managed low 13-second quarter-mile times while its Japanese multi-cylinder competition was hitting the mid-12s. The powertrain is entirely blacked out except for the rocker boxes, pushrod tubes, and timing cover. Adding to the CR's uniqueness is its siamesed exhaust system; the headers flowed into a crossover and then exited on either side of the rear wheel.

680 Although the 80-ci Shovelhead debuted in mid-1978, it was optional until 1980 when it became standard equipment on FLHs. The 80-ci version used the same cylinders as the 74, but they were bored out to 3½ inches while the stroke was increased to 4-1/4 inches (this is actually 81.6 ci). The 80-ci Shovelhead cylinders have one less fin than the 74-ci cylinders. The original 74-ci Shovelhead was built to run on premium leaded fuel but the new 80-ci was built to run on premium unleaded fuel. It also averaged a 49-mpg fuel economy that, even with its larger displacement, was less than the 74's 36 mpg. FX models were available with either a 74-ci or 80-ci engine until the entire Big Twin lineup went to the larger engine in 1981. 2,525 FLH-80s were produced that first year and another 8 were ordered in 75th anniversary trim.

681 The 1980 FLT Tour Glide debuts with Harley-Davidson's first rubber-mounted drivetrain. This greatly reduces vibrations in the 80-ci Shovelhead, allowing it to live up to its name as a long-distance cruiser. A new 5-speed transmission bolted directly to the engine instead of mounted to the frame as a separate component also makes its first appearance. The long-range performance potential of the Tour-Glide's powertrain is immediately evident and soon finds its way onto other Big Twin models.

682 In mid-1978, Shovelheads received a handful of updates to both the 74-ci and 80-ci engines. The new cylinder heads replaced the small-lip O-ring with a flat band with no lip to seal the intake manifold to the head. These heads also used new valves and valve guides to eliminate valve sticking.

683 The 1978 model year was the last that a Big Twin was available with a kickstart-only ignition. Of the 19,875 (total) Super Glides and Low Riders sold in 1978, only 1,774 were the base model FX Super Glide. The kickstart-only option in Sportsters barely lasted one more year; only 141 XLCH kickstart-only Sportsters were built in 1979.

684 The Kevlar drive belt now used on all H-Ds first appeared in 1980 and made owning a Harley significantly easier. A belt drive needs fewer adjustments over time because it doesn't stretch as much as a chain and, partially because of that, it doesn't need to be checked as often. And, belt drives are quieter. Even though the Shovelheads of the 1970s had some issues with oil leaks, the 1980s Shovels and certainly the Evolution and Twin Cam engines are oil tight. Because you don't have to oil a belt (as you do a chain), no extra oil or grease is under the bike, so everything is kept much cleaner.

685 In 1974, the Department of Transportation mandated that all motorcycles must be left-side shift and right-side brake. For the upcoming 1975 model year, Harley-Davidson had to make some quick changes to the Sportster, which was left-side brake and right-side shift to make it more effective as a flat track racer. The temporary solution was to run a second shift shaft underneath the frame and connect it to a longer shift lever. That same year, turn signals became mandatory on all motorcycles.

686 The 1979 Sportsters received the siamesed, dual-exit exhaust system seen only on the XLCR during the two previous years. AMF executives decided that the system's sleek look, as well as the fact that it was good for an additional 5 hp from the 1,000-cc engine, made it an obvious choice. Like the 1979 frame change, enthusiasts hated everything about it. Most of these exhausts were discarded in favor of drag-style dual pipes before the bikes even left the dealership. In fact, many dealers replaced them before the Sportsters even hit the showroom floor! For 1980, Sportsters were once again available with the traditional dual shorty exhaust system.

687 By 1982, low-octane, low-lead, and no-lead fuels had forced their way into pumps all across America thanks to a pair of fuel crises and stringent new EPA requirements. To run better on the new fuel offerings, engineers reduced the Sportster's compression ratio from 9.0:1 to 8.8:1 by using thicker head gaskets. With the new gas and lower compression, top speed dropped from about 110 to about 100 mph, and quarter-mile runs increased by nearly a second. The late 1970s and early 1980s were difficult times for all American engine manufacturers.

688 The Linkert carburetor was eliminated in 1967 and replaced with a Tillotson pumper carburetor. It used a great new feature called an accelerator pump that gave an immediate shot of gas into the manifold when the throttle was twisted. This gave the motorcycle near-instant acceleration, and it started much easier and faster, too.

689 By 1968, all Shovelheads were sold with electric start as indicated by the B at the end of the call letters. It is also the same year that Harley-Davidson began using a new, more-powerful Homelite starter and an uprated, 53-amp-hour 12-volt battery. In 1974, electric start was available on the FX line with the introduction of the FXE. However, the first few years of FX models were kickstart-only; this is sort of a step backward, but it was also an appeasement to the hardcore faction of Harley riders.

690 By 1975, there was very little demand for the low-compression FL engine, even among police departments, which had historically preferred low-speed usability. Only about 1,000 FLs were ordered in 1973 followed by 900 police orders in 1974 and 1975. In 1976, only the FLH-1200 was available and Harley riders began itching for a new top dog Big Twin.

691 In the days before cruise control, riders depended on the ability to set the throttle and relax their right hands. That's why Harley-Davidson developed the jam screw mechanism, which some riders, forgoing safe practices, leave tight for some old-school cruise control. However, in 1974 the U.S. government mandated that all motorcycles have a self-closing throttle. H-D began using a single sheathed cable with a return spring to work the carb instead of the old spiral control inside the handlebar.

692 The 1980–1982 FXB Sturgis is one of only two Harley-Davidsons ever to use a belt-drive primary. Most Big Twins switched to a belt final drive in 1980 as well, giving the FXB the distinction of having twin belt drives. The FXB's final run was in 1982, allowing it one year to wear the commemorative fender badge proudly while simultaneously removing the little AMF insignia from its gas tank. For its badass Willie G. styling, as well as the incorporation of new technology, the FXB (especially the 1982 version) is one of my favorite Harley motorcycles!

693 The Shovelhead engine remained in only a handful of models for 1984: the FX series and FLH series. But only one H-D

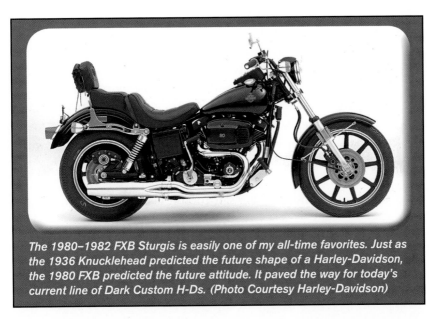

The 1980–1982 FXB Sturgis is easily one of my all-time favorites. Just as the 1936 Knucklehead predicted the future shape of a Harley-Davidson, the 1980 FXB predicted the future attitude. It paved the way for today's current line of Dark Custom H-Ds. (Photo Courtesy Harley-Davidson)

model can lay claim to being the last Shovelhead: the FLHX. The FLHX used a solid-mounted Shovel backed by a good old 4-speed. Harley-Davidson produced the full-dress FLHX in limited numbers and it was available in black and white only; a few more than 200 of each color were built. Red and gold pinstriping with spread-wing eagle and a USA shield on the fairing set the FLHX apart. But it's really the wording on the side of the saddlebags and front fender, "Harley-Davidson Motor Co. Special Edition Electra Glide," that make it a collector's item today.

694 Project Nova, which eventually became today's liquid-cooled V-Rod, was put into motion after the Pinehurst retreat in 1976. It was a complete alternative to the air-cooled Big Twin. Because The Motor Company didn't have the capability to develop two engines at the same time in-house, especially one as advanced as the liquid-cooled Nova, the design project was farmed out to Porsche Design in Germany. The initial Porsche concept was a V-4, but it was "modular" in the sense that it could easily be adapted into a V-twin and a V-6. Even though the Nova could have been a great motorcycle, the project was scrapped when the bottom fell out of the motorcycle market in 1982.

695 The Nova's chassis had to be built around the needs of the liquid-cooled powerplant. The bike's air intake system was hidden underneath the faux fuel tank (just like on a V-Rod) while the radiator was hidden underneath the seat. The sport-touring version is the best known of the Nova iterations thanks to its prominent location in the Harley-Davidson Museum. An FLT-fairing tourer and naked cruiser were also in the works. The Nova fairing, which went on to find its way onto the FXRT, FXRP, and FXRD, had two functional intake scoops on the Nova version, one side routing air to the intake and the other side routing air to the radiator.

Harley-Davidson's Nova line of motorcycles could have been an incredible asset to the company in a time of strict environmental standards and high-quality motorcycles coming in from overseas. It also could have been the biggest bust of all time. What do you think of the H-D that never was?

696 In 1975, Harley-Davidson engineers took on the challenge of building a high-tech, modern powerplant; the only rule was that it had to be a V-twin. What they came up with was the OHC 1100, which used overhead, chain-driven cams, identical front and rear cylinders, rubber mounting points, and an under-seat fuel tank with an electronic fuel pump. The OHC 1100 marked the first time Harley-Davidson experimented with any of these modern design elements. It was essentially a V-Rod 30 years before its time; and the technology compares to what most Japanese V-twin motorcycles use today, but without water cooling. The motorcycle's style was unmistakably Harley-Davidson. However, the advanced power-plant would have cost too much to produce on a large scale, and it's likely that it would have failed on the showroom floors.

697 I'd be remiss if I didn't mention one of the most legendary aftermarket Harley-Davidson engine variations built, the 45 Magnum. Randy Smith of Custom Cycle Engineering built the first 45 Magnum using a 45-ci WR bottom end with a set of OHV 900-cc Ironhead cylinders mounted to it. The conversion works because the rod length, stroke, and deck height are identical on both a 45 and an Ironhead. The end result is a 55-ci engine that could easily put out three to four times more horsepower than a stock 45.

698 Although it wasn't introduced until 1989, many Shovelhead owners have opted to swap their stock carburetor to the later, much better Harley-Davidson CV carb. The conversion is straight-forward and provides quicker throttle response, more power, and more accurate throttle control. The conversion simply requires a carburetor boot to hold the new carb; it slips onto the boot rather than bolting directly to the manifold. It also requires a new two-cable throttle system. Although it's possible to retain the single throttle cable, the two-cable setup is faster acting and safer.

699 In 1973, the U.S. government began requiring gasoline without lead to comply with provisions of the Clean Air Act. Harley-Davidson had not yet begun updating engines for unleaded fuel and owners of machines not yet retrofitted for the new fuel experienced numerous problems. Vehicles newly equipped with catalytic converters were damaged from using the wrong fuel. High-performance engines were unable to run at their prescribed high-compression settings on unleaded fuel; even stock valves and seats required the lubrication that leaded fuel provided. Some experts believe that an original Shovelhead run on unleaded fuel will require a top end rebuild in less than half the time as the same engine using leaded fuel.

700 Harley-Davidson upgraded the Shovelhead's oil pump toward the end of the 1981 model year, and that design was used well into the Evolution engine's reign. This final Shovelhead oil pump improved oil delivery capacity by 33 percent over the previous version. It was a big, but necessary jump to compensate for the 80-ci displacement and higher performance of the later engines.

PEOPLE AND POP CULTURE

701 Robert Craig "Evel" Knievel began performing motorcycle stunts in 1965, but it wasn't until December 12, 1970, that he got his act together and began using Harley-Davidson XR-750s. He had two XRs with him at every event; one was geared lower to make pre-show wheelies easier and, thanks to its higher gearing, his jumping XR achieved speeds of 90 to 100 mph upon takeoff. He upgraded to the new, more powerful XR-750 in 1972 and lightened it to around 300 pounds by using more aluminum and fiberglass.

Perhaps no other entertainer has ever put more on the line than stunt jumper Evel Kneivel. Imagine coming down off a 100-foot-plus jump with this thing. If you think your stock Harley shocks are bad now, imagine what each landing must have been like for him!

702 In 1971, Evel Knievel launched his XR-750 129 feet over 19 cars, a record-setting jump that was featured in the movie *Evel Knievel* starring George Hamilton. His longest successful jump, however, came at the Kings Island theme park outside Cincinnati, Ohio. On October 25, 1975, he jumped 14 Greyhound buses totaling 133 feet. He landed successfully on the safety platform above the 14th bus and earned the record for the longest jump on a Harley-Davidson, a record that stood for 24 years.

703 The 1971 movie, *Evel Knievel*, features Knievel reflecting on his life before his big jump (at the end of the movie) at Ontario Motor Speedway in Ontario, California. This was where he set the record, jumping his XR-750 129 feet over 19 cars. Evel Knievel went on to star in the 1977 film, *Viva Knievel!* and the 1988 documentary *The Last of the Gladiators*. Many films have been made about the legendary stuntman; one of the more recent is the 2004 TV movie, *Evel Knievel*.

704 Evel Knievel holds the Guinness World Record for the most broken bones. The official record was set in 1975 by which point he had suffered 433 fractures. However, he was injured again in 1976 in an attempt to jump a tank full of sharks on live television. He broke both of his arms and, for the first time in his career, a bystander was injured when a cameraman lost an eye after being struck. A year later, the *Happy Days* episode featuring Fonzie jumping a shark on water skis aired, and gave life to the expression "jumping the shark" as a sign of the downhill slide of a career or television show.

705 Evel Knievel's life was honored with an exhibit at the Harley-Davidson museum in 2010 called True Evel: The Amazing Story of Evel Knievel. It was a collaboration between the museum and Evel's oldest son, Kelly, and contained artifacts from his career including his iconic leather suits, several motorcycles, and X-rays from his various hospital visits. The exhibit then went on a year-long tour of Europe.

706 In an effort to get away from its outlaw image, The Motor Company sponsored the television show, *Then Came Bronson*, in 1969. Michael Parks stars as the main character, Jim Bronson, who travels around the country on his Sportster meeting and helping people along the way. Bronson, wearing his traditional black leather jacket, is always the levelheaded pacifist who helps the antagonists realize that the solution to their woes lies within themselves. Harley-Davidson lent a hand by promoting the show it in its dealer showrooms as well as supplying the motorcycles.

707 Bronson's 1969 XLH-1000 Sportster quickly became the star of the show, and is one of the more recognizable Harleys in showbiz. It uses an XLCH gas tank that, along with the bobbed front and rear fenders, is painted in "Bronson Red." The custom headlight and front end was always covered up by Bronson's massive bedroll, which contained his belongings. But the real identifier of the Bronson Sportster is the Eye of Providence decal on the side of the gas tank. Bronson's custom Sportster became so popular that The Motor Company provided a dealer bulletin about how to convert a stock XLH into an exact replica of Bronson's bike. For 1970, Bronson Red was available as an option on Sportsters.

708 Michael Parks did all of the riding scenes in *Then Came Bronson*, but Bud Ekins, one of the most famous Hollywood stuntmen of all time, handled the stunts. Bronson managed to dump, crash, or in some way damage his Sportster a lot throughout the show's one-season run. Bud Ekins had his work cut out for him coordinating, and often taking part in, the stunts. Even though Ekins' most famous scenes come from the silver screen, he earned a reputation as the go-to guy when it came to motorcycle stunts.

709 To honor the U.S. bicentennial, as many around the country were doing in 1976, Harley-Davidson unveiled the Liberty Edition motorcycles. The biggest 1976 Liberty Edition began life as a fully loaded FLH with fairing, Tour-Pak, and saddlebags. It was painted black metallic with silver flake and had a huge Eagle's Wings decal on the fairing that included the Bar & Shield logo. It

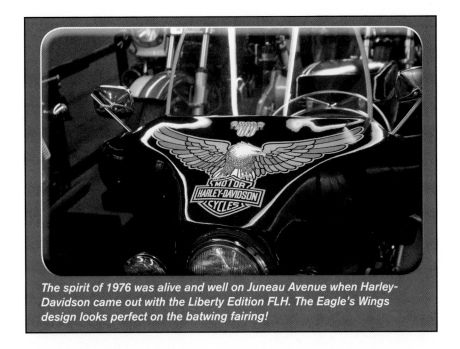

The spirit of 1976 was alive and well on Juneau Avenue when Harley-Davidson came out with the Liberty Edition FLH. The Eagle's Wings design looks perfect on the batwing fairing!

also had Liberty Edition and Made In The USA decals. The top of the Tour-Pak sported a Liberty Edition emblem. At a time when Japanese motorcycles had become the norm on American roads, the Liberty Edition proudly proclaimed Harley-Davidson as THE American motorcycle. The Sportster and Super Glide versions wore similar trim, but without the touring components.

710 Easily Harley-Davidson's most controversial option package, the Confederate Edition was offered in 1977, in a bid to ride the success of the 1976 Liberty Edition. The Confederate Edition consisted of Metallic Gray paint with confederate flag decals on either side of the tank and an army general sleeve braid decal on the front fender. Most models were available with Confederate Edition trim, although few were actually ordered. Total production was 359 Sportsters, 228 Super Glides, and 59 FLHs, which makes the Confederate Edition Harleys some of the rarest ever produced. It is difficult to disavow their existence, because people actually own them, but good luck finding any reference to one in modern Harley-Davidson literature, or even finding one on display in the museum!

711 From September 1979 to March 1982 the U.S. government mandated that speedometers on motorcycles and automobiles could only go as high as 85 mph, no matter how capable the vehicle was of surpassing that number. Apparently, the idea was so that people would save fuel by staying under 85 mph. However, there was one flaw with the government's genius plan. Vehicles could still go faster, you just wouldn't know how much faster. To give you an idea of the sheer idiocy of this mandate, my 1982 Honda CBX, a 100-hp 6-cylinder sport tourer redlines at 10,000 rpm but has a speedometer that only goes to 85 mph. Yes, that's second-gear cruising speed. Of course, this also affected H-Ds and although it's not a big pain for FL owners, FX and FXR riders could easily spend time cruising the ton. After the mandate was lifted, H-D speedos went to a 150-mph-max speed reading, which is probably further from max speed than 85, but at least you could tell what that speed was.

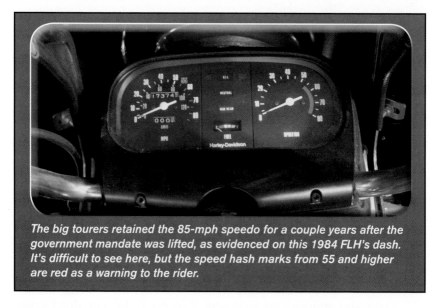

The big tourers retained the 85-mph speedo for a couple years after the government mandate was lifted, as evidenced on this 1984 FLH's dash. It's difficult to see here, but the speed hash marks from 55 and higher are red as a warning to the rider.

712 Harley-Davidson built its first Shrine Edition in 1979. Shriners International (commonly called The Shriners) is a charity organization that uses synchronized performances with motorcycles (and other vehicles) to raise awareness for its causes. Their motorcycles require gearing similar to police motorcycles, but they need to be flashy, attention-getting machines. The 1979 Electra Glide Shrine featured H-D's enclosed chain-drive setup, which keeps oil and grease off the bikes. It was almost unnecessary because Shriners traditionally keep them exceptionally clean and well polished. The tradition of building a special edition motorcycle for The Shriners continues to this day.

713 It seems strange to say, but riding around the world these days is hardly an oddity. It was, however, a very big deal in 1989 when Dave Barr rode his 1972 Super Glide 83,000 miles over the course of 3-1/2 years, hitting every continent except Antarctica. Perhaps even more impressive than riding a nearly 20-year-old Shovelhead around the world is that Dave did it as a double amputee, having lost both of his legs in combat. By the time Dave retired the 1972 Super Glide, it had more than a quarter of a million miles on it! And if that trip of a lifetime wasn't enough, he then rode a 1996 883 Sportster with sidecar 9,375 miles through Europe and Russia, in winter, staying mostly within the Arctic Circle on ice roads.

714 "I pulled in to Nazareth, feelin' 'bout half-past-dead." These classic lyrics by The Band elicit instant serenity for any Harley rider. The iconic motorcycle film, *Easy Rider*, not only defined a whole generation of motorcyclists but also continues to inspire riders to this day with its ultimate tale of the freedom found on a Harley-Davidson out on the open road. Peter Fonda produced and starred in the 1969 film along with Dennis Hopper and Jack Nicholson but the real stars, according to most Harley riders, were the choppers, *Captain America* and the *Billy Bike*, both of which were based on Panheads.

715 Have you ever heard of the "Motorcyclin' Gran'ma?" Hazel Kolb earned that nickname after she embarked on a 15,000-mile solo trip around the perimeter of the United States in 1979 on her Electra Glide. At a time when most H-D publicity was either about poor build quality or outlaw culture, Hazel utterly destroyed both stereotypes by racking up that much mileage in one long trip. At the same time, she spoke to and made friends with as many other motorcyclists as she could on her journey. Harley-Davidson's public relations department set up newspaper and television interviews for her along the way. She even appeared on *The Tonight Show with Johnny Carson* and *Good Morning America!* Obviously, the people who came up with the slogan "You meet the nicest people on a Honda," never met Hazel Kolb. And, naturally, painted onto the back of her Tour-Pak was, "Say Hi to the Motorcyclin' Gran'ma."

716 In 1983, The Motor Company's 80th year, it created what could possibly be described as its second-greatest product: the Harley Owners Group, known as H.O.G. 33,000 H-D riders signed up in that first year; it was apparent that Harley riders were desperate to ride and get together with like-minded enthusiasts without the stigmas often associated with a "club." Today, H.O.G. has more than a million members, making it the largest manufacturer-sponsored riding organization.

717 The expression "one percenter" appeared around the mid-1960s referencing the supposed 1 percent of Harley-Davidson owners who lived the outlaw lifestyle. Either way, outlaw culture nearly became the definition of Harley-Davidson into the late-1960s and through the 1970s. At the same time, The Motor Company's archnemesis, Honda, was attracting the "friendliest people" in droves with its CB750 and CB450. H-D management ran itself ragged trying to come up with ways to distance itself and its iconic V-twin from motorcycling's outlaw element. Rumor has it that the company even offered to buy Hondas for one-percenter club members to get them to stop using Harleys! Whether or not it's true, it obviously didn't work.

718 Even though history shows that the late 1960s were a difficult time for Harley-Davidson sales, the 1965 model year brought in $30 million in sales, nearly double the $16 million from 1959. So what was the problem that nearly led the company to bankruptcy by 1971? You guessed it: Honda. From 1959 to 1965, Honda sales rose from $500,000 to $77 million, followed by $106 million in 1966. Harley-Davidson's sales were up, but its biggest enemy became not just the market, but also the market share.

719 On Friday August 13, 1971, President Richard Nixon announced, among other things, a 10 percent surcharge tax on imported goods, which included Japanese motorcycles Honda and Yamaha (among others). There's no evidence that the "Nixon Shock" had a direct effect on H-D sales because it also included a mandatory wage freeze and widespread economic uncertainty. However, it more than likely slowed competitor sales until at least December when the surcharge was lifted and the Japanese two-wheelers really began to fly out of showrooms.

720 In 1977, six years before the Harley Owners Group began, California enthusiast Carl T. Wicks had an idea for an all-inclusive H-D owners' club and called it the Harley-Davidson Owners Association. At a time when The Motor Company was having some serious technical (and consumer loyalty) issues, Wicks' goal was to bring the company, dealers, and riders together to improve the product and the overall ownership experience. The HDOA was taken over by Harley-Davidson in 1983 and turned into H.O.G., which is run by the company.

721 Prior to President Ronald Reagan's April 15, 1983, signing of the Japanese heavyweight motorcycle tariff order, a group that included the Japanese motorcycle manufacturers came together and offered Harley-Davidson a $200,000,000 loan and technical advice in lieu of the tariff. Harley-Davidson declined the offer.

722 Just about every major motorcycle museum has the original *Captain America* chopper from the movie *Easy Rider*, but which one is the real one? None of them. Both Peter Fonda's and Dennis Hopper's choppers are no longer in existence, which is unfortunate because builders Cliff Vaughns and Ben Hardy so perfectly nailed the look of the 1960s-era chopper. However, most of the museum collection replicas, including the one on display at the Harley-Davidson Museum, are top-notch machines that allow visitors to be a part of the *Easy Rider* cultural experience.

723 Every modern Harley-Davidson anniversary since the 75th in 1978 has featured a special logo designed to mark the occasion. In every instance (except 1978), those logos appeared on the special anniversary-edition motorcycle. In 1978, the logo appeared only on commemorative merchandise. Executives must have realized the marketing and promotion potential of the unique logos; for every five-year anniversary since 1978, the anniversary logos have appeared on just about everything.

724 Stunt jumper Evel Knievel rode only a Harley-Davidson, except when it came to his failed September 8, 1974 attempt at jumping Snake River Canyon. That machine was the X-2 Sky-Cycle, which had three wheels and was actually registered in Idaho as an aircraft, not a motorcycle. Even though it didn't have the usual V-twin H-D power that Knievel preferred, it did have the stars and stripes No. 1 Harley-Davidson logo on the vertical stabilizer as a nod to his regular jumpbike brand. Although it would have likely ended in a fatality, Knievel probably would have gotten farther on his XR-750. The SkyCycle's parachute deployed on takeoff and caused the machine to float hopelessly to the bottom of the canyon.

725 Joe Geiger, Harley-Davidson's longest-serving employee, retired in 1982 after working for the company for 63 years 11 months. Originally, Joe worked directly for Bill Harley, and, in case you're wondering, that record includes all four founders, as well as any of their offspring. By comparison, Willie G. Davidson worked at The Motor Company for 49 years, officially retiring in 2012, although he still is active in the Harley-Davidson Museum on a daily basis. Even with that, he still has a decade left of working to match Joe Geiger!

MILITARY, POLICE AND RACING

726 One of the greatest American motorcycle racers of all time, Cal Rayborn rose to true superstardom with back-to-back Daytona 200 wins in 1968 and 1969 with the Harley-Davidson factory team. Riding a 750 KR, he became the first rider to average over 100 mph on the course of the 1968 200-miler. That speed helped him beat the most internationally diverse field of skilled racers Daytona had yet witnessed. His 1969 win was just as satisfying for the all-American; he outlasted and outraced the latest two-stroke speed demons from Japan.

727 Mert Lawwill joined the Harley-Davidson Class C flat track race team in 1964 and achieved his first AMA national win at the Sacramento Mile on September 19, 1965. However, it wasn't until 1969 that he came into his own: He won the AMA Grand National championship and was also voted the AMA's most popular rider of the year.

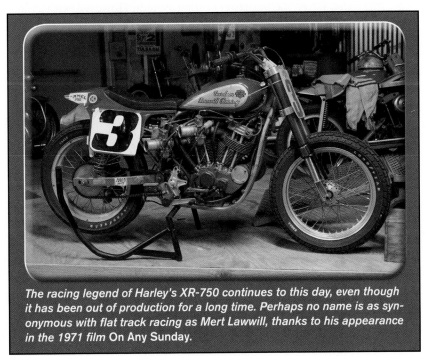

The racing legend of Harley's XR-750 continues to this day, even though it has been out of production for a long time. Perhaps no name is as synonymous with flat track racing as Mert Lawwill, thanks to his appearance in the 1971 film On Any Sunday.

728 By the time he retired in 1977 (because of an inner ear disorder that affected his balance), Mert Lawwill had racked up 17 national championship wins in TT, Short Track, Half Mile, and Mile classes. His 15-year career saw him finish 161 total AMA

Grand National races, making him one of the winningest riders in AMA Grand National history.

729 Even with the numerous two-wheeled legends that rolled out of the Harley-Davidson factory, the XR-750 stands as one of the most elite models. But based on what the factory produced in 1970, you'd be hard-pressed to guess that. The first XR-750 to replace the 750 KR quickly earned a reputation as being heavy, slow, and unreliable. Based on an 883-cc Sportster engine, but destroked from 96 to 82 mm, the first XR-750 was actually a stopgap model that was rushed to market so it could campaign when AMA rules finally allowed OHV engines. The first XR-750 used aluminum heads, cast-iron cylinders, a magneto instead of a generator, and an improved (over the Sportster) oiling system. However, with evenly matched riders, it was no match for Japanese two-strokes and British twins.

730 The look of the XR-750 is unmistakable and just about anyone who's ever felt the thrill of two-wheeled transportation can pick one out of a lineup. The fiberglass 2-1/2 gallon fuel tank and fender have defined the "dirt tracker" look. A Ceriani front fork and a pair of Girling rear shocks kept the 19-inch spoked wheels on the ground. The seat snaps down over a foam cushion, furthering the XR-750's spartan appearance. Initially, 200 XRs were built for homologation purposes and sold for $3,200 apiece.

731 The XRTT version of the XR-750 was a completely different beast altogether. It carried a 6-gallon fiberglass fuel tank and a large, aerodynamic fiberglass bump seat tail section on its backbone. A full fiberglass fairing covered the entire engine area and had a clear windshield on top; the bike's unique triangular oil tank on the left side was not covered. The TT boasted some serious braking power over its dirt track brother in the form of a hydraulic disc brake in the rear and a huge Fontana four leading-shoe drum brake in the front.

732 Even though Cal Rayborn failed to get a national win in 1970, he still managed to bring glory to the United States and the Harley-Davidson Motor Company. At the Bonneville Salt Flats in Utah, the famous land speed racing grounds, he piloted a Sportster-powered streamliner to a new American and International record. Rayborn took the 700-pound 16-foot-long machine to 265.492 mph even after experiencing several high-speed crashes in the finicky behemoth.

733 The truly legendary XR-750 was actually built in 1972 to campaign in a variety of races that year. To solve an overheating issue, aluminum cylinders were swapped into the existing design, which helped produce more power. But the biggest changes are what define the look and performance heritage of the XR-750 today. The heads were redesigned to allow for dual, rear-facing intake manifolds and Mikuni carburetors on the right side and dual, forward-exiting, high-mounted exhaust pipes on the left side. This incredible improvement in airflow, and the all-aluminum engine's ability to handle the power, made the XR-750 the winningest racing motorcycle of all time. It went on to win 29 of 37 AMA Grand National Championships between 1972 and 2008 when production finally ceased.

734 Cal Rayborn's last great success as a road racer occurred outside the realm of the H-D factory team and outside the borders of the United States when he went to England to compete in the invitation-only Transatlantic Match Races in 1972, which pitted the best British riders against the best American riders. With no factory support and therefore no access to the much-improved 1972 XR-750 racer, he used an outdated and outgunned iron-cylinder XR-750 owned by Walt Fault, a Harley-Davidson employee. Rayborn had never raced in England. He received help from another American motorsports legend, Don Emde, who drew up maps of the various tracks on cocktail napkins for Rayborn to study. You might think that Cal Rayborn didn't stand a chance against the stiff competition from the British racers. Wrong. Rayborn won three of the six races, finished second in the other three, and tied for the top score, making him an instant hero in England and boosting his prominence back at home.

735 The Harley-Davidson factory team earned its last road race win on July 23 at the 1972 AMA Grand National road race at Laguna Seca Raceway with an XRTT piloted by Cal Rayborn. It was the Monterey, California, track's first time holding an AMA Grand National road race. The win cemented Harley-Davidson's name into the world-renowned facility's history. Sadly, it was also Rayborn's final national win. He was killed in 1973 (age 33) at a club race in New Zealand when his Suzuki's engine seized and he careened into a guardrail at more than 100 mph. Even though he last raced for Suzuki, he will always be remembered as one of Harley-Davidson's most legendary racers.

736 In 1975, rider Gary Scott kicked off four consecutive years of Harley-Davidson winning the AMA Grand National Championship on the dirt track. In that same year, rookie Jay Springsteen won the AMA Rookie of the Year award for his performance and was signed to the H-D factory team for the following season. But Springsteen's accolades didn't stop there. He went on to win the AMA Grand National Championship in 1976, 1977, and 1978.

737 Jay Springsteen became the first rider to achieve 30 AMA Grand National wins by 1982. Today, motorcycle racers are generally considered old by their mid-20s, but Springsteen raced competitively until age 46 (in 2003), when he retired from flat track racing. In a career of almost 30 years, he became one of the winningest AMA flat trackers in history with 43 total Grand National victories out of a record 398 starts. He even scored two podium finishes the year he announced his official retirement, although he continued racing in various other forms and in vintage events. In 1994, *American Motorcyclist*, the AMA's magazine, gathered a panel of 30 experts to decide who was the best dirt track racer of all time. To no one's surprise, they decided on Jay Springsteen.

738 The legend of Jay Springsteen doesn't exist only out on the dirt, but also on America's most famous road race track, Daytona. Riding Mark Brelsford's previously crashed and blown-up XR road racer, rebuilt and punched out to 1,000 cc, Springsteen rolled up to the starting line against the best riders on the latest Ducati motorcycles in the 1983 Battle of the Twins race at Daytona. And won.

739 From 1966 through 1969, Harley-Davidson didn't have a specific model for police use, but that was the intent of the lower-compression FL with the police package. Except that the role of motor officers had changed through the years, and cops didn't want to give up 5 hp in exchange for low-speed comfort. It really didn't make sense for cops to be on bikes that were slower than just about any other vehicle on the road. Instead, most motor officers opted for the high-performance FLH.

740 When most folks think of the great racing two-strokes of the 1970s, visions of Yamahas usually appear. From 1974 to 1976, the only place visions of Yamahas were appearing was in H-D/Aermacchi racer Walter Villa's rearview mirror, that is, if he had one. Villa raced the RR250 and RR350 two-stroke twins built at the Aermacchi factory to three (technically four) championships in a row. He won the 250-cc class in 1974 and 1975 and then both the 250- and 350-cc classes in 1976. The 5-speed 230-pound 250RR produced 50 hp and revved to 10,000 rpm. Later, it was upgraded with water-cooling, allowing it to hit 58 hp at 12,000 rpm. The 350RR was the real monster of the group, able to hit 70 hp with the same chassis.

741 Harley-Davidson began manufacturing practice bomb casings for the Department of Defense (DoD) in 1982, a division of the business that generated $125 million in revenue during some of the toughest financial years the company had ever seen. As Vaughn Beals stated in the April 1988 issue of *American Motorcyclist*, "for the next couple of years [post 1983], our Defense Department contracts showed the biggest profits . . ." At a time when the banks were mere breaths away from foreclosing on Harley-Davidson, every bit of profit was vital to survival. The company's other DoD contract was for a small, liquid-fueled rocket engine that it sold to Beech Aircraft, which initially used them in drones.

742 When you think of fast motorcycles, you probably think of Japanese and Italian four-cylinder bikes, but it's Harley-Davidson power that holds the longest official land speed record. On July 14, 1990, Dave Campos rode a twin-Shovelhead-engine streamliner to 322.150 mph, breaking the 318.598 record held by a twin-engine turbo Kawasaki. Campos' record held for 16 years, until 2006.

743 The XR-750 wasn't the only Harley-Davidson taking checkered flags in the mid-1970s. One of the greatest, and also least-known, Harley-Davidson victories occurred on June 13, 1975, on Mexico's Baja peninsula in the Baja 500. On that unlucky Friday (for the competition), Bruce Ogilvie and Larry Roeseler won the 250-cc motorcycle class on an SX-250. They also claimed the overall motorcycle win against much larger displacement imports and took a second-place overall out of 375 total competitors. Ogilvie, Roeseler, and their SX-250 are the only Harley-Davidson team to ever win at Baja.

744 Scott Parker earned his pro racing license in 1979 at the age of 17, making him the youngest rider up until that point to turn pro. He certainly deserved it. He achieved eight top-10 finishes that first year aboard his H-D and, even more impressive, won two mile-long Nationals at Du Quoin and Indianapolis. That scored him yet another "youngest" notch as the youngest to win an AMA Grand National race. He finished his rookie season in ninth place overall and earned the coveted Rookie of the Year award.

745 By the late 1960s and early 1970s, Harley-Davidson had begun to lose its controversial grasp on the American Motorcyclist Association, of which founder Arthur Davidson was the president from 1944 until his death in 1950. By this time, foreign motorcycles were more and more common on the streets and racetracks of the United States, and the AMA was under pressure from its members and the other OEMs to make the rules fair for everyone, not just Harley-Davidson. One of its most outlandish rules, which nearly cost the AMA everything, was the refusal to sanction road racing of any sort. If you were caught road racing, you weren't allowed to compete at any AMA event, which, of course, applied entirely to high-performance Japanese and British motorcycles.

746 Harley-Davidson factory rider Bart Markel finally broke one of Joe Leonard's records when he won his 28th Grand National victory on June 27, 1971. He hadn't won a championship since 1966, the year he was awarded the AMA's Most Popular Rider of the Year Award. He took five wins in 1968, only a couple in 1969, and then only a single victory in 1970 and 1971. He raced for the last time on September 10, 1972, and came in 12th. However, his record number of wins was unbeaten for another decade.

747 AMA Hall of Famer Pete Hill rode his "world's fastest Knucklehead" to five International Drag Bike Association (IDBA) and AMA Dragbike Top Fuel championships more than 30 years after his engine originally left the factory. Hill built his first dragracing motorcycle as a teen in 1948, using a Knucklehead engine. In 1981, he won

Pete Hill's daily rider is a dual-carb Knucklehead bobber with a Coors keg mounted to the sissy bar to hold extra fuel. From left to right: Buzz Kanter, Pete Hill, and Dale Walksler.

his first IDBA championship title as well as the AMA Dragbike Top Fuel title aboard the 1947 Knuck; he went on to win another four IDBA and AMA championships aboard that bike. He beat and set 15 records over the course of his career, including the one for the world's fastest Knucklehead: 1/8-mile ET of 4.75 seconds, set in 1988. His wife, Jackie, served as his crew chief throughout his career, and even handled the important job of mixing fuel. Pete joked that he was always especially nice to her, because even the slightest miscalculation in fuel mixing could lead to an immediate explosion.

748 Even under the showroom onslaught by the Japanese motorcycle brands, Harley-Davidson's XR-750 continued to dominate on the flat track. Honda wasn't happy about this, and had tried to campaign a flat tracker with little success in the late 1970s and early 1980s. So it did the only thing it could. Honda bought an XR-750 (which were readily available to anyone at the time) and reverse engineered a Grand National champion. Honda's RS750, first campaigned in 1984, used identical bore and stroke figures as the XR, except that it added an overhead cam on each cylinder and used four-valve heads. The added performance allowed the RS750 to win four consecutive national championships from 1984–1987.

749 The last time Harley-Davidson offered a hand/shift, foot/clutch motorcycle was on the 1978 Police edition FLH. Police versions were available this way for so long because slow-speed maneuvering was easier with a foot clutch, as opposed to the heavy (by today's standards) hand clutches in use then. Not needing to fully grasp the clutch lever allowed the motor officer to hold something in his left hand, like a radio. Or a gun.

750 Joe Smith of West Covina, California, became the first motorcycle drag racer ever to run the quarter-mile in less than 9 seconds. His motorcycle was based on a 108-ci Shovelhead with S&S Cycle flywheels and carburetor, Burkhardt cylinders, and a Leinweber camshaft. Smith did all of the machining and headwork himself to accomplish his 1971 record. He went on to set another record of 8.20 seconds in 1974 on his double-Shovel drag racer.

Chapter 7

Evolution Era 1984–1998

THE MOTOR COMPANY

751 After years of financial hardship and a looming turnaround, Harley-Davidson had a lot to celebrate at its 85th anniversary in 1988. For the 85th, The Motor Company unveiled three limited-edition anniversary models that wear unique paint schemes and badging. Enough of these motorcycles were built so that each dealer was allotted one of each model. The Softail Springer was black with eagle decals on either side of the gas tank; the 85th badge sat on the front fender. Although each Springer was labeled #### of 1450, only 1,356 were actually produced. The FXRS Low Rider and the FLHTC Electra Glide Classic sported a black and Champagne Gold paint scheme with the 85th markings on the side of the tank. 850 were made of each. All three models also wore the words "MADE IN AMERICA" and "1903–1988." As part of the celebration, President Vaughn Beals rode an 85th Anniversary FLHTC on a cross-country trip, "The Milwaukee Ride For MDA," to celebrate the brand's comeback. And, about $600,000 was raised for the MDA (Muscular Dystrophy Association). More than 60,000 enthusiasts showed up in Milwaukee to pay tribute and participate in the festivities.

752 In its July 1986 initial public offering (IPO) on the American Stock Exchange, shares of Harley-Davidson were listed publicly for the first time since the 1969 AMF merger. Initial expectations were for 1.43 million shares to be sold at between $9 and $11. The IPO was more popular than expected, and 2 million shares were sold at $11 per share on its first day of trading. The money raised went toward paying off debts, providing working capital, and financing expansions. On July 1, 1987, a rejuvenated Harley-Davidson began trading on the New York Stock Exchange (NYSE) with the ticker symbol HDI. H-D executives celebrated the occasion by riding from a dealership in Queens to the NYSE building on Wall Street in Lower Manhattan, marking the first time a motorcycle appeared on the trading floor. The parade included 25 motorcycles, 10 limousines, 2 H-D tractor-trailers, and a Holiday Rambler motor home. On August 15, 2006, the HDI symbol was traded for a more fitting symbol: HOG.

Harley-Davidson President Vaughn Beals accompanies a Heritage Softail to the company's official listing on the New York Stock Exchange (NYSE). With the exception of those old monitors, the famous floor of the NYSE hasn't changed much. Beals must have felt on top of the world when this picture was taken. (Photo Courtesy Harley-Davidson)

753 Harley-Davidson acquired the Holiday Rambler Corporation and its subsidiaries in December 1986 for $155 million, doubling the size of The Motor Company. Holiday Rambler is best known for its high-end recreational vehicles (RVs); it pioneered many creature comforts that are standard today, including built-in refrigerators and holding tanks. Vaughn Beals and other executives believed that their company needed diversification as it continued to grow. Soon after, however, demand for motorcycles increased significantly, and the company decided to put all of its effort into the core business. After only 10 years, Holiday Rambler was sold to Monaco Coach for $50 million.

754 The Fat Boy, introduced in 1990, quickly became a favorite of riders and nonriders alike and remains one of the most popular models to this day. It is also one of the more controversial models ever produced, and leads to numerous debates every time bikers gather. The styling of the all-silver 1990 Fat Boy, with its yellow cylinder head rings and winged logo on the gas tank, bears a remarkable similarity to a particular pair of World War II B-29 Superfortress bombers: the *Enola Gay* and *Bockscar*. These aircraft each featured large, striking physiques that were covered with polished metal plates, giving it a silver appearance. Their propeller tips are yellow, and the Army Air Corps logo on the fuselage resembles the Fat Boy logo on the gas tank. Of the 3,970 B-29s built, only a handful received this treatment. The *Enola Gay* and *Bockscar* earned their notoriety by dropping the atom bombs, *Fat Man* and *Little Boy*, on Hiroshima and Nagasaki, Japan, during WWII. After two decades of Japanese motorcycle domination in the United States, followed by the Harley-Davidson resurgence, many believe that the Fat Boy's name originates as a combination of the two atom bombs. Of course, The Motor Company has denied this, and likely always will, leaving this as a source of debate among enthusiasts for many years to come.

755 A prototype Fat Boy was created in 1988 that nearly matches the version that hit showrooms two years later. H-D management did things a little differently back then. With a beautiful, edgy prototype sitting at Harley-Davidson headquarters, Willie G. decided that he wanted to ride that motorcycle from Milwaukee to Daytona Beach, Florida, for Bike Week. So, two years before the Fat Boy was introduced to the public, Willie G. was actually cruising around Daytona and talking to consumers about his prototype motorcycle. So, if you think back and swear that you saw the Fat Boy before it was officially introduced in 1990, were you at Bike Week the previous year? Here's something else: Willie G. was known for commuting to work on many of the prototypes that his team designed. That sort of thing is completely taboo today, but that's just part of what makes him a legend among the Harley community.

756 The mid-1990s saw the major expansion of Harley-Davidson's operations. In 1996, the company opened a 250,000 square-foot facility in Franklin, Wisconsin, to serve as its parts and accessories distribution center; by 1997, all inventory from Juneau

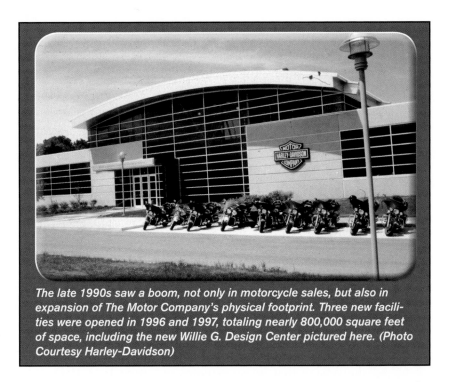

The late 1990s saw a boom, not only in motorcycle sales, but also in expansion of The Motor Company's physical footprint. Three new facilities were opened in 1996 and 1997, totaling nearly 800,000 square feet of space, including the new Willie G. Design Center pictured here. (Photo Courtesy Harley-Davidson)

Avenue was moved to the new location. In 1997, H-D opened a new, 217,000 square-foot product development center dedicated to Willie G., located next to the Capitol Drive plant in Milwaukee. A new, 330,000 square-foot Kansas City plant rolled out its first complete Sportster in 1997, while Big Twin engine and transmission production moved to the newly-purchased powertrain operations facility in Menomonee Falls, a suburb of Milwaukee.

757 The Motor Company took another huge step into the future with the opening of its first operations outside the United States in Manaus, Brazil. The facility served as a base for all of South America; it produced and sold motorcycles as well as housed executive offices. One of the main reasons for choosing Manaus is its status as a free economic zone. This meant that companies there paid little to no taxes in an attempt to spur economic development for its inner Amazonian location.

758 In 1993, Harley-Davidson bought a 49 percent minority interest in the Buell Motorcycle Company. Founded 10 years earlier by former H-D engineer Erik Buell, the brand installed modified Sportster engines into high-performance frames and chassis; typical Harley buyers weren't interested in this type of motorcycle. The Motor Company looked at Buell as a gateway to a new, youthful market with a product that already had high-performance and name recognition. Based in East Troy, Wisconsin, 35 miles from Milwaukee, Buell was a perfect fit for dealerships across the globe. Harley-Davidson bought another 49 percent interest in Buell in 1998, and Erik Buell was named chairman.

759 Harley-Davidson celebrates its 90th Anniversary in Milwaukee with a Family Reunion in June 1993. An estimated 100,000 people show up in Milwaukee to take part in the grand celebration. A massive parade of motorcycles shuts down Milwaukee highways and streets in what has now become a five-year anniversary tradition. Anniversary models were available in mostly black and silver paint schemes with special tank badges honoring the 90th.

760 By 1987, the steps that management took to improve quality, efficiency, and sales worked big time. Productivity was improved by 50 percent, quality was up by 68 percent, parts and materials inventories were reduced by 75 percent, and the heavyweight market share increased by 97 percent. United States revenues increased by 80 percent, international revenues by 170 percent, and operating profits increased by $59 million. After only four years of the tariff on Japanese heavyweight imports, Harley-Davidson petitioned the United States Government to lift its tariff protection, one year ahead of schedule.

761 More than 140,000 riders head to Milwaukee in 1998 to celebrate Harley-Davidson's 95th anniversary. Anniversary models are available on every H-D chassis and each features a two-tone Midnight Red and Champagne Pearl paint scheme with a special cloisonné tank emblem that resembles the winged Fat Boy emblem. Each anniversary model is also numbered for uniqueness.

762 In 1984, money began rolling into the troubled Harley-Davidson Motor Company with the release of the Evolution engine. A turnaround was imminent, and it appeared to all as though the company might finally be on the right track to future success. Citicorp, the company's lender, agreed and decided that it was the perfect time to liquidate. This left Vaughn Beals (and others) a year to find a new lender, or prepare for bankruptcy. The actions of Vaughn Beals and Chief Financial Officer Rich Teerlink proved nothing short of heroic as they worked to find and secure a new lender and pushed the deal and paperwork through the required process over the Christmas and New Year's holidays to beat the January 1 bankruptcy deadline.

763 Thanks to the massive popularity of the Evolution engine and Softail platform, The Motor Company sold 38,741 motorcycles in 1984, placing it just behind Honda and Yamaha in 850-cc-plus sales. Industry-wide, motorcycle sales were down, but not for Harley-Davidson, which sold even more motorcycles in 1985 than it did in 1984, this time surpassing Yamaha and securing second place in heavyweight motorcycle sales to Honda. By 1987, Harley-Davidson owned 38 percent of the 850-cc-plus market share, officially placing it ahead of Honda.

764 Not unlike today, many first-time motorcyclists in the 1980s wanted the biggest, baddest Big Twin The Motor Company offered, but didn't have the necessary riding experience to handle a machine of that caliber. The logical decision was to spend a couple of years riding a Sportster and then trade up. But a lot of people didn't want to have to buy two bikes back to back and then lose all that money by trading in the first one. Harley-Davidson introduced an ingenious marketing campaign in 1987. The plan allowed 883 Sportster buyers to trade in their motorcycle for a Big Twin within two years and get the full $3,995 paid for it toward the new purchase. Of course, The Motor Company lost some money by paying top dollar for a used Sportster, but the tactic forced buyers to get that new Big Twin sooner than they might have otherwise.

765 Harley enthusiast and engineer Bill Davis of St. Louis, Missouri, originally designed and patented what he called the Sub Shock frame in the mid-1970s. An August 1976 meeting with Willie G. Davidson ended with Harley-Davidson not purchasing the concept, even though Willie G. made it clear that he was still interested. Davis improved his design by moving the suspension from under the seat to under the frame, which allowed for the standard H-D horseshoe oil tank to be retained. Finally, in 1982, Jeff Bleustein (who later became president and CEO) contacted Davis and worked out a deal for the Sub Shock. To many folks at the time, the new Softail looked as though it had no suspension at all and the frame looked like something last seen in 1957. Closer inspection reveals a pair of horizontally mounted shock absorbers underneath the transmission that actuate the tube-style swingarm. An immediate hit, the Softail showed that modern Harley buyers cared more about the heritage and retro feel of a Harley-Davidson, and less about having the latest and greatest in technology.

766 Harley-Davidson discovered the financial benefit in licensing its name, logo, and other likenesses to be used on products developed by others. One of the best-known and most collected items is Harley-Davidson beer, which was brewed by Pabst. Today, just about any item you can think of has a version with the Bar & Shield logo on it, which provides not only advertising, but also royalties for The Motor Company.

767 What does a high-end golf resort in North Carolina have to do with the company's legendary turnaround? In April 1976, senior management went on a retreat to Pinehurst Country Club where they were joined by new AMF hires Vaughn L. Beals and Jeffrey Bleustein. The mission was to figure out the best way to move The Motor Company forward to compete in the modern motorcycle arena without jeopardizing its heritage. From that retreat came the idea for a new, liquid-cooled engine, dubbed the NOVA project, which was to be developed at the same time as an air-cooled, 45-degree V-twin engine, called the Evolution.

768 AMF, still Harley-Davidson's parent company in 1976, was unsure about the Pinehurst proposal of moving forward with two vastly different engine platforms at the same time. AMF certainly didn't like to think of the costs associated with such a plan, so it brought in the Boston Consulting Group (BCG) to do a study and give an opinion on the plan. BCG had previously completed a study for the British government regarding how to move forward with its dying motorcycle industry. BCG endorsed the two primary engine plan, pointing out that the traditional V-twin would eventually be a thing of the past. The good news for Beals and Harley-Davidson was that AMF agreed to fund both projects as intended. The bad news for those privy to the study was that the air-cooled V-twin might not be around much longer. Looking back, if BCG was so wrong about the V-twin, what else could it have been wrong about?

769 Thanks to the incredible efforts of Beals and Teerlink, Heller Financial became The Motor Company's financer, and proved to be a friendly business ally. Ironically, the Japanese Fuji Bank had recently acquired Heller. Some people have suggested a link between the money and the early discontinuation of the tariff on Japanese heavyweight motorcycles. H-D had reached serious levels of success by the time the tariff was dropped so it's very likely just a coincidence. Also noteworthy regarding the refinancing arrangement is that the state of Wisconsin pitched in $10 million from its employee pension fund to keep jobs and a major company in Wisconsin.

770 Attractive paint has always been an important part of the Harley-Davidson motorcycle and today its paint is one of the best in the entire transportation industry. The excellent paint tradition began in 1992 with the opening of a new paint facility at the York plant, which debuted an entirely new process for automotive paint. It used a clear powdercoat applied over the paint, which was then baked to harden. This creates an incredibly tough finish that can stand up to thousands of miles of bugs, gravel, and anything else the road throws at a motorcycle.

771 When originally setting out to develop the FXR, one of the team goals was to keep the motorcycle as "all-American" as possible. Therefore, the FXR development team turned to Monroe for the rear shock absorbers, after Monroe went above and beyond to help develop a prototype. When it was time to place the production order, Harley-Davidson asked for only 5,000 pairs for the first-year FXR, which was well below Monroe's minimum order requirement. The Motor Company then turned to Showa, which was supplying all the other shocks, and ordered from that company. Harleys have used Showa shocks ever since.

772 Harley-Davidson initiated a company-wide contest to name the company's newest FX variant, what we now know as the Dyna. When all of the entries were submitted, marketing settled on its favorite: Dyna Glide. And with that, Harley-Davidson's FXD family was born.

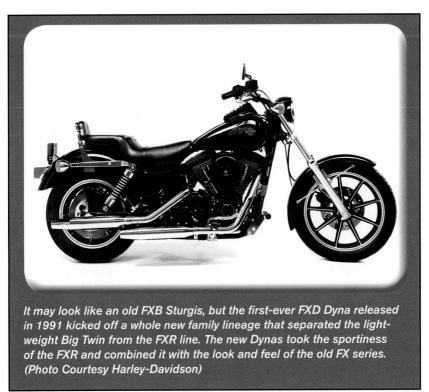

It may look like an old FXB Sturgis, but the first-ever FXD Dyna released in 1991 kicked off a whole new family lineage that separated the light-weight Big Twin from the FXR line. The new Dynas took the sportiness of the FXR and combined it with the look and feel of the old FX series. (Photo Courtesy Harley-Davidson)

773 One of the most collectible pieces of merchandise from Harley-Davidson anniversaries is the 90th anniversary belt buckle from 1993. The front uses brass, black, and pewter to form the official 90th logo with the words "THE REUNION" on the top between the Eagle wings. The backside of each belt buckle is individually numbered out of 4,000 and reads "For Ninety Years — The Proud Tradition of an American Legend." Interestingly, the engraved copyright reads 1992, which gives some indication of how far in advance The Motor Company plans its celebrations.

774 It is well known now that the Evolution powertrain and chassis was a top-notch product right out of the gate. But in 1984, people needed some convincing to upgrade from a Shovelhead or return to The Motor Company from a foreign brand. To do this, Harley-Davidson had to actually get people onto the new motorcycles, and it did that with the Super Ride demonstration program that was launched at the same time as the motorcycles. Each dealer had demonstration models and encouraged as many riders as possible to try out the new Evo, especially the Softails. Today, H-D trucks tour the country with a full load of new motorcycles and prospective owners have the opportunity to spend time sampling each one. H-D quickly realized that nothing sells a Harley-Davidson like a Harley-Davidson.

775 Although unionizing the company was severely frowned upon at the time, Harley-Davidson had come to be a shining example of organized labor putting out a top-quality product in the United States by the time the Evolution engine was launched. In 1985, Harley-Davidson motorcycles received a specially awarded seal of quality from its two unions, the Allied Industrial Workers of America and the International Association of Machinists and Aerospace Workers. This award, first suggested by the workers, denoted the highest level of quality in manufacturing to prospective buyers. Once more, the buying public could have confidence in America's only motorcycle brand.

THE CHASSIS

776 To launch the all-new FX-derived, Evolution-powered Dyna family in 1991, Harley-Davidson brought back the tried-and-true Sturgis nameplate. The new Dyna model, labeled the FXDB, had all of the mean, back alley–brawling attitude of the original, but with none of the early-1980s Shovelhead quirks. The Dyna family was developed when faithful FX riders pointedly did not switch to the FXR platform, in large part because of "the look." That same look has been making H-D engineers' lives difficult and salespeople's lives easy since the 1920s. It meant that riders accepted a lower-performance model that had the classic long, low look. Harley-Davidson gave the people what they wanted, but with a few updates including a rubber-mounted engine and a strong, rectangular-backboned frame. Only 10 years after the original, the FXDB Sturgis carried a sticker price of slightly more than double of the original FXB Sturgis.

777 Harley-Davidson answered the call of those seeking the retro look and feel of its heyday offerings by introducing a model called the Heritage Softail, which debuted in 1986. Based loosely on the stylish 1949 Hydra-Glide, the FLST has full-coverage FL fenders, a beefy FL front end, and 16-inch spoke wheels with 140/90x16-inch tires front and back. To fit an FL front end, engineers had to decrease the angle on the Softail family's current FX-style triple trees and lengthen the fork about 1-1/2-inches for the optimal ride quality. Plenty of chrome and a comfortable set of floorboards round out the retro ride. An FLSTC Heritage Softail Classic was also available; it included a windshield, black leather saddlebags, and a passenger backrest. The Motor Company's ode to a simpler time never lost popularity or fell out of vogue. After 30 years, the FLSTC remains a staple in the H-D lineup.

778 Launched as a mid-year 1988 model, the FXSTS Softail Springer immediately became a legendary motorcycle. It marked the first time Harley-Davidson produced a springer front end on a Big Twin since the 1948 Panhead. The new leading-link springer front fork had little in common with its ancestors, including how it was designed: computer-aided design and analysis. A modern suspension damper up front greatly increased the amount of control and performance of the springer design. 1,356 Softail Springers were produced for 1988, 132 of which were equipped with an evaporative emission system for California use. All were

Only Harley-Davidson could get away with building a new motorcycle with 40-year-old technology and then watch it become one of the hottest bikes on the street. Although the Softail Springer may look old, Springer owners maintain that the sprung front end handled better than a typical hydraulic unit. That's not surprising because it was so heavily over engineered. (Photo Courtesy Harley-Davidson)

black with gold and red pinstriping and featured an eagle graphic with the Bar & Shield on the gas tank as well as an 85th anniversary emblem on the front fender. Everyone who purchased a Springer was given a certificate of authenticity and a supplemental owner's manual.

779 Harley-Davidson released the all-new FLSTF Fat Boy as a 1990 model and it immediately cemented its place in motorcycle history. A modern departure from what the company was doing at the time, the Fat Boy took residence in the hearts of enthusiasts and has been a best-seller ever since. Initially, it was only available in gray, which, along with its matching painted frame and oil tank, led to its nickname, "the gray ghost." The Fat Boy had a mean, street-pounding look that was accentuated by its 16-inch solid cast wheels and fat tires. A big FL front end and headlight nacelle helps give it that freight train appearance. The 1990 model is unique with its gray paint scheme and matching frame, as well as the yellow trim on the cylinder heads. The winged Fat Boy graphic on the side of the gas tank is seen on every Fat Boy, making it one of a handful of models that has its own special logo.

780 1987 marked the 30th anniversary of the Sportster, and Harley-Davidson celebrated the occasion with a black and orange 1,100-cc special edition XLH-1100. Commemorative graphics on the gas tank and a black and chrome engine set the 600 anniversary models built apart from the rest of the 14,000 Sportsters sold that year. Black and orange went on to be some of the most popular Sportster colors to this day, no doubt thanks to its XR-750 heritage.

781 Even though the FXRT was introduced in 1983 with a Shovelhead engine, most enthusiasts are familiar with the more performance- and touring-friendly, Evolution-powered Sport Glide. With the Nova project now gone, The Motor Company still wanted to make a sport tourer, and quickly found the FXR chassis to be a worthy entrant into the class. Saddlebags were fitted to the machine, but the biggest visual update is the (insert your own adjective here) fairing, which was pulled from the Nova. Who better to build a sporty Harley than Erik Buell, who was put in charge of the project. In 1986, the company introduced the uprated FXRD Grand Touring which cost $1,000 more than the FXRT and $100 more than the FLHT; it included a better seat, chrome saddle-bag protectors, additional gauges, and handlebar-mounted controls for the stereo.

782 One of the technological features on the new FXRT and Evo Touring bikes that followed, which has unfortunately disap-peared from the H-D lexicon, is the air-adjustable front suspen-sion designed by Erik Buell. The bike also used air-adjustable rear shocks, but those are still used on most Touring bikes today. Not only did the air-filled front forks resist brake dive, but the pre-load could be altered depending on exactly what kind of riding you were doing and how much weight was on the bike. With the front and rear adjusted separately via Schrader valves, a Sport Glide rider could tune his motorcycle's suspension for a one-person, spirited ride or a two-up cross-country jaunt.

783 The first official Harley-Davidson Road King became avail-able in 1994 and replaced the Electra Glide Sport. An easily detachable passenger seat and windshield allowed owners to take full advantage of the two-person touring comfort of the larger machines when needed, but could also revert to stylish one-per-son cruising, too. The 1994 King paid homage to its storied past by wearing whitewall tires, chrome tank console (with speedo, igni-tion, and indicator lights), and standard spotlights. It's that classic style and grace that makes the Road King one of The Motor Com-pany's perpetual favorites to this day.

784 I can remember one of the first Harleys I got up close to and heard run and rev right in front of me. It was my friend's dad's all-black 1998 Softail Custom, which he bought while on vacation in Puerto Rico; getting that bike at that time required a long waiting period in the United States. If there was ever a contest for the bad-dest Harley ever, without a doubt the Evo-powered Softail Custom would be in the running with its raked front end, 21-inch spoked front wheel, bobbed rear fender, and slotted disc rear wheel. The Custom remained in the H-D lineup until its last iteration in 2010.

785 Five different Sportsters were available in 1996. It was a group that included the all-new XL1200S Sport and XL1200C Custom, proving once and for all that Sportsters were more than just inexpensive Big Twin alternatives. While quite similar at first appearance, the ride was vastly different. The S featured adjustable rear shocks with piggyback reservoirs and an adjustable Showa cartridge-style front end. Dual disc brakes up front and cast wheels added to the performance aspect of the Sport. The Custom used conventional suspension that set the bike 2 inches lower. A 21-inch spoked wheel up front and a slotted disc wheel in the back gave the bike a style reminiscent of the larger Softail Custom. Taller handlebars on the Custom provide a more laid back riding style. From this point forward, the Sportster lineup provided diverse models to suit any Harley rider.

786 Harley-Davidson introduced the Softail Bad Boy in 1995 sort of as of a Springer-equipped version of the Softail Custom. Designed by Willie G., one of the bike's unique styling features was the fact that it came only in black, but with the three optional graphics colors of purple, turquoise, or yellow on the gas tank and rear fender.

787 To mark the 50th anniversary of the 1948 springer-equipped Panhead, and the final year of the Evolution engine, The Motor Company came out with one of its classiest, most beautiful bikes ever: the 1999 Heritage Springer, released in 1998. Every styling cue found on previous models came together for the Evolution Softail's final incarnation. A big, chrome springer front end with chrome spotlights flanking the headlight leads the way. The front fender mounts to the wheel in almost exactly the same way it did in 1948. Leather fringed saddlebags and seat with chrome conchos look straight out of the 1950s as does the tombstone taillight and tall, pullback handlebars. And so, it's only appropriate that the regular-production (noted as such because of the 2000 CVO

FXR4) Evolution era ends with the classically-styled Softail, which not only kicked off the era, but kickstarted The Motor Company's heart.

788 Launched in 1993, although not as a silver and black anniversary model, the Heritage Softail Nostalgia has its own unique features that make it a collectible model today. Usually referred to as the Moo Glide, the black and white Nostalgia features Holstein fur inserts down the center of the saddle and passenger pillion as well as across the leather saddlebags. 2,700 were built and sold immediately; a numbered plaque under the ignition switch shows the bike's build sequence and exclusivity. What else would you expect from a Wisconsin company?

Only in Wisconsin would something like this be possible. You can see the Holstein fur inserts on the seat, backrest, saddlebags, and the dash trim on this 1993 Heritage Softail Nostalgia. This unique trim package makes this bike a great collector's item, although I'd be nervous about riding it around the state.

789 You'd think that the first 1984 FXST Softail would have been completely designed from the ground up to work with the brand-new frame design. Not so, and in fact, just about everything on that first Softail was a carryover from the FXWG Wide Glide, the most chopper-esque model that Harley-Davidson offered at the time. Just about the only new parts on the Softail were the frame, rear shocks, seat, oil tank, and fender struts. The Wide Glide already had the 2-inch-longer fork tubes, skinny 21-inch front wheel, bob-tail rear fender, and 5-gallon gas tank that epitomized the look of the factory chopper. Willie G. and his design team simply used the parts they already had to develop a seemingly all-new motorcycle.

Remember that I said the 1936 Knucklehead set the stage for every Big Twin that followed? The first-ever 1984 FXST Softail is the proof. Compare the chassis, engine, oil tank, and gas tank on the first Softail to the first Knucklehead and you'll see that nearly 50 years of history has come full circle. (Photo Courtesy Harley-Davidson)

790 Showa, a Japanese suspension firm, had been building Harley-Davidson's shocks for several years when Softail development started. One of the most difficult areas for original Softail designer Bill Davis was developing a shock that worked in extension rather than compression; at the time, no companies offered one. Davis has said that that single aspect of the project was one of the most difficult. It was easy for The Motor Company; the big purchaser simply sent the specs to Showa and Showa developed and built exactly what was needed.

791 With the introduction of the hot new Evo engine, braking power became that much more important, so the existing 10-inch front brake rotor was upgraded to the 11-1/2-inch size found on most models today. A single new rotor could actually stop faster than a pair of the old 10-inchers could.

792 The process of designing a front end that could hold an 800-pound motorcycle but perform like a 400-pound sportbike required creative thinking from Harley-Davidson's Department 43. Ray Miennert designed the initial fork for the FLT by reducing the angle relative to the steering head and then setting the fork tubes behind the steering head. In addition, all of the weight, including the large fender, was centered around the steering axis. This created an extremely light front end, but provided little feedback. The production version increased trail geometry a little over Miennert's design to provide the feedback that consumers wanted.

793 FLT fans may have had quite a scare in 1997 when no model with a frame-mounted, twin-headlight fairing was found anywhere at the model launch. Never fear, Willie G. was hard at work developing a motorcycle, the likes of which had never been seen: the factory custom bagger. In 1998, the FLTR Road Glide made its debut in both carbureted and fuel-injected versions of Evolution power. A completely redesigned batwing fairing was rounder and more aggressively shaped, and sat lower than the previous FLT fairing. A lower windshield added to the aggressive look, as did a completely clean front fender, devoid of any trim. The 1998 Road Glide was available in 95th Anniversary trim, in addition to the standard trim for that year.

794 You have to love some of the nicknames that folks come up with for different Harleys. Before the well-known *Moo Glide* came the FXRC Low Glide that featured a Candy Orange and root beer paint scheme and a root beer-colored seat; it was nicknamed

Candy Glide. It was one of the loudest and most intense colors that The Motor Company had used up to that time. However, it's a far cry from custom paint jobs of today!

795 With the nearly guaranteed success of just about any special edition that The Motor Company introduces, launching a 30th Anniversary Sportster in 1987 seemed a no-brainer. Based on an XLH 1100, the 30th Sportster wore a black and orange paint scheme (also a great selling feature) and special graphics. Each of the 600 built was fitted a serial plate that showed its special collector number.

796 Indicator lights (not to be confused with turn signals) are a necessary ugliness that has plagued Harley-Davidsons since Knucklehead instruments were changed from analog to lighted indicators. The release of the 1991 Dyna was the first step in the right direction toward the small, blended-in indicator lights on today's Harleys. The indicator lights on the 1991 Dyna Sturgis were tucked into the rectangular cover on top of the headlight eyebrow piece. Along with a numbered plaque indicating the bike's production number out of 1,600 units (although only 1,546 are recorded as built) are small, round indicators for high beam, neutral, turn signal, and oil pressure.

797 When it was time to construct the new springer front end for the 1988 Springer Softail, nobody at The Motor Company had even been around when springers were taken out of production, or was even familiar with the actual design principles. And, of course, all of the design prints were lost during the AMF years. To give the springer design team a crash course in this lost suspension concept, former engineer John Nowak was called in to teach them how to do it. After he showed them how they built a springer front end individually, by hand, the way it was done when he was there, it was up to the current engineers to figure out how to mass-produce it on a modern scale.

798 Even though it may seem as though a springer front end was taking a step backward in terms of performance and comfort, the opposite was actually true for the 1988 FXSTS Softail Springer. Even though the front end uses exposed springs and weighs more than a comparable hydraulic front end, moto-journalists of the day actually preferred the characteristics of the springer! Although the journalists, who generally prefer the latest and greatest technology, weren't keen on the springer front end's looks, they agreed that it worked better than most telescopic front ends from other motorcycle manufacturers.

799 Electra Glides were updated with a new fairing for 1996 that, from the front, didn't look a whole lot different, which is typical for Harley-Davidson. Actually, the ergonomics and user-friendliness of the new fairing were vastly improved. The inner dash was completely reconfigured to make the stereo and gauges easier to read without taking eyes off the road. The inner fairing molding was now more rounded to better flow with the style of the big Touring models. Instead of one big center gauge, the new fairing received the now-familiar 4-inch speedo and tach front and center with 2-inch fuel, oil pressure, voltage, and ambient air temperature gauges on either side. The accessory switches were placed at an angle that made them easily accessible and highly visible. Redesigned, round speakers were placed farther outboard on the fairing and angled in toward the rider to make better use of the entire inner fairing. In addition, a low-fuel warning light was placed on the tach face while the standard indicator lights display was placed in the center. The number of parts and hardware used to mount the Electra Glide fairing was reduced from 42 to 14, which made servicing the instruments much easier.

800 What goes better on a classic Harley-Davidson than some long, black, leather fringe? Everyone has their preferences, including Germany's motor vehicle department, which actually had a maximum length for cosmetic trim as part of its safety requirements. Because the Heritage Springer Softail, built in 1997 and 1998, was slated for European export, The Motor Company had to work with German authorities to agree upon a legal length of fringe for the leather saddlebags. Even though the saddlebags ended up with an attractive amount of fringe, speculation says that The Motor Company wanted even more!

THE POWERTRAIN

801 The 1984 V2 Evolution engine was launched in 1983 after seven years of development. It changed the game forever and helped bring The Motor Company into a new period of prosperity. The 80-ci engine is a direct descendant of the previous Big Twins, but it was redesigned from the case up. After years of high-performing, dependable Japanese imports, riders in the 1980s were used to trouble-free performance with little maintenance and would accept nothing less. The all-aluminum engine provided impressive weight savings and greatly improved heat dissipation. With a reliable 8.5:1 compression ratio, it made about 77 ft-lbs of torque and produced more power at every speed than its predecessor. For the Touring

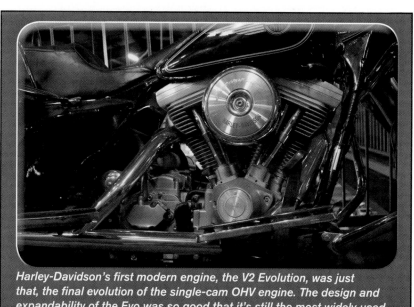

Harley-Davidson's first modern engine, the V2 Evolution, was just that, the final evolution of the single-cam OHV engine. The design and expandability of the Evo was so good that it's still the most widely used engine in aftermarket applications. Today, it's not uncommon to see 100-ci-plus Evo-style engines in custom motorcycles.

models, which included the Dyna (released in 1991) and the FXR, the Evolution engine was rubber-mounted to the frame. However, it was solidly mounted for the Softails, which sometimes caused tooth-chattering vibration. The squared-off head design prompted some riders to nickname it "Blockhead," although most people just call it the Evo.

802 With the new Evolution engine powering Big Twin models, the old Ironhead sitting in between the Sportster's frame rails seemed even more antiquated than it already was. In 1986, Harley-Davidson changed the game for its entry-level XL by introducing an all-new, all–aluminum alloy, 883-cc Evolution engine. Retaining its basic high-revving four-cam design with a 45-degree angle, 3-13/16-inch stroke, and 3-inch bore, the new Evo was new in every way. Aluminum alloy heads, hydraulic lifters, more efficient porting, lighter pistons, and a new three-piece crankshaft added up to a lively and dependable engine. Shortly after the launch of the 883, the company introduced a reengineered version of its 1,100-cc engine for the XLH that used the traditional 3-13/16-inch stroke, but had a bigger 3.4-inch bore. This gave it an actual displacement of 1,101 cc, compared to its predecessor's 997 cc. Both use the 34-mm Keihin carburetor. However, the more powerful engine combined a solid-mount setup and 4-speed transmission that left riders itching for another gear, and itching from the massive vibration.

803 The 1988 Sportster received another displacement increase; the new 3-1/2-inch bore produced the familiar 1,200 cc (actually 1,198 cc, or 73.11 ci)) of today. The size of the current Sportster engine almost matches the 74-ci engine size of the Big Twins just 10 years earlier.

804 Harley-Davidson's 1995 Touring models made a huge technological leap forward with the introduction of an optional electronic fuel injection (EFI) system. Produced by Magneti-Marelli, this open-loop system uses a throttle position sensor (TPS) to gauge the correct air/fuel mixture and timing. This system, used until 2001, is identified by its side-by-side butterfly valves. Models equipped with EFI received the "I" designation at the end of their model call sign. For example, an EFI Ultra Classic Electra Glide is FLHTCUI while the carbureted version is FLHTCU. The addition of EFI increased power output from 77 ft-lbs of torque on carbureted models to 83 ft-lbs, with peak power hitting 500 rpm sooner. Simultaneously, fuel economy increased from 50 to 52 mpg on the highway.

805 The Sportster received a couple of major improvements for the 1991 model year, the most well received of which was a new 5-speed transmission that improved cruising comfort. It also marks the first appearance of a rear belt drive; it's only available on 1200s and the 883 Deluxe. Considering the Sportster's perceived role as somewhat of a starter bike in the H-D lineup, riders no longer had to worry about maintaining a chain. The new belt drive is also quieter and cleaner, making for a more pleasant ride. By 1993, belt drive was standard on all Harley-Davidson models.

806 Many enthusiasts refer to the last Shovelhead as heralding the end of the era, and it did, in its own way. In 1986, another great Harley-Davidson tradition bit the dust when the last kickstarter and 4-speed transmission rolled off the assembly line attached to the Wide Glide. All Harleys had been electric start for the past decade, so it's unlikely that kickstarters were getting much use any more; only 1,200 were sold.

807 Unlike previous engines that H-D developed, especially the Flathead and Knucklehead, the Evolution engine simply couldn't afford to use customers as test dummies. It had to be perfect from the get-go and make a statement: Harley-Davidson motorcycles were dependable, powerful, and easy to operate. Over the course of testing, H-D engineers logged 1,000,000 miles on test bikes, and tackling each concern as it arose.

808 I'm sure that countless Harley riders are grateful for the introduction of cruise control to Touring models, which first appeared in 1989 on the Tour Glide and the Electra Glide Ultra

Classic. However, it was hardly the same system that we know and love today. The first-generation cruise control was a glorified (and safer) throttle lock. It still had to be adjusted for inclines and declines, but it provided enough assistance to give a rider's right arm a rest. Electronic cruise control was introduced along with fuel injection in 1995. It adjusted to a set road speed rather than remaining at a constant throttle position. Another useful feature, self-canceling turn signals, appeared on tourers for the first time in the 1989.

809 In 1993, the oil tank on Touring models was moved from underneath the seat to a new, larger oil pan underneath the engine and transmission as on Dyna models. Cooling was improved somewhat because of the direct airflow around the pan versus the hidden tank. In addition, the bike's overall center of gravity was lowered. Interestingly, the biggest improvement because of the new oil pan was the fact that the battery could be placed securely and comfortably underneath the seat. This was a necessary move given the increasing amount of electronics on Touring models in the following years. Unfortunately, the engineers put the oil pickup and

If you've never seen a pre-1993 Evo Touring bike, you might wonder what this massive, boxy tank hanging off the left side of the bike is. It's the oil tank that was shaped to clear the passenger footrest; it does take up space in the right-side saddlebag.

return lines right next to each other, and directed the hot oil back into the engine instead of sending the cooler oil that's been sitting in the pan longer. The 4-quart capacity and pickup/return locations remain through the 2016 models, even though the engines put out twice as much power.

810 The Sportster Sport, released in 1996, was the best-handling Sportster yet. Unfortunately, like the XLCR of the late-1970s, it didn't have additional power to back up the handling. That changed in 1998 when H-D management decided that the Sportster Sport should have a little more sport in it. The 1998 model received an additional pair of spark plugs, making it one of the only (if not *the* only) times a Harley-Davidson arrived with twin plugs straight from the factory. Hotter cams and a higher-compression piston rounded out the performance package that added up to 15 percent more peak torque.

811 Initial testing of the powerful Evolution engine quickly sent the rocker boxes, cylinder heads, and jugs flying off their cases because the aluminum parts dislodged from the base studs. To remedy this, Evo engineer Hank Hubbard took some notes from the automotive world and used extra-long, steel base studs that ran all the way through the cylinders and heads, and then tightened in the rocker boxes. As the aluminum top end parts expand with heat, they actually tighten the parts together. As a bonus, this design, along with the new three-piece rocker covers, allows easy disassembly and removal of the top end with the Evolution engine still in the frame!

812 "It's got a Hemi!" was a popular phrase among Mopar enthusiasts of the 1960s, but Harley-Davidson had been using hemispherical heads on its Big Twins since the 1936 OHV Knucklehead. At least, they were until the Evolution engine was launched at a time when efficiency and heat-transfer were more important than raw power. Evos were built with flattop pistons and a lower combustion chamber height. Another addition to the Evo head was a squish shelf on the side of the combustion chamber; it essentially squishes air to improve circulation and overall burn.

813 An entirely new valve configuration was adapted with the new non-hemispherical combustion chamber design. Contrary to what you may think, testing at the time showed that smaller valves flowing the same amount of air actually provided more low-end grunt than larger valves, which is perfect for a Harley-Davidson. They also ran cooler because of less exposed surface area and more airflow, which was also perfect. Because of the flatter combustion chamber roof, the angle between the valves was lessened from 90 degrees to 58 degrees.

814 Some people like the high-performance, rugged look of external oil lines found on 1963 and later Big Twins and Ironheads. Especially for a high-performance custom built today, a set of stainless braided lines running alongside the pushrods looks like something straight from NASCAR. By the late-1970s, it was getting a little ridiculous that The Motor Company couldn't figure out how to run oil internally, and more leak-resistant. As part of the Evolution's design mantra (no leaking or misting oil!) engineers eliminated the external lines.

815 So how did oil get from Point A to Point B, and then back to Point A again? Again, engineers turned to the automotive world and built oil passages into the cylinders so that oil could return from the rocker boxes back to the crankcase. To get oil up to the heads, it was fed up through the hydraulic lifters, then through new, hollow pushrods and rockers, and from there it lubricated the other moving parts hidden underneath the rocker box covers.

816 As Harley-Davidson continued to inch its way closer to suites of computer-controlled engine functions and fuel injection, engineers came up with the V-Fire III electronic ignition. The really cool about the V-Fire III was its ability to adjust automatically between two different ignition timing modes based on a vacuum-operated switch. Under high-vacuum conditions, such as open-highway cruising, the V-Fire III advanced timing for better fuel economy. It stayed in this mode in most constant-throttle situations, regardless of speed. At idle and under heavy acceleration,

V-Fire III's timing was retarded more to provide the most power possible.

817 How could anyone ever forget the "ham can" air cleaner that late Shovels and Sportsters used as a cheap solution to the EPA's noise restriction requirements? If you haven't actually seen one on a bike, you've no doubt seen them at swap meets. Because everything from that era of The Motor Company continues to increase in value and many of these air cleaners were trashed, they are, ironically, actually worth something now. Note: never throw away your stock parts! At the time, H-D knew that a bulky air cleaner over the beautiful new Evolution engine would be a deal breaker for many buyers, so they designed with a nice round, chrome air cleaner cover shaped similarly to those used on Knucks and Pans. Beautiful, yes? But there's no way that little cover can keep noise down far enough (it didn't). Behind it, hidden in the V of the engine, is an ugly plastic air box that handles that task. And, in true Harley-Davidson spirit, it most certainly robs the engine of horsepower and torque. Evo-powered Touring models continued to use the ugly big breathers for additional power to move their weight, and with all the extra Touring parts, they weren't as noticeable as on the smaller FX and FXR models. The "ham can" was removed on all models by 1986.

818 Nearly everything on the Evo-powered bikes had been updated and modernized for a diverse motorcycling public. First-year Evos, however, retained the same dry clutch format that was relatively unchanged since 1936. Apart from requiring some serious muscle to operate, it was still perfectly functional. The exception was that as the primary drive continued to improve and receive better lubrication, it became increasingly difficult to keep the clutch pack dry. They finally made the (obvious) decision to use a wet clutch, which worked well with the oil bath primary. The problem was that wet clutches weren't typically as strong as dry clutches, and for a variety of reasons (see Fact No. 861), The Motor Company couldn't introduce a new clutch that was weaker than the previous clutch. The new wet clutch was put into production partway through the 1984 model year run. It came pretty close to the capacity of the previous dry clutch. Using a single diaphragm spring instead of several coil springs reduced lever pull strength significantly.

819 Ever hear the phrase "49-state legal" or wonder why every aftermarket part sold in the state of California has to be compliant with the California Air Resources Board (CARB) standards? Emissions equipment, which had been choking cars of horsepower since the mid-1970s, finally became a requirement for Harley-Davidsons sold in California in 1985. The first system used an Evaporative Emissions Controls System (EVAP), which used a charcoal canister and had three functions. Fuel vapor from the gas tank passes through a vapor valve and hoses and then moves into the charcoal canister, which is supplied with clean air from the carburetor; both the vapor and the air are cleaned in the canister. Finally, the clean air/vapor mixture flows back into the carburetor and combustion chamber to be burned. So, since 1985, Harley owners have another useless part to remove from their motorcycles.

820 With all of the grand, modern new technology and processes taking residence at the Harley-Davidson factories you'd think production was pretty much perfect by 1987, three years into the Evolution's reign. It was, for the most part. Except when it came to the five-piece crankshafts that had to be individually checked and trued on the assembly line. To true them, technicians had to hit with big copper hammers! Engineers redesigned the cranks on Big Twins, in favor of a forged three-piece unit. The flywheel and mainshaft became one piece that was then machined to the proper specs.

821 Chrome engine covers on a black Harley-Davidson engine is a favorite look for many enthusiasts. This style is popular on many models today, but was first used in regular production on the 1986 FXSTC Softail Custom. The heads and cylinders were covered in crinkle black, which made the chrome stand out even more.

822 Harley-Davidson engines may look like they're perfectly vertical, but unless you use a long fork with no steering head modifications, some of them aren't. The new Dyna chassis, which debuted in 1991, sets the engine with a two-degree tilt rearward while FLT and FXR engines each have a two-degree forward tilt. Softail engines are the only ones actually positioned with zero degrees of tilt in the chassis.

823 The barrel keys: love them or hate them, they're a pretty necessary part of your motorcycle. The new Dyna was the first to use the "Coke-machine" style of steering-head lock and ignition key. However, changing the type of key used wasn't exactly high on The Motor Company's to-do list. The change was only made because the company decided to compete in several foreign markets that required steering-head locks on motorcycles and keys with a certain minimum number of combinations.

824 Evolution engines are the last ones to use what are now referred to as Evo-style engine mounts. While that may seem obvious, what that term actually means is that a frame with Evo mounting points will also fit a Shovelhead, Panhead, and even a Knucklehead. However, because the cylinder and head height is taller with each subsequent engine, newer engines won't fit into older frames without modification.

825 When Harley-Davidson bumped the displacement of the lightweight Sportster up to 1,200 cc, it became one of the fastest vehicles you could buy in 1988. The XLH-1200 could hit 60 mph in 4 seconds and clear the quarter-mile in just about 13 seconds! Not bad for less than six grand, right? Compare that to the $180,000-plus race-bred V-12 Ferrari Testarossa, undoubtedly one of the fastest cars available that year. You wouldn't want to go up against a Sportster in a street race; the 1988 Red Head did 0–60 in about 5.2 seconds and the quarter-mile in 13-1/2 seconds, although it could continue to pull strong until about 180 mph, which helped in avoiding embarrassment at the next traffic light.

PEOPLE AND POP CULTURE

826 The handful of Sturgis models that Harley-Davidson has introduced through the years are pretty well known by enthusiasts, which makes sense because the Sturgis Rally is attended mostly by Harley riders. However, many folks have questioned The Motor Company's love for America's other major rally, Daytona Bike Week. Perhaps not as brand-centric as Sturgis, Daytona is attended by tens of thousands of Harley riders from around the world. The company honored the annual run to the sun rally with a special-edition Dyna for 1992, in honor of the Daytona 200's 50th anniversary (which was actually in 1991). Only 1,700 Daytonas were built and they carried a two-tone Gold Pearl-Glo and Indigo Blue paint scheme as well as a special graphic on the tank. The 1992 Daytona was the first Harley-Davidson to use a pearl paint.

827 Politicians have often used Harley-Davidson motorcycles as a way to seem relatable to the public. Although some are true enthusiasts, none is more of a true H-D enthusiast than former Wisconsin state senator Dave Zien. Senator Zien rode his 1991 FXRT Sport Glide more than one million miles, frequently flying large U.S. and Wisconsin flags on the back of his bike. Throughout his career in politics he championed motorcyclists' rights both in Wisconsin and on a national level. Thanks to the work he did promoting and defending the sport of motorcycling, Harley-Davidson honored him in 2009 by giving him a brand-new Road Glide and putting his FXRT on display. The senator's million-mile Sport Glide is now in permanent display at the Sturgis Motorcycle Museum where it sits untouched since its last ride.

828 All manner of celebrities rushed to Harley-Davidson dealerships after the Evolution's introduction. Of course, there were the typical "bad boys" like Billy Idol who rode a black Springer and Jon Bon Jovi who rode a red and white Heritage Softail. But did you know that Elizabeth Taylor and Malcolm Forbes rode Harley-Davidsons? In fact, Forbes gave a customized lavender-colored Sportster to Taylor as a present and, written on the top of the gas tank was "Elizabeth Taylor's Passion." The two of them attended many motorcycle events together and may have been just the image the public needed to start considering a Harley-Davidson motorcycle as a fun husband and wife activity.

829 In the 1989 film, *Nam's Angels*, a group of one percenters (originally Hells Angels, until a lawsuit requested the club logo and name not be used) go to Vietnam as government mercenaries. George Christie, former president of the Ventura chapter of the Hells Angels, led the suit against the film, which showed the club members riding only Yamahas. George Christie commented, "Everybody knows that the Hells Angels don't ride anything but Harley-Davidsons."

830 Even though the film itself lost millions of dollars and maybe ruined a couple of careers, there's no debate about how good those motorcycles looked in the 1991 film *Harley Davidson and the Marlboro Man*. The better known of the Harleys in the movie is Mickey Rourke's FXR chopper named *Black Death*. Bartel's Harley-Davidson in Marina Del Ray, California, built four versions of *Black Death* after Mickey Rourke sketched the bike on a cocktail napkin. He used *Black Death* no. 3 and no. 4 in the movie after no. 1 and no. 2 were stolen. *Black Death* no. 4 was used for most of the filming scenes. Some scenes required a faster, throatier motorcycle than the standard 80-ci could muster so they used *Black Death* no. 3, which was fitted with a 98-ci Sidewinder stroker kit from S&S Cycle. Stuntman and actor Chuck Zito later crashed it near Pelham Bay.

831 You might think that the 1947 Hollister Rally would want to be brushed aside and never brought up again. That wasn't the case when the city celebrated the 50th anniversary of the rally in 1997, dubbed the Hollister Independence Rally. 60,000 riders descended on the small town to celebrate an important part of American motorcycling history. Among them were Buzz Kanter and Jim Babchak, the editor-in-chief and classics editor, respectively, from *American Iron Magazine*. They rode up the California coast to the rally, Kanter on a 1946 Indian Chief and Babchak on a

1947 Harley-Davidson Knucklehead. These two motorcycles might very well have been in attendance at the original rally.

832 Larry "SuperJew" Freedman, Special Forces hero in Vietnam, Delta Force commando, CIA paramilitary officer, and posthumous recipient of the Intelligence Star, loved motorcycles and especially his Harley-Davidson FXRT, which he rode to rallies all over the country. He earned his fame, and his Intelligence Star, on his final mission, which involved conducting reconnaissance prior to the U.S. military's 1992 amphibious landing in Somalia. He volunteered with the understanding there would be no support in the hostile area. Throughout his deployment to the North African country, he wore a tan Harley-Davidson hat. He was wearing it when he was killed on December 23, 1992, the first casualty of the Somali conflict. He is memorialized on a plaque on a picnic table below Mt. Rushmore that reads, "In Memory of Larry Freedman," placed there because it was one of his favorite stops to make while attending the Sturgis Rally every year.

833 Many people have considered motorcycles, especially Harley-Davidsons, to be works of art. The two-wheel transporter received a special nod in 1998 with The Art of the Motorcycle exhibit at the Solomon R. Guggenheim Museum in New York City. The exhibit, which ran from June 26 to September 20, 1998, featured 114 motorcycles, including eight Harley-Davidsons from a 1911 single to a 1989 Buell. The exhibit was later displayed at the Las Vegas Guggenheim and featured five additional Harley-Davidsons.

834 Regardless of how good a company says its product is, sometimes there's just no substitute for a good magazine review to back up the claim. As part of the 1984 model-year Evolution launch, Harley-Davidson made sure that the press had access to the new bikes so that they could run the article at the time of the official launch. As a magazine man, I like to think that *Cycle* magazine's frequently quoted review from November 1983 had an impact on the buying public. In that review, *Cycle* dyno'd the 1984 FXRT at

54.64 hp at 5,000 rpm and 68.16 ft-lbs of torque at a very convenient 3,500 rpm. But *Cycle*'s big finding was that after a 1,000-mile ride, the Evo-powered FXRT burned only 12 ounces of oil and not a single leak was found anywhere. The review noted a slight misting at the clutch actuating arm, but nothing serious. Knowing how magazine editors test bikes, if there were a problem, they would've found it.

835 1986 marked the 100th anniversary of the raising of the Statue of Liberty on Liberty Island in New York City. To commemorate the occasion, Harley-Davidson introduced Liberty Editions in almost every model family. These featured a Blackberry and silver two-tone paint scheme with Lady Liberty graphics on the gas tank and on the front of the fairing of the FLHT. The Motor Company donated $100 from the sale of every Liberty Edition to the restoration efforts of the Statue of Liberty. So, that meant that 810 FLHTC Libertys, 202 FLTCs, 954 XLH 1100 Sportsters, and 744 FXRS Low Riders, added up to $271,000 for the Statue of Liberty–Ellis Island Foundation.

836 To further celebrate the occasion, Vaughn Beals and his wife, Eleanore, led the Liberty Ride from Los Angeles to New York City on a Liberty Edition FLHT. Upon arrival, the bikes, all Liberty editions ridden by the company's executives, were auctioned off to raise even more money for the cause. A couple years after the event, Beals learned that the winning bidder had backed out of the sale. Then the number two and number three bidders also backed out, leaving the bike ownerless in New York City. So, Vaughn Beals bought the bike and rode it regularly for many years.

837 The comfortable, performance-oriented FXRT was supposed to appeal to a new type of touring customer, thereby simultaneously being unattractive to the "outlaw" customers that had been riding FX models and choppers. To The Motor Company's surprise, its first customer was Sonny Barger, leader of the Hells Angels. Barger, 45 years old at the time, wanted something that was both fast and comfortable.

838 On the other end of the FXRT-riding spectrum is The Motor Company's targeted convert, Chuck Irwin, who was president of the Suzuki owner's group. Whether as a marketing ploy, a real test, or maybe he just wanted a joyride on a new Harley-Davidson, Irwin suggested that they provide him an FXRT to go head-to-head against his Suzuki GS1100G. At the end of his testing, which covered more than 3,000 miles, Irwin relinquished his position with the Suzuki owner's group and purchased an FXRT. Harley-Davidson jumped at this most unlikely of converts and featured him in magazine ads.

839 Rolling Thunder. The very words exude a power that can only be achieved by hundreds of thousands of Harley-Davidsons riding in unison. Or the massive, explosive sound from the onslaught of American bombers over Southeast Asia. Both factor in the annual Rolling Thunder run that takes place in Washington, D.C. in a show of support for those still missing in action in Vietnam. The first run took place on Memorial Day in 1988 when 2,500 riders showed up to demand accountability for every single MIA/ KIA in Vietnam. Today, the event totals nearly one million riders and doubles as a show of support for those lost in Vietnam and conflicts since then.

840 The American Motorcyclist Association (AMA) created the American Motorcycle Heritage Foundation in 1982. It, in turn, created a Hall of Fame to tell the history of motorcycling through the eyes of the people who lived it. On August 16, 1990, the AMA took this goal to new heights when it opened the Motorcycle Heritage Museum right next to the AMA's Westerville, Ohio, headquarters. Here, motorcycles and memorabilia were displayed and enjoyed by the public. The AMA and its museum moved to a larger facility in Pickerington, Ohio, in 1999; this is its current home. Many of the greatest Harley-Davidsons ever to race are available for viewing there.

841 One of the most memorable scenes in Harley-Davidson cinema history has to be Arnold Schwarzenegger jumping a 1990 Fat Boy into the Los Angeles River in 1991's *Terminator 2: Judgment*

Day. That scene was actually shot with his stunt double, Peter Kent. The crew used massive cables to lower Kent and the Fat Boy down the approximately 12-foot jump safely. Of course, the cables were digitally erased during editing. The Fat Boy used in the film is now on display at the Harley-Davidson Museum, where it still shows all the wear and tear of a Hollywood stunt bike.

842 By The Motor Company's 85th anniversary in 1988, it had truly become a prime example of American quality, ingenuity, and corporate citizenship. As part of its anniversary celebrations, the company raised more than $600,000 for muscular dystrophy. And, during the presidential campaign that year, both presidential candidates (George H. W. Bush and Michael Dukakis) said that The Motor Company was a company that others should strive to emulate.

843 The 1985 film, *Mask*, was one of the first to portray a H-D– riding motorcycle club in a positive light. Starring Cher, Sam Elliott, and Eric Stoltz, and based on a true story, the movie revolves around a boy with a skull deformity who is shunned by society, yet treated with love and friendliness by his mother's boyfriend's motorcycle club. As the boy's condition continues to worsen, he dreams about and begins planning a motorcycle trip across Europe where he hopes to ride a 1974 Shovelhead with a suicide shift.

844 After taking the unprecedented and publicly applauded move of petitioning for an early termination of the import tariff, Harley-Davidson President Vaughn Beals invited President Ronald Reagan to the York final assembly plant. President Reagan made his official visit on May 6, 1987, when he took a complete tour of the plant. He also met with a small group of employees before giving a speech hailing the fortitude of the American worker and especially the effort put forth by H-D employees from the factory floor to the Juneau Avenue offices to make The Motor Company competitive again. While on his visit, President Reagan personally fired up a newly built 30th Anniversary Sportster. If you own one of these machines, there's a possibility that President Reagan started it for the first time!

Presidents don't just go around visiting every company in the United States, and you wouldn't think a heavyweight motorcycle manufacturer would be on that list, either. Harley-Davidson's American success story of the 1980s was so powerful that it clearly warranted recognition from the most powerful man on the planet. (Photo Courtesy Harley-Davidson)

845 Before The Harley-Davidson Museum was even being discussed, The Motor Company built a scaled-down, traveling museum in 1988 that attended events around the country to show off the storied past that was 85 years in the making. The massive tractor-trailer was painted black, and had orange stripes running the entire length, with Bar & Shield logos all around. Harley-Davidson was written in huge letters on the sides of the trailer. Inside the rig sat a beautiful display of motorcycles from 1907 to present that elicit the same feelings of romanticism that visitors feel when touring the current museum.

846 To honor Vietnam veterans during the 50th running of the Sturgis Rally in August of 1990, Harley-Davidson sponsored the exhibition of the traveling Vietnam Veterans Memorial. The

Moving Wall was set up at the Rushmore Plaza Civic Center and was available for viewing by the 300,000 motorcyclists in attendance that year.

847 As a company that has historically shown an incredible amount of support to veterans and active-duty military and their families, Harley-Davidson continued that policy during Desert Shield and Desert Storm in 1990–1991. The Motor Company announced that leave would be granted immediately and honored for its employees who served in the Reserves and were called to duty in Iraq. The company had one of the best leave programs in the country for service members in Desert Storm. In addition, many dealerships and dealers associations printed up military-themed Harley-Davidson shirts and they were worn to show support for fellow Americans overseas.

848 After Karen Davidson, Willie G.'s daughter, took charge of the MotorClothes division, she expanded the offerings for fashionable clothes for off-the-bike wear. The popularity of MotorClothes took off rapidly, and the first non-dealer store opened in Kansas City's Bannister Mall in 1990. Jewelry, accessories, and all sorts of riding and casual wear were available in the first test location. It must have been a success because similar locations are now open around the country. Perhaps one of the better-known locations today is inside Milwaukee's General Mitchell International Airport, where visitors and locals alike are greeted with the familiar hometown Bar & Shield.

849 Among the plot twists and turns of the television show *Twin Peaks* which aired from 1990–1991, was only one character that provided a break from the daily drama: James Hurley's (played by Actor James Marshall) 1978 FLH-80 Electra Glide. It played a prominent role throughout both seasons in trimmed-down form with just a small set of leather saddlebags thrown over the seat.

850 Plenty of corny movies have been made that feature America's favorite V-twin motorcycle. Perhaps none is as much fun, and features so many great Harley scenes, as 1991's *Stone Cold* starring Brian Bosworth. In the movie, The Boz, rocking his signature skunk-tail hairdo, rides a customized FXR that he uses in a drag race, a high-speed chase that ends in a fiery explosion, and, of course, to save the day at the end. If you can get over the hair, it's actually a pretty enjoyable movie that features loads of great, 1990s-era customs.

MILITARY, POLICE AND RACING

851 The Motor Company's strong history of road-racing dominance was absent in recent years, so The Motor Company initiated the VR-1000 program to compete in the AMA World Superbike series. All previous factory racers were modified versions of street bikes. But unlike the factory racers before it, the VR-1000 was an entirely new design, from the ground up. Although the project was initiated in 1988 to compete in the 1991 season, the VR-1000 didn't see a live racetrack until the 1994 season. By then,

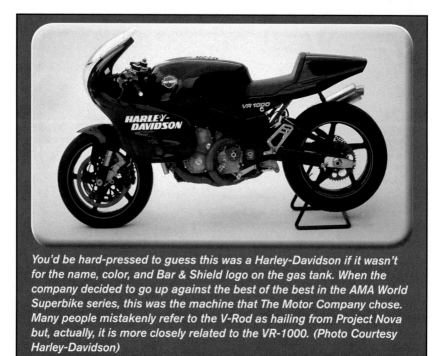

You'd be hard-pressed to guess this was a Harley-Davidson if it wasn't for the name, color, and Bar & Shield logo on the gas tank. When the company decided to go up against the best of the best in the AMA World Superbike series, this was the machine that The Motor Company chose. Many people mistakenly refer to the V-Rod as hailing from Project Nova but, actually, it is more closely related to the VR-1000. (Photo Courtesy Harley-Davidson)

it was already behind the curve, compared to the other established teams. The VR's biggest strengths were its impeccable cornering ability and the all-star riders brought in to race it.

852 A completely new 996-cc liquid-cooled 60-degree V-twin powered the VR-1000 Superbike; NASCAR's Roush Racing in North Carolina developed it. It has a high-performance double overhead cam (DOHC) design and four valves per cylinder. Fuel and air are mixed via a Weber USA electronic fuel injection system. With a 98-mm bore and a 66-mm stroke, the racing machine created around 150 hp, but it still wasn't enough to compete with the top dogs on the straights. Initially, the VR-1000 Superbike was to be an all-American racer, using equipment from the best suppliers in NASCAR and Indy racing. In addition to the Roush engine, Penske built the suspension, and Wilwood supplied the brakes. Before racing even started, the team swapped in an Ohlins front end and, when the program was terminated in 2001, the VR-1000 was actually running a Showa front end.

853 Harley-Davidson was certainly trying some new things in the 1980s. In 1987, it purchased the British motorcycle manufacturer Armstrong, which was known for its off-road, Rotax-powered, single-cylinder MT500. This machine had proved its capabilities in the 1982 Falklands War. In 1987, Harley-Davidson purchased the production and design rights for the Rotax engine for its dirt track racing teams.

854 With the introduction of the FXRP as a first-year Evolution, 1984 model, Harley-Davidson finally gave the police market something to counter the fast and light Japanese motorcycles that many were using. Because motor officers spend hours at a time on their bikes every day, the low vibration aspect of the rubber-mounted engine was a major plus as was the 5-speed transmission that delivered low cruising RPM and an acceptable top speed. The use of a rear belt drive made the motorcycle generally quieter and cleaner. The story behind the first FXRP is that it was essentially a warehouse parts bike; it had little in common with a showroom

The FXRP was the ultimate law enforcement highway cruiser. It had everything a motor officer needed for a hard day out on the road including tons of storage, an entire suite of communications and lighting equipment, and all-day comfort. Moreover, the FXR chassis and hopped-up Evo could run with almost anything out on the road. That's the same fairing found on FXRT models, with the exception of air scoops replacing the red flashing lights.

FXR of the same vintage. When they were instructed to make a great police bike, H-D techs used whatever parts they could find in the factory warehouse to come up with the best product they could. The Police model has floorboards, special panniers (saddlebags), dual-disk front end, crinkle black trim instead of chrome, and unique tires. Early FXRPs were also fitted with the project Nova fairing, which was modified with spotlights on either side of the headlight.

855 The FXRP's big test came when Harley-Davidson invited the California Highway Patrol (CHP) to compare the new

Pursuit Glide against the Kawasaki machines they'd been using for a decade. The FXRP was good enough for the CHP to order 152 of them that first year. The motor officers loved them; in 1985, 161 more were ordered. And then, if the FXRP was good enough for the demanding CHP, it was good enough for any police department. The orders for the Pursuit Glide began to flow in from all over the country.

856 Like many racing series, AMA rules required homologation for its Superbike class, meaning that a minimum number of street legal variants had to be produced. The problem for Harley-Davidson was that it was too complicated to make the VR-1000 emissions-legal in the United States. Therefore, in 1994, it released the minimum required 50 VR-1000s for sale only in Poland with a price tag of $49,490. The road-going version weighed about 400 pounds and put out 135 hp. Its unique paint scheme was black on one side and orange on the other, with a white stripe down the center separating the two. To make it street legal, H-D added a one-piece plastic bracket to the rear of the fender that included a pair of orange turn signals, a red taillight, and the license bracket. In the front, matching orange turn signals were mounted on the fairing, as was a pair of black mirrors on either side of the windshield. A battery and an electric starter were also new to the street version. Don't give up hope of ever seeing one just yet. Many of the original VRs have made their way to the United States.

857 National dirt track champion Chris Carr and road racers Miguel Duhamel, Pascal Picotte, and Scott Russell all lent their skills to the VR-1000 program, giving the team a fighting chance against its more modern competition. In 1996, Carr took the pole position at Pomona, the first for the VR-1000, and went on to accumulate five top-10 finishes for the season. Also in 1996, new rider Tom Wilson took second at Mid-Ohio, the first VR-1000 podium finish, and achieved three top-5 finishes for the season. Picotte gave the VR project its last hurrah in 1999 with two podiums: a second at Pikes Peak and a third at Sears Point, making four top-5 finishes that season. In 2001, The Motor Company pulled the plug on the

VR program and announced that it would participate in NHRA Pro-Stock drag racing.

858 A military, police, and civilian market for the MT platform still existed so Harley-Davidson continued producing the MT500 (used by the Canadian and Jordanian armies) before introducing the newly-designed MT350E that featured disc brakes and electric start. The smaller displacement lessened the heat radiation, which is visible at night through infrared scopes, as did the placement of large panniers on either side up front. Unfortunately, the upgrades weren't enough to make it useful for the U.S. military. Its other major downfall was its use of gasoline instead of diesel, which also removed it from consideration. MT models produced during its ownership have "Harley-Davidson" in raised lettering on the bike's sidecovers. A small number of civilian versions were sold until 2000 and, like many of The Motor Company's quirky, low-production offerings, they are valued collector's items today.

859 One of the pitfalls of the VR-1000 was that, unlike the other race-team motorcycles, there was no corresponding relationship between the bike on the track and the bikes in dealer showrooms. Harley-Davidson remedied that problem with its support of the AMA's Continental Tire 883 Championship, in which every racing machine was a Sportster 883. The championship series put the Sportster to the test. Half of the races took place on road courses (known as TwinSports racing) and the other half took place on dirt ovals. Points were tallied up to include a total combined championship as well as a dirt-only championship. This series kicked off at Daytona Bike Week in 1993.

860 The best part of the Sportster 883 series was that the relatively stock motorcycles were used in extraordinary ways. Similar to the Hooligan dirt track series today, it's fun to see "your" bike competing in a way you'd only ever dream about. The 883 Championship Sportsters were allowed to make changes to the exhaust systems, seats, suspension, foot control location, brakes, and a few other areas. However, neither the engine nor the frame could be altered in any way. In fact, the tires were required to be DOT-approved street legal! One modification that riders could take advantage of was a factory replica XR-750 seat and tank decals that labeled the bike as an XR883R. All in, Harley-Davidson advertised the total cost of the race-ready package AND a brand-new Sportster to be about $7,500.

861 Harley-Davidson was preparing to change from the old dry clutch system to a new wet clutch to make the entire primary system much less complicated. The California Highway Patrol (CHP) had some concerns, however. It was worried about the new clutch being strong enough to push stalled cars off the highway. Apparently, the CHP had been using its Harleys for this purpose, and early wet clutch experimentation proved it barely capable of overcoming the weight of a sidecar! Therefore, the engineers had to develop a wet clutch capable of handling these tasks. This is just another example of the Harley-Davidson motorcycle putting function and durability first for its customers.

862 An FLHTP was available beginning with the 1983 model year. In 1986, the police line grew to include both a fairing model and a nonfaired, windshield-equipped model in addition to the FXRP, which was offered until 1994. Beginning in 1993, Police models began using the crinkle-black and chrome-covered engines used on the high-end civilian models.

863 Harley-Davidson factory rider Scott Parker set the lofty goal for himself of winning 10 national races in one season. He accomplished that goal on October 7, 1989, when he won at the Sacramento Mile; it was in the season following his first Grand National title win.

864 Scott Parker continued to dominate Grand National racing by winning the championship trophy from 1988 to 1991, matching Carroll Resweber's four-season winning streak set 30 years earlier. As part of that final winning season in 1991, Parker became the all-time winningest racer in Grand National history with his 41st win, beating Jay Springsteen's previous record.

865 Even after failing to secure series championships for two years in a row, Scott Parker nearly doubled his wins from 1994–1998 and broke almost every record in AMA history. He won 39 national races in those five years and secured the Grand National Championship every year, earning the outright record for most consecutive winning seasons. By the end of the 1998 season, he had amassed 9 series championships and 91 career victories.

866 Scott Parker's final career win came after he officially retired from the sport after the 1999 season, in which he only won twice. He hopped back onto an XR-750 in 2000 to race for the last time at his favorite track: the Springfield Mile. In one of the greatest retirement sendoffs in sports history, he took the checkered flag in his final race, and cemented his name in the history books.

867 After the Honda team's third consecutive flat track championship with the RS750 in 1987, the AMA restricted the faster Honda racers with weight and carburetor restrictions. Believing that Harley-Davidson was behind the move, Honda quit its factory involvement in flat track racing after the 1987 season, leaving Harley-Davidson to continue winning. The last time that a Harley-Davidson failed to win a Grand National title with a V-twin was in 1993 at the hands of Ricky Graham and his Honda RS750.

868 Who says racing is for men only? The only woman in the Battle of the Twins racing division was Danbury, Connecticut, native Nancy Delgado. She acted as racer, mechanic, and crew chief, and she also recorded her experiences in a series of columns in *American Iron Magazine*. Riding a 500-pound race bike surely made for an interesting perspective.

869 At the 1988 Transamazon Rally, Charles Peet rode his 1985 Harley-Davidson FXRP 9,000 miles from Cartagena, Columbia, to Buenos Aires, Argentina. Almost the entire trek was off-road through jungle, swamp, mountain, and any other kind of terrain and climate zone imaginable. Because it was the first (and only) Transamazon Rally, no one had any idea of what to expect. Entrants could use any vehicle they wished to make it to the finish line first, and most chose Jeeps, Land Rovers, Toyota Land Cruisers, and other four-wheel-drive vehicles or off-road motorcycles. "Harley Charley" and his trusty FXRP was one of only 12 finishers out of 175 competitors. His motorcycle resides at the Harley-Davidson Museum in as-raced condition, dirt and all.

870 In 1989, Lou Gerencer campaigned an absolutely monstrous XR-750 hillclimber to become national hillclimb champion that year. The bike used an extended swingarm that nearly doubled its entire length to keep it from rotating around the back tire and flipping over backward. Gerencer built up his XR-750 using mechanical fuel injection to mix incoming air with nitro methane. The bike is believed to produce in excess of 150 hp, possibly making it the most powerful XR-750 ever.

871 Harley-Davidson ceased production of the XR-750 in 1985, but even as of this writing, it's still the preferred powerplant for flat track racing. Toward the end of its run, most customers were replacing the frame and equipment with aftermarket parts that performed better, so The Motor Company just stopped building frames and sold just the engines, which included information about to how to build your own racer. In 1991, the XR engine was improved with new cylinder heads and a tougher bottom end.

872 Harley-Davidson has always done what it could to make its police bikes stand out from the crowd and that they are equipped to handle the rigors of daily police duty. In 1985, when the California Highway Patrol swapped its fleet to the FXRP, the Evo motors they received were hopped up from the factory with .050 inch taken off the heads and .015 inch off the cylinders. These engines used a higher-lift cam and shorter pushrods, as well. In addition, it seems strange that this would happen in California, but none of the FXRPs were equipped with smog-control devices. For the proper ignition sequence in these warmed-over engines, they used the E ignition curve that worked beautifully with the higher compression and allowed the FXRPs to rev up to 5,800 rpm. Many

Evo owners have upgraded to an E curve on their own bikes for more performance and a higher rev limit.

873 When Harley-Davidson stopped building complete XR-750s, a variety of aftermarket companies stepped in and competed for business. This caused a bit of a problem because of the AMA rulebook; flat track racing was supposed to be a stock class. Now, with so many engine and chassis parts to choose from, the chances of finding two bikes exactly alike were slim to none. The AMA adjusted the rulebook before legalities could kill flat track racing. The new rules said that as long the engine was from Harley-David-son, the bike weighed at least 315 pounds, and the wheelbase was 57 inches, a garage-built XR could race. However, this actually evened out competition; the H-D factory team had to buy aftermarket parts just like everybody else, instead of developing its own parts then distributing them.

874 Harley-Davidson went to Talladega in July 1983 in a race against the clock, and the durability of its new Evolution engine. To celebrate The Motor Company's 80th Anniversary, company marketers decided to run a brand-new Evolution-powered Tour Glide for 8,000 miles at the famed Alabama superspeedway. It ran at 80 mph, without any maintenance procedures including changing the oil or the tires. To cover their backs for any subsequent advertising campaigns, riders actually ran the Tour Glide at 85 mph, just in case a problem popped up, it could be solved and the bike returned to the track to keep the 80 mph average. The Evolution engine and the Tour Glide ran strong at 85 mph for the entire 8,000 miles without so much as a hiccup.

875 In 1985, Erik Buell took a factory-built Sportster XR-1000 street engine and built one of the greatest racing machines of the day, which unfortunately never saw a whole lot of track time. The bike was the RR1000 Battletwin, and it was meant to take on Ducati in the AMA's Battle of the Twins series as a replacement for the venerable Lucifer's Hammer. To do that, Buell also had to build 50 street-legal versions for homologation purposes. In the

Battletwin's first practice run at Daytona, it was running about 30 mph faster than its predecessor, but a transmission issue caused the bike and its rider, Gene Church, to crash. A subsequent trial at Road America resulted in another crash, after which Church retired from racing. The Battletwin's racing history was a short one, winning some races in New Zealand, Japan, England, and the United States. Except for a few owners that still race their Battletwins, the black and orange racer was pretty much relegated to collector's item status from day one.

Chapter 8

Twin Cam Era 1999 to Present

THE MOTOR COMPANY

876 Harley-Davidson collaborated with Ford Motor Company in 2000 to bring to market the Harley-Davidson edition F-150 pickup truck. 8,197 of the high-end trucks were built; they featured 20-inch wheels, black monochromatic styling, and a specially tuned exhaust. Ford had a Harley-Davidson trim package every year until 2012, when the partnership discontinued. Each year saw changes and different truck models offered, but two constants remained: unequivocal Harley-Davidson styling, and lots of tire-shredding power!

877 Harley-Davidson dealers began offering the Rider's Edge Academy of Motorcycling in 1999. The announcement came at the same time as the launch of the Buell Blast, a small-displacement beginner's model that made up the Rider's Edge fleet until

The new Street family of motorcycles provided the perfect platform to improve global reach, instruct new riders, and welcome entry-level riders into the Harley-Davidson world. Behind that massive plastic radiator cover in the front is The Motor Company's newest racing platform. (Photo Courtesy Harley-Davidson)

2014. Learning how to ride on a "Harley," at a dealership greatly improved customer loyalty and the overall Harley-Davidson experience. The last Blast was built in 2009, and it continued its tour of duty as a Rider's Edge staple until the launch of the Street 500 in 2014 (as a 2015 model). The Street training version has hi-viz orange protective covers that minimize risk of injury and damage during a drop. It uses an ECU flash that limits speed to 18 mph in first gear and 25 mph in second gear. Along with the new motorcycle came the rename of Rider's Edge to the Harley-Davidson Riding Academy, which went global at the same time.

878 If you thought that the sporty FXR was history by 1995, you might be excited to learn about the 1999 FXR2 and FXR3 models used to kick off The Motor Company's new Custom Vehicle Operations (CVO) program. Unlike later CVO variants, which show off future company offerings, the FXRs used 80-ci Evolution engines and a chassis design that hadn't been used in five years. However, enough customers still wanted one more taste of the FXR to warrant the production. Only 900 examples of each were built and used a special paint scheme with billet and chrome accessories. The FXR2 sported a 21-inch spoke front wheel while the FXR3 ran a cast 19-inch front wheel. Harley-Davidson released 1,000 FXR4s as part of its CVO lineup in 2000; this model was the last that was powered by an Evolution engine.

879 One of new CEO Keith Wandell's first orders of business was looking into the viability of the Buell brand. With a poor economy, and Harley-Davidson's future in question, Wandell took the hardline approach of putting the company's money into the products with the highest returns: cruisers. On October 15, 2009, the company ceased production of Buell motorcycles, opting to no longer sell the brand. H-D/Buell dealerships still currently offer servicing and parts, and some kept the Buell name on their building. Perhaps the best example of this is Wisconsin's oldest existing H-D dealer, Uke's, which is visible from Interstate 94 in Kenosha, just south of Milwaukee.

880 Sometimes it's easy to forget that the Milwaukee company producing the motorcycles we love is a successful Fortune 500 business. This was made especially clear when The Motor Company was featured on the cover of the January 7, 2001, issue of *Forbes* after having been voted Forbes Company of the Year!

881 The 23,000-pound Bar & Shield logo that sits 80 feet above the entrance to the Harley-Davidson Museum took Poblocki Sign Company of nearby West Allis six months to create. The always-lit sign is 22 feet 8 inches wide and deep, and 17 feet 6 inches tall. The massive brick wall at the entrance to the museum (with Harley-Davidson written on it) was built using 20,800 gray and black bricks.

882 The Harley-Davidson Museum officially opened its doors on July 12, 2008, the same year that The Motor Company

The Harley-Davidson Museum is one of Milwaukee's greatest treasures and attracts tourists from all over the world, many of whom don't even ride a motorcycle! The quality displays, friendly staff, and Bar & Shield immersion provide an unforgettable experience for any visitor.

celebrated its 105th anniversary. The museum took decades to grow from an idea to a finished product, and the concept was carried out to perfection. It sits on 20 acres in downtown Milwaukee's Menomonee River Valley area surrounded by the Menomonee River on three sides, which provides a private, yet middle-of-the-city backdrop for daily visitors and year-round events.

883 The long-fork chopper craze took the country by storm in the late 1990s and early 2000s, and The Motor Company wanted in on some of that action. You might be familiar with some of the chopper-esque models introduced during that period including the Softail Rocker and the more widespread Deuce. Some folks at Harley-Davidson wanted to take the chopper look even further, so they developed the Bandit concept motorcycle in 2004 It used a lowered Peanut tank, lengthened Deuce forks, and a Softail chassis. A 250-mm rear tire sat out back beneath a Bobtail fender. Anything on the bike that wasn't chromed was painted bright orange, including the frame; the fenders and gas tank wore silver tribal markings with some purple mixed in. It looks remarkably similar to bikes that were rolling out of custom bike shops at the time and visible during Daytona Bike Week. Unfortunately, the Bandit never made it into production.

884 The Motor Company celebrated its milestone 100th anniversary in 2003 and the festivities in Milwaukee certainly lived up to the hype and the magnitude of the occasion. Reports estimate that 300,000 riders showed up for the event in Milwaukee, with a total of one million people participating in events worldwide. As part of its 100th anniversary, Harley-Davidson organized a group ride through the city; the ride was limited to the first 10,000 motorcyclists signed up. Every Milwaukeean who saw it will always remember it. Cars pulled over everywhere, including along the highway and on all the overpasses to watch the Harley-Davidsons rumble by. Lots of people waved American flags and showed signs of support.

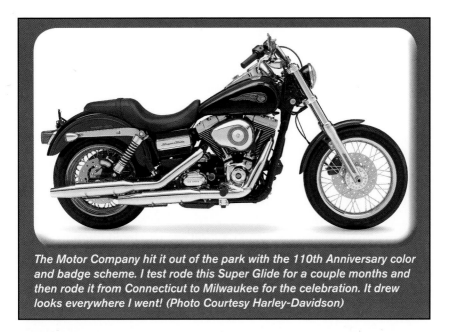

The Motor Company hit it out of the park with the 110th Anniversary color and badge scheme. I test rode this Super Glide for a couple months and then rode it from Connecticut to Milwaukee for the celebration. It drew looks everywhere I went! (Photo Courtesy Harley-Davidson)

885 In July 2001, Harley-Davidson announced its plans to build an entirely new, 350,000-square-foot manufacturing facility on the York campus. The $145 million project added 275 more employees to the York workforce and a huge increase in parts and motorcycle production. As part of the major expansion announcement, The Motor Company also expanded its Tomahawk facility and the Juneau Avenue Product Development Center. In September, it announced that all Dyna model production, 15 percent of its motorcycle output at the time, would be moved to the Kansas City, Missouri, facility in order to devote more space in York to Touring models, Softails, and CVOs. This move brought an additional 300 jobs to that facility.

886 Harley-Davidson kicked off its century-mark anniversary with a 10-city, worldwide series of events called the Open Road Tour. Its events were not just weekend get-togethers; each event was like a full-blown rally! The Open Road Tour kicked off in Atlanta on July 20, 2002 for six North American events, then went international to Sydney in March 2003, Tokyo in April, Barcelona in June, and ended in Munich in July. Each stop consisted of live music with some of the world's top names performing as well as numerous exhibits and displays of Harley-Davidson's storied past. Of course, the final stop on the tour was Milwaukee; the Open Road Tour organized rides from all around North America to the city where it all started.

887 The Motor Company took a giant step forward in its international business by opening the first Harley-Davidson dealership in Mainland China in 2006 (a dealership had been in Hong Kong since 1995). Beijing Feng Huo Lun received the appointment to open the dealership, Beijing Harley-Davidson, and it functioned as a full-fledged dealership right off the bat. In addition to selling motorcycles and providing service for them, the dealership also offered MotorClothes, various merchandise, as well as genuine parts and accessories. Harley-Davidson's Rider's Edge training could be done right at the dealership. In addition, like American dealerships, Beijing H-D also organized rides, events, and activities for customers. As of this writing, China has 18 Harley-Davidson dealerships.

888 Following the downturn in the U.S. economy, Harley-Davidson began expanding its export business to maintain the number of sales and hedge against future downturns in any one marketplace. In 2011, it expanded operations around the globe to best handle the unique markets of each continent. To improve its sales and management in Asia and the Pacific islands, including Australia, The Motor Company opened the Asia Pacific headquarters in Singapore in 2011. This office handles all the sales, support, marketing, and development functions that had previously been handled at Juneau Avenue. A similar facility was also opened in Oxford, England, to support the operations of Europe, the Middle East, and Africa. To handle operations in Latin America, H-D opened a headquarters in Miami, which handles the major markets of Mexico and Brazil and other South American countries.

889 Harley-Davidson opened its Bawal Assembly Plant in India in 2011 to build some motorcycles for the Indian, European, and Asian markets. Among the most notable motorcycles built there is the nimble, export-minded Street family of motorcycles, introduced in 2014. Quite a bit of controversy arose when the Street 500 and 750 were first introduced and then announced that they were built in India. The Bar & Shield faithful did not like the idea of American motorcycles being built in India and then shipped to the United States. Harley-Davidson made it clear from the beginning through its Street marketing effort that any Street intended for the North American market would be built at the Kansas City plant.

890 To capitalize on its customers' seemingly endless desire to customize motorcycles to individual taste, Harley-Davidson launched the H-D1 Factory Customization program with the 2012 Sportster 1200 Custom. H-D1 offered the ultimate personalization to customers by allowing them to equip a brand-new 1200 Custom with more than 2,600 combinations of parts directly from the assembly line. Paint, wheels, chrome, controls, handlebars, and seat can all be exchanged for something different, and it's all done as the motorcycle is being built. Customers can simply change one thing, check all the option boxes, or just leave it bone stock. It's all done on a computer screen, at home or at the dealership, so the customer can actually see the mock-up of the bike before ordering. For 2013, H-D1 expanded to include the Street Bob, and the number of available combinations has increased each year since then.

891 In 2013, Harley-Davidson went retro. But, unlike its heyday of the 1930s, 1940s, and 1950s, it went straight to the late 1960s and 1970s by offering Hard Candy Custom paint options. Hard Candy Custom paint uses a big-metal-flake base and bright colors with names such as Candy Big Red Flake, Hard Candy Lucky Green Flake, and Hard Candy Coloma Gold Flake. Today, many more 1970s retro paint colors are available to match the groovy stylings of bikes including the Sportster Seventy-Two, Forty-Eight, Street Bob, and Blackline.

892 Ten different models were available in 110th Anniversary trim for 2013, including, for the first time, three CVOs. The 110th package on the standard models revolved around the stunning

Anniversary Vintage Bronze/Anniversary Vintage Black paint scheme and solid bronze fuel tank cloisonné. Each was equipped with all of the available options as part of the package as well as a numbered plaque and several special 110th Anniversary badges sprinkled over the bike and engine. CVO versions featured an equally mesmerizing Diamond Dust and Obsidian paint scheme to further set them apart. Each of the ten models was produced in limited quantity; the most was the Limited with 3,750 examples and the least were the CVO Road King and CVO Road Glide Custom with only 900 examples.

893 In 2014, Harley-Davidson unleashed the biggest update to its Touring family since the introduction of the Twin Cam when it announced Project Rushmore. Project Rushmore was a several-year-long project that revolved around customer input to make Touring models even more user-friendly, while also redesigning the bodywork for the first time in 20 years. It involved the four primary areas: control, infotainment, feel, and style. With these refinements, The Motor Company could continue its reign as the ultimate long-distance motorcycle. And the name? According to H-D execs at the time, it was because a Harley-Davidson gives you a rush, and the new Touring models give you more of it.

894 Harley-Davidson figuratively "shocked" the world when it introduced the Project LiveWire concept bike in June 2014. As its name suggests, LiveWire is The Motor Company's first completely electric motorcycle. Designed from the ground-up, LiveWire uses a lightweight, sportbike-style chassis with a mono-shock rear end and an inverted fork up front. When it comes to instant-torque electric motorcycles, the LiveWire is no exception to the insane acceleration of which these machines are capable. With only one speed (fast) at a rider's disposal, clutching and shifting aren't necessary. It *is* necessary for the rider to hold on when releasing the throttle at high speeds because the bike will feel as though the brakes are being applied. Many riders have compared the sound of a full-throttle LiveWire to that of a jet fighter taking off from an aircraft carrier, and I can say from first-hand experience that it will do an outrageous burnout!

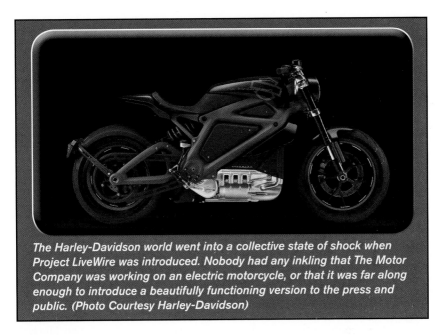

The Harley-Davidson world went into a collective state of shock when Project LiveWire was introduced. Nobody had any inkling that The Motor Company was working on an electric motorcycle, or that it was far along enough to introduce a beautifully functioning version to the press and public. (Photo Courtesy Harley-Davidson)

895 In 2011, Polaris Industries announced that it had purchased the Indian name, and, in 2013 it began producing Indian motorcycles for the first time in 60 years. It, along with Polaris' other motorcycle brand, Victory, produce all motorcycles in the United States, marking the first time since the 1930s that three American motorcycle brands have competed with each other on the streets, showrooms, and, as of 2016, on the race tracks, of America.

896 In 1999, Harley-Davidson introduced electric heated apparel to its MotorClothes line of riding gear. Although Harleys had been used year-round in many states from the very beginning, by the introduction of the Twin Cam engine, riders were traveling farther and faster through rain, snow, and freezing temperatures because they finally had a motorcycle that could confidently take them through it. Today, the heated gear lineup includes just about everything a rider could think of, including plug-in socks!

897 Many Harley-Davidson employees didn't think that a certain motorcycle would last long enough to warrant an update from the old 1950s Flathead to the four-cam design. But the Sportster celebrated its 50th anniversary in 2007. To mark the special occasion, Harley-Davidson released a 50th Anniversary edition 1200. It's a fitting year, too, whether planned or otherwise; 2007 marked the first Sportster EFI system, which couldn't be any further from what was offered in 1957. The 50th version was limited to 2,000 examples with a serialized handlebar clamp that used a specially designed logo. Other special features include a gold tank badge of the 50th logo, as well as a logo on the seat, and the original XLCH "H" silk-screened onto the sidecovers. The entire powertrain and suspension was chromed out, and the bike used a dual-gauge setup for speedo and tach.

898 Harley-Davidson had proven just how good a motorcycle could be when it brought out the Evolution engine along with the state-of-the art chassis and equipment that came with it. In fact, the entire package was so good that many riders ran their Evos to the mileage limit and wanted to keep going! In 1999, Harley-Davidson announced its engine-remanufacturing program. This involved sending an Evo, and later a Twin Cam, engine back to Milwaukee for an entire teardown and rebuild, then sending it back to the dealer within two weeks. What came back was essentially a brand-new engine, with all of the original case numbers and a one-year warranty. While rebuilding the engine, owners could opt to have Screamin' Eagle performance parts installed at the factory and, in the case of Twin Cams, a big-bore kit. Each engine is tested before being returned, all for around $2,000. The Longblock Program replaced this reman program in 2014; only the left case has to be sent to Milwaukee in exchange for an almost new engine. S&S Cycle in Viola, Wisconsin, took over the reman business for those who want to retain their original engine components.

899 As of July 2010, The Motor Company officially stopped taking new orders for sidecars, but it did honor orders already on the books. It built and sold its last sidecar in 2011 following several years of declining demand for the sidehacks. In addition, dealerships continued to provide service, parts, and other technical support to sidecar owners. Harley-Davidson had built sidecars for just shy of 100 years; do you remember what year The Motor Company started building them?

900 Possibly one of the easiest model years to identify is 2003, with the 100th Anniversary editions. The silver over black paint scheme is unique in its severe contrast, but it portrays the ironclad nature of a company that has, almost impossibly, survived for 100 years, with the last 20 being pure domination. To satisfy the absolutely overwhelming demand for these models, The Motor Company extended production of 2003 models by two months, to 14 months, so that it could build enough of them. Unlike other years before and since, 100th Anniversary editions had no production limit and every single model that year came with special badging, regardless of whether or not the unique color combination was ordered.

THE CHASSIS

901 With the rollout of the new Twin Cam engine came a response to sportier Big Twin riders still lamenting over the loss of the FXR: the FXDX Super Glide Sport. The $13,000 no-frills performer is still considered to be one of the best Dynas ever produced. Dual front disc brakes; tall, adjustable front and rear suspension; sticky tires; a low, XR-style handlebar; mid-controls; and tachometer made it ripe for ripping around curvy backroads. But the FXDX also screams "style" with its completely blacked-out powertrain, 13-spoke mag wheels, low-profile dash console, and modern Harley-Davidson lettering on the gas tank. This is one of those Harleys that makes it very difficult to ever swing a leg over another brand again.

902 In the same way that the sporty FXR led to the sport-touring FXRT and FXRD, the FXDXT T-Sport found its way into the H-D lineup for 2001. A chrome exhaust system gave it a more traditional look, as did a different Harley-Davidson gas tank letter-job, but it was otherwise the same as far as performance. The big additions to the T-Sport were quick-detachable nylon saddlebags and a big, comfy, two-passenger seat. A small quarter-fairing quickly identifies the T, and it uses a height- and angle-adjustable windshield.

903 The Buell Blast was released in 2000 as Harley-Davidson's first single-cylinder motorcycle since the Sprint, which was last produced in 1974. The Motor Company decided that an entry-level motorcycle was necessary to bring new riders into dealerships, and eventually hooking them on a Harley-Davidson. Truly made for the beginner, the bike's bodywork is made of color-injected Surlyn, which is also the outer coating of golf balls. The body is nearly impervious to the H-D Rider's Edge new rider program. Weighing in at 360 pounds with a low-profile seat height of 25½ inches it was the perfect machine to hook new riders at a Harley-Davidson dealership.

904 Who says Harley-Davidson can't make a great sportbike? The Motor Company launched the all-new XR1200 at the

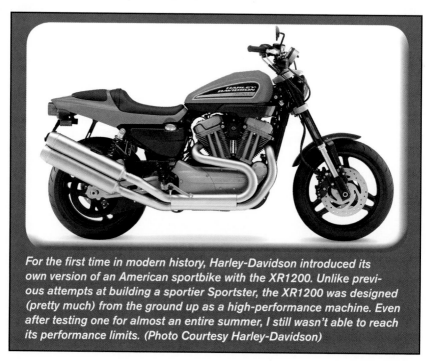

For the first time in modern history, Harley-Davidson introduced its own version of an American sportbike with the XR1200. Unlike previous attempts at building a sportier Sportster, the XR1200 was designed (pretty much) from the ground up as a high-performance machine. Even after testing one for almost an entire summer, I still wasn't able to reach its performance limits. (Photo Courtesy Harley-Davidson)

International Motorcycle Show in Cologne, Germany, on October 10, 2006. Some parts were from a Sportster, but they were few and far between, and what was referred to (internally) as Project Steroid, was clearly in a league of its own. The styling cues on the plastic gas tank shroud and bump-seat tail section were certainly from the XLCR of the late 1970s, yet the 43-mm inverted Showa front end was brand-new. Dual four-piston Nissin brakes up front and a more aggressive riding position made pushing the bike's 39- and 40-degree right and left lean angles all the more fun. Although it was also available in Vivid Black and Brilliant Silver Denim, the XR-750–style Mirage Orange Pearl was the most popular color among XR1200 buyers, who, unfortunately, only lived in Africa, Europe, and the Middle East beginning in 2008. The North American Markets sat on pins and needles for a year waiting to see if it would ever have a shot at a real Harley-Davidson sportbike. Wishes do come true; it was unveiled in the United States in 2009.

905 The Sportster lineup received its big generational change in 2004 with an all-new frame that uses rubber mounting points for the engine; every Sportster built since then is now referred to as a "rubbermount." With the new frame also came a new, smoothly styled oil tank cover on the right side and a new battery/electronics cover on the right side, which hid the battery completely for the first time. The other major addition to the Sportster family that year was the Fat Bob–style, 4½-gallon gas tank that was standard on Custom models. The larger gas tank made a world of difference in the appearance of these bikes to the point that they resembled Dynas more closely than the Sportsters of earlier years. A larger, 150-mm rear tire also helped bulk up the look of the Sportster line.

906 Among the many parts that only appear on the V-Rod, one of the most prominent is the angled headlight that flows along the forks and is meant to blend in with the overall appearance of the bike. To develop a headlight with just the right angles and shapes, and, at Willie G.'s insistence, use glass instead of plastic, Harley-Davidson spent a reported $500,000 in tooling expenses.

907 The XR1200 was made even better in 2011 and given the name XR1200X. It used Showa adjustable piggyback rear shocks and was only available in Black Denim and White Hot Denim; both are attractive colors, but the original orange version will be the one that is long remembered after the XR1200's final run in 2012. I was in possession of *American Iron Magazine* Editor-in-Chief Buzz Kanter's XR1200X for a couple of months one summer and I didn't want to give it back. Of course, his was hopped up with racing parts, and that only made it even more fun.

908 The bullet-style turn signals and taillights that are standard equipment on most Harley-Davidson models today were first used in 2002. They blended in with the overall motorcycle much better than the previous bulky turn signals that stuck out like a sore thumb. Lenses were orange originally. The Motor Company began using the bullet lights as run/turn/taillights in 2007 with the introduction of the Nightster, when the lenses became red. Through the years, many owners have opted for red lenses in the rear for better visibility, or used smoked lenses all around for less visual obtrusiveness.

909 In 2000, Harley-Davidson introduced one of its most popular and attractive models to ever roll out of the factory: the FXSTD Softail Deuce. The Deuce, like several other Softails before it, was the right motorcycle at the right time to introduce the powerful, technologically advanced Twin Cam engine to the Softail family. The Deuce relied on traditional Softail style that The Motor Company wouldn't dare mess with, but it had a muscular, modern appearance that wasn't exactly like the retro Softails of the previous year. A 21-inch spoked wheel led the way, followed by a fully chromed front end, handlebar, and dash console. The chrome engine, exhaust, and oil tank also make the bike stand out, as does the chopped fender in the rear. Unlike previous retro Softails, the Deuce's sleek, plain black seat and a cast rear wheel let onlookers know that this was a brand-new motorcycle. Moreover, the 34-degree lean angle and endless torque of the new Twin Cam, with optional fuel injection, reassured the rider that this was no throwback wannabe.

910 It took until 2002 for Harley-Davidson to finally update the chassis in its Touring models from the mostly unchanged 1980 design. Over the course of those 20 years, Touring riders had pushed their bikes farther, faster, and harder than the 80-ci Shovelheads were capable of and the frame began to show its weak spots. So, for 2002, The Motor Company developed a new swingarm that was physically beefier and had a stronger connection with the transmission housing to reduce flex. New rubber mounts for the engine were also used to better handle the Twin Cam's additional power. New air shocks were tuned to the heavier, better-handling chassis.

911 When Harley-Davidson introduced the VRSCA V-Rod for the first time in 2002, the collective motorcycling world dropped its jaw in confusion, excitement, and, above all, curiosity. "Is it possible that this could be a Harley-Davidson?" was the question that everyone was asking. Long, low, and mean as can be, it had the Bar & Shield attitude, but was like a glimpse into the future. The all-new Revolution engine sat within a trellis-style tube frame that was painted body color to match the bright silver panels. A chrome front end, shapely chrome exhaust pipes, and chrome handlebars and controls blended in perfectly with the silver motorcycle while solid, polished cast wheels gave the V-Rod a look all its own.

912 The first *modern* use of a high-performance upside down fork was on the 2006 VRSCR V-Rod Street Rod. The Street Rod was Harley-Davidson's attempt at a corner-carving machine, and it was given taller rear shocks, the performance front end, a bump seat, and foot pegs set higher and farther back to improve clearance and lean angle. It served as Harley's go-fast model until the XR1200 was released, and was then discontinued after the 2007 model year. Following the styling success of the inverted front end on the Street Rod, the V-Rod Muscle was introduced in 2009 with the same front end, followed by the rest of the V-Rod lineup in 2012. In 2016, The Motor Company put its first inverted front end on a production Big Twin when it launched the CVO Pro Street Breakout.

913 Harley-Davidson introduced the FLSTNI Softail Deluxe in 2005 as a throwback cruiser based on the design of the 1939 Knucklehead. At first glance, the Deluxe may look like a stripped Heritage but it actually has a personality all its own. Low beach-style handlebars place the hands in a very comfortable and relaxed position while the sculpted solo saddle with chrome trim sits the rider at a low 24-1/2-inches off the ground, 1 inch lower than the Heritage. Running without the small, easily detachable passenger pillion reveals even more of the Deluxe's signature chrome luggage rack, which hovers over the rear fender. The optional two-tone paint schemes suit the Deluxe perfectly and set off the wide white-wall tires, spoked wheels, and chrome everything. It's the only Harley today that uses the 1930s-era Tombstone taillight. In 2014 and 2015, the Deluxe received the CVO treatment that included sporty, detachable leather saddlebags and windshield with a built-in GPS navigation system. Crazy paint options, even more chrome, and that thundering 110-ci Screamin' Eagle B-engine rounded out the CVO version.

914 For the first time since the last Servi-Car rolled off the assembly line in (it's believed) 1974, Harley-Davidson again began producing its own three-wheeler in 2009, ushering in the Tri-Glide family. Unlike the Servi-Car, however, the all-new Tri-Glide Ultra Classic is meant for on-road enjoyment for those who, for any number of reasons, want to enjoy that open-air experience on three wheels instead of two. Modeled after the Electra Glide Ultra Classic, the Tri-Glide adds a 4-1/2-cubic-foot rear trunk, Hayes disc brakes at each rear wheel, and a built-in parking brake. To make steering the wide beast easier, engineers increased the rake from 29.25 degrees to 32 degrees, lengthened the fork tubes by 1.775 inches, and included a steering damper to cancel jarring bumps in the road. The whole setup makes for 25 percent less steering effort than with the standard Electra Glide front end.

915 First launched in 2006 as a blacked-out, budget, Big Twin bobber, the no-nonsense Street Bob was an instant favorite among younger riders because of its low price tag and seemingly endless customization potential. The 10-inch mini ape hangers, solo seat, and mid controls are that model's calling card. The whole package was improved further in 2013 with the addition of a new chopped rear fender and dual bullet run/brake/turn lights, an even-more blacked-out powertrain, black triple trees and fork lowers, and a nifty side-mount license plate. Basically, Harley-Davidson gave it all of the stuff that previous Street Bob customers were already adding.

916 Through its Custom Vehicle Operations (CVO) Harley-Davidson has often brought back defunct models with new

Even the standard-issue Breakout carries on the CVO's pro street, ground-pounder style with a fat rear tire, raked front end, and drag bars. The bobbed rear fender, run/brake/turn taillights, and a side-mounted license plate are all components usually found on custom-built motorcycles. It gave riders the opportunity to enjoy that custom feel but with a factory price. (Photo Courtesy Harley-Davidson)

features and custom equipment, but only once has it launched an entirely new model as a CVO. The Motor Company couldn't have picked a more suitable motorcycle for such a release as the CVO Breakout, introduced as a 2013 model. The CVO Breakout is all about details: the little *and* the big ones. These include a raked front end with a 21-inch wheel and 130-mm front tire and a 18-inch wheel with massive 240-mm rear tire. Everything is chromed, and each paint scheme includes a matching painted frame. Not since the 1971 Super Glide had a stock Harley-Davidson looked so much like the bikes that the top custom builders were bringing to bike shows around the world. Six months later, The Motor Company released a toned-down, but still entirely badass, standard version of the Breakout.

917 Of the many big changes to Harley-Davidson's Touring family that were part of Project Rushmore (launched for the 2014 model year), perhaps the most shocking was the incredibly advanced and user-friendly infotainment system available on many of the Touring models and CVOs. The new color-screen Boom! Box 6.5GT system was the first in the motorcycle industry to feature voice recognition, Bluetooth, touchscreen technology, GPS navigation, text-to-speech technology, and a radio, all in one single unit in the fairing. Vehicle information displays were available right on-screen, including tire pressure monitoring on CVOs; the optional helmet-mounted microphone allowed voice control of everything. Every feature that was available in a state-of-the-art luxury car was available on a Harley-Davidson. One of the coolest features was the "find dealer" menu that allowed the rider to quickly start turn-by-turn guidance to the nearest Harley dealer. To make smartphone and iPod connectivity even easier, a Jukebox compartment in the fairing securely holds a music device or phone and plugs it directly in to the system.

918 Project Rushmore also involved the redesign of the Touring 6-gallon gas tank, saddlebags, Tour-Pak, and even the front fairing on both Road Glide and Ultra/Street Glide models. Opening and closing the saddlebag lids and Tour-Pak was easily doable with

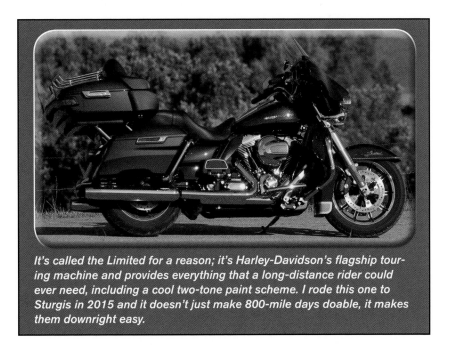

It's called the Limited for a reason; it's Harley-Davidson's flagship touring machine and provides everything that a long-distance rider could ever need, including a cool two-tone paint scheme. I rode this one to Sturgis in 2015 and it doesn't just make 800-mile days doable, it makes them downright easy.

one hand instead of two. The new batwing fairing received a redesigned windshield; a vent below the windshield could be opened to reduce head buffeting by 20 percent, or closed to keep out cold air. The Road Glide system used three vents, one underneath the windshield and one on either side of the dual headlights, which had become one solid unit instead of two separate lights. At the same time, Tour-Pak capacity increased by 4 percent and passengers received an additional 2 inches of saddle space with improved ergonomics.

919 In 2009, Harley-Davidson began using a completely redesigned chassis for its Touring models. The new frame uses half the number of individual pieces as the old frame; that means half as much total welding. Unlike the previous frame, the new swingarm is bolted directly to the frame instead of the transmission for improved rigidity and frame strength. The rubber isolator system was improved all around. The most significant upgrade was up front; the single isolator was replaced with double isolators on a single tie link for reduced vibration at idle. The trail and overall wheelbase were increased by about 1/2 inch for improved highway comfort; this allowed the saddlebags to be moved back 1/2 inch for more passenger legroom. A 180-mm rear wheel also became standard. Overall, the 2009 Touring models have a 70-pound increase in carrying capacity; the saddlebags and Tour-Pak capacity each increased by 5 pounds.

920 The last Harley-Davidson to use a springer front end was the Softail FLSTSB Cross Bones that was in production from 2008 until 2011. The previous springer-equipped Softails were meant to represent the finest machines that The Motor Company produced in the 1930s and 1940s. The Cross Bones represented what guys were doing in the 1950s in their garages with a torch and rattle-can black paint. The Cross Bones had wide-set ape hangers, a bobtail rear fender, and 16-and 17-inch spoked wheels with fat tires front and rear. In addition to the blacked-out, sprung front end, the Cross Bones also used a sprung solo saddle; two springs provided extra comfort for the rider. 1950s-style pinstriping wrapped around the gas tank, which held the classically styled cat's eye dash console. Although a handful of appropriate colors were available, Black Denim was the ultimate iteration of this bad-to-the-bone retro classic.

921 When Harley-Davidson unveiled the fresh new lineup of Project Rushmore Touring models, a familiar sight was noticeably absent: a Road Glide with the shark nose–fairing. As was the case when the Tour Glide went missing in 1997, it roared back from the dead as a better-than-ever 2015 model. Like the Street Glide, it appeared in Road Glide and Road Glide Special varieties, the latter with the color touchscreen infotainment system and improved suspension. H-D engineers spent an extra year fine-tuning the frame-mounted, double-headlight fairing for the ultimate aerodynamic capabilities. Hundreds of hours were spent in Wichita State University's wind tunnel for it to cut through the air, reduce head buffeting, and feed as much air to the engine as possible. The new fairing is 1.4 inches narrower than the previous fairing and aerodynamics are improved by using a one-piece headlight with single plastic lens. The Road Glide Ultra also appeared in 2015, but only as a

CVO model. The 2016 CVO Road Glide Ultra was the first regular-production model to debut with a price tag of more than $40,000 ($40,299). 2016 also brought a standard Road Glide Ultra with all the bells and whistles of its Limited stablemate.

922 For years, custom builders had been competing to see who could wrap a chopper's rear fender closer to its rear tire. In 2008, Harley-Davidson joined in that competition with its Rocker and Rocker C Softails. The Rockers marked the first time that The Motor Company built a bike with a swingarm-mounted fender. The fender was an engineering marvel that gave the bike the appearance of the hottest custom hardtail; the fender moved right alongside the wheel and swingarm. The seating setup was equally trick because it mounted to the frame and sat mere inches above the rear fender. The solo seat itself is also deceptive; a passenger seat actually folds out of the bottom for two-up riding. The Rocker's components were all brushed metal while the Rocker C was its chromed-out twin. Production on the Rocker ceased after the 2009 model year and the Rocker C ended after the 2011 model year.

923 In 2006, Harley-Davidson paid tribute to one of the motorcycles credited with keeping the company afloat during the difficult times of the 1970s when it launched the FXDI35 Dyna 35th Anniversary Super Glide. The 35th version was limited to 3,500 examples, each with a special serial number, and the unique red, white, and blue paint scheme that was first seen on the 1971 Super Glide Night Train. Special anniversary features included labeled covers on the air cleaner, battery box, and gas tank caps, as well as the classic "#1" Harley-Davidson logo on the top gas tank strip. Unfortunately, the company didn't feel like bringing back the boattail rear fender, but unlike that massive piece of fiberglass, red, white, and blue will always look right on a Harley-Davidson.

924 Only Harley-Davidson could manage to make something so cool by not changing it very much. Enter the Street Glide in 2006, which became The Motor Company's best-selling motorcycle in every single demographic category. It's the details that count on the Street Glide, and for every major component removed, there's a unique detail added for a modern, custom look. The Electra Glide lost the spotlights, fairing lowers, fender lights and trim, Tour-Pak, full-size windshield, and an inch of suspension height. What the Street Glide gains is minimal lighting on the flared rear fender, a smooth front fender, low, smoked windshield, color matched saddlebag latches, a sporty seat, and a custom-style Harley-Davidson badge on the sides of the gas tank. Every now and then The Motor Company builds exactly the right bike at exactly the right time. The Street Glide is certainly one of those bikes.

925 To provide the best possible motorcycles for the broadest range of customers, Harley-Davidson began offering "low" models beginning with the Fat Boy Lo. This model carried completely different trim than its taller sibling. The suspension was 1.15 inches lower, which made it a selling point for shorter or new riders who appreciated the extremely comfortable support. The low theme continued in 2015 with the release of the Ultra Classic Low and the Ultra Limited Low. They shared all the features of the standard height versions, except that they were modified for shorter riders. Low-profile seats, shorter suspension, pullback handlebar, narrower primary housing, and smaller-diameter grips all lend themselves to the perfect ride for those with shorter inseams.

THE POWERTRAIN

926 The 1999 Dyna and Touring models received the brand new, 88-ci Twin Cam. The biggest design change, obviously, is the use of dual camshafts, which allow more efficient valve operation and can safely achieve higher RPM. The new Twin Cam features a reshaped combustion chamber, single-fire ignition system, and more efficient airflow in the valvetrain. A twin gerotor, dry sump oil pump is used for optimal lubrication efficiency. The CV Keihin carburetor was used on Dynas and some Touring models until 2006. The Magneti-Marelli EFI system also carried over from the Evolution era, and was only used on Touring models until the introduction of the Delphi system in 2002.

927 Softail enthusiasts rejoiced in 2000 when the Twin Cam engine finally became available (a year after Dynas and Touring models), and sported a new counterbalancing system. Unlike the other Big Twin families, Softail engines remained solidly mounted to the frame, which, in the case of the Evolution engine, caused tooth-chattering vibration at idle. To eliminate this source of consumer complaints, the engineers developed a chain-driven gear system (driven by the crankshaft gear) that spins gears forward and aft of the flywheel. These gears have weights attached at different positions, so that they rotate in the opposite direction of the flywheels. These weights smooth out the engine, thereby creating less vibration through the frame. Softails used a Keihin carburetor until 2006, but some models began using the new Delphi EFI in 2002. Counterbalanced Twin Cams are referred to as "B" motors.

928 Don't make the mistake of considering the 1,200-cc V-twin in the XR1200 just another Sportster engine. This XR engine uses a high-flowing downdraft throttle body that sucks air in through an inlet that's part of the plastic gas tank body. An external oil cooler keeps the whole engine cooler, but a unique set of heads also provides more oil flow for cooling; the engineers called this "precision-cooled." A stronger valve train, including a set of hotter cams, allowed more power to be made in the upper RPM ranges. In addition, that range could be extended to 7,200 rpm by using a stronger crankshaft. A tuned dual exhaust with crossover allowed the engine to exhale freely, and with a sound usually only heard at racetracks. To monitor performance, the XR used an analog tachometer and a smaller, digital speedometer mounted next to each other on the handlebars. For even more oomph, and possibly to compensate for the engine's high powerband, it used taller gearing. It's noticeable accelerating out of a corner, and doesn't affect highway comfort until you're doing about 90. But that's not really what the bike is for, is it? The XR1200 engine was updated in 2011 as the XR1200X with a full blackout treatment.

929 The 2004 Sportster frame update also included a mostly new engine to go with the smoother running frame. The biggest change came in the bike's 5-speed transmission housing, which no longer has a transmission trapdoor; the trapdoor had allowed easy servicing of the gearbox. To fix or replace a rubbermount transmission, the entire engine must be split at the case. In addition, the ham can air cleaner was given a rounder, modern appearance along with an exposed intake tract on the bottom. The exhaust system's crossover pipe was placed back by the mufflers and hidden out of sight, instead of cutting across the engine underneath the air cleaner.

930 Sportsters became fuel-injected across the board in 2007; it provided better fuel efficiency and snappier throttle response. Hiding the ECU components on such a small motorcycle proved somewhat problematic, so they were integrated into the rear fender, underneath the seat. This proved even more problematic for owners when they wanted to switch to an aftermarket seat. The Motor Company didn't consider this a problem until it designed the Forty-Eight with a barebones seat; a portion of the rear fender where the ECU was positioned was now exposed. To fix the problem, the engineers pleased all Sportster customers by tucking the ECU down near the battery and oil tank; this allowed for a wide array of aftermarket seat options and also allowed for the smooth production of its hot new throwback bobber.

931 For the 2006 model year, the Dyna family was the only one to receive the new Cruise-Drive 6-speed transmission. However, for 2006 only, it retained the 88-ci Twin Cam engine, making those bikes the only ones in Harley-Davidson history to ever have both an 88-ci engine and a 6-speed transmission. In 2007, all of the Big Twins were upgraded with the new 96-ci Twin Cam engine and the 6-speed Cruise Drive that had appeared on the Dynas the year before.

932 Harley-Davidson introduced its first production liquid-cooled engine with the launch of the VRSC V-Rod in 2002. The Motor Company dubbed it the Revolution engine; it's about as far from the traditional 45-degree, air-cooled V-twin as possible. The Revolution engine was bred from Harley's VR-1000 racing program and the defunct Nova program, and, like those, Porsche in Germany designed it. The first iteration of the 60-degree, DOHC Revolution engine displaced 1,131 cc (3.94-inch bore and 2.83-inch stroke) and produced 115 hp at 8,250 rpm. Air and fuel are fed through a downdraft throttle body under the faux gas tank shell that actually hides a large air cleaner. The gas tank fits neatly under the seat where it's accessed by lifting up the rider's seat. Of course, as much as Harley-Davidson tried, there's no hiding that huge radiator on the front of the frame downtubes. Air goes in through the intake ducts on either side of the front wheel while a plastic cover sits in the middle protecting the radiator from road grime coming off the wheel. A 5-speed transmission backs the whole thing.

933 Even though the power output of the first-gen V-Rod was fine, The Motor Company gave the Revolution powertrain some upgrades for the 2007 model year. The biggest update was an increase in fuel capacity from a measly 3.2 gallons to a usable 5 gallons. Fuel economy on the V-Rod is less than impressive, but it's a fair price to pay for all that horsepower-fueled fun. When that change was made, the Revolution's displacement was bumped up to 1,250 cc by boring the cylinders out to 4.13 inches, giving it another seven ponies to play with. However, the first V-Rod to use the 1,250 was the 2006 VRSCSE2 Screamin' Eagle V-Rod, which has the appearance of a street-legal Destroyer.

934 In 2010, The Motor Company responded to some customer concerns about a loud, whining sound when in first and fifth gears of the Cruise Drive transmission. It replaced the straight-cut fifth gear with a helical gear like gears two, three, four, and six. Although the straight-cut gears are stronger, which is why they were used in the (takeoff) first gear and the (highway passing) fifth gear, the angled teeth on the helical gears last longer because of less friction, which also makes them quieter. This change was made for all Big Twins.

935 When Harley-Davidson first launched the Tri Glide Ultra Classic in 2009, it received a lot of attention from riders who would never (they say now) throw a leg over a trike. What were they looking at? The Motor Company equipped the massive Tri Glide with a 103-ci Twin Cam that had only previously been available in police bikes and CVOs, and therefore eluded most of the buying public. The big Big Twin put out 101 ft-lbs of torque through the usual 6-speed Cruise Drive, which transferred power to the ground via a belt drive and solid rear axle. Tri Glide buyers had the option of including an electric reverse system in the rear differential; a handlebar-mounted module controlled it for an extra $1,195. And then Harley riders everywhere waited for the announcement that the TC103 would be available in their favorite Big Twin model.

936 Those who wished that the TC103 was available in a standard two-wheel package only had to wait until 2010 when the Ultra Limited was introduced as Harley-Davidson's new flagship motorcycle. With 102 ft-lbs of torque, the TC103 delivered 10 percent more power than the TC96 it replaced. The following year saw the first use of the factory term "PowerPak," which was a package that includes the TC103, ABS, and Smart Security System. The Power-Pak was standard on the Limited, Road Glide Ultra, and Road King Classic and could be ordered from the factory on the Street Glide and Road Glide Custom. In 2012, it was announced that every Big Twin model (except the Dyna Super Glide and Street Bob) would receive the 103-ci Twin Cam, although it was only rated at 100 ft-lbs of torque that year. The 2012 Touring models received the added cooling benefits of an oil cooler, something that was seen on police bikes for years.

937 The first bigger-inch version of the 88-ci Twin Cam engine came just one year after its arrival when a 95-ci version appeared in the 2000 Screamin' Eagle Road Glide. The 1,550-cc Twin Cam comprised all street-legal Screamin' Eagle parts including big-bore cylinders that bumped the bore from 3.75 to 3.87 inches while maintaining the same 4-inch stroke, flattop pistons, hotter cams, high-flow air cleaner, and special tuning. This particular 95-ci engine made about 10 percent more horsepower and 14 percent more torque than the 88-ci version. The 88 to 95 upgrade remains an easy and popular modification for owners of TC88s. The Screamin' Eagle Road Glide was also the first Twin Cam–powered motorcycle produced by CVO and, since then, a Touring model has always been in the CVO lineup.

938 Harley-Davidson's first 103-ci engine appeared in the 2003 Screamin' Eagle Road King, which also made it the first H-D engine to put out 100 ft-lbs of torque. The 103-ci engine size was created by using the 3.87-inch bore of the uprated 95-ci engine while also stroking it up by 4.37 ci. In addition, the compression ratio was decreased from the 95: from 9.4:1 to 9.0:1, giving the 103 slightly friendlier road manners. Even though 2003 also saw the first-ever CVO Softail with the Screamin' Eagle Deuce, that lighter model retained the 95-ci package. The Softail line received its first introduction to the 103-ci mill with the 2006 Screamin' Eagle Fat Boy, which was counterbalanced for riding pleasure. However, the Softail version maintained its regular 8.6:1 compression ratio, which only puts out 96 ft-lbs of torque.

939 The counterbalanced 103 only made it into one Screamin' Eagle Fat Boy for one year, because the following year, 2007, all Screamin' Eagle models received the 110-ci Twin Cam. For those interested in one-year-only H-Ds, the 2006 Screamin' Eagle Fat Boy is the only Softail to ever use a 103-ci engine with a 5-speed transmission. The Screamin' Eagle 110 increases the cylinder bore to an even 4 inches while maintaining the 103's 3.37-inch stroke with 9.3:1–compression pistons. The 110 puts out an arm-ripping 115 ft-lbs of torque at 3,000 rpm, which is felt way more in the 695-pound SE Dyna than the 888-pound SE Ultra Classic Electra Glide.

940 With the 2011 Softail lineup, Harley-Davidson began updating the ignition and electrical systems from the J1850 data bus system to a new CAN bus system. The bike's computer, switches, and engine-monitoring equipment worked much faster with smaller parts and much less wiring with the CAN bus system. The 12-mm oxygen sensors in the headers replace the larger 18-mm sensors; all of the bike's functions were essentially moved

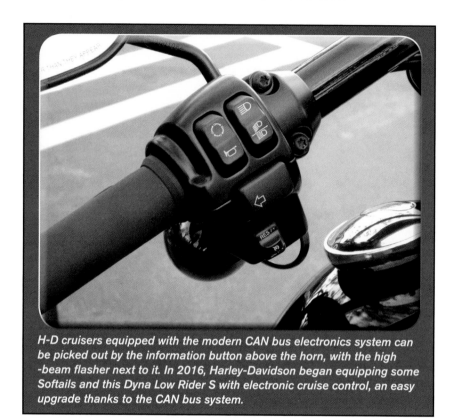

H-D cruisers equipped with the modern CAN bus electronics system can be picked out by the information button above the horn, with the high -beam flasher next to it. In 2016, Harley-Davidson began equipping some Softails and this Dyna Low Rider S with electronic cruise control, an easy upgrade thanks to the CAN bus system.

from their individual locations to a central computer. This change is immediately obvious in the new handlebar switches. These new switches require only the softest touch for engagement. Unlike previous switches, for which each function had its own wire, the entire switch housing operates off a single wire that goes to the central computer. The CAN bus moved to the Dyna line for the 2012 model year, and to the Touring models and Sportsters in 2014. One of the handiest updates for models that didn't already have it is the trip/display switch that is now located on the left handlebar switch housing; it has a new gear and tachometer display built into all CAN bus speedometers.

941 The control switch of the H-D cruise control system on the right-hand side could be slightly annoying to engage while simultaneously controlling the throttle. Obviously, many riders voiced the same concern to The Motor Company. As part of Project Rushmore, the cruise control switch was moved to the left side where it is easily controlled while riding, as is the infotainment system's features.

942 As more and more couples ride together (on one bike), The Motor Company made many of its 2009 Touring frame updates with a passenger in mind. To reduce the heat felt by a passenger, the entire exhaust system was reworked to curve to the left side in front of the transmission; it moved the exhaust pipe away from the passenger's left leg so that it runs underneath the bike and then underneath the saddlebag. In addition, a new, one-piece heat shield replaced the previous two-piece heat shield that had a sizable gap in coverage. On models equipped with a catalyst, that system was moved to be within the collector/crossover pipe farther up in the system. With the Touring line's added weight capabilities, the rear sprocket was increased from 66 teeth to 68 teeth for improved acceleration.

943 Along with the major chassis and comfort updates that were part of the 2014 Project Rushmore was an uprated version of the 103-ci Twin Cam, the High Output Twin Cam 103. The development team's goal was improved passing power; they achieved that by using new cams with greater bottom-end torque and a higher-flowing air cleaner. The Motor Company claims a 5-percent torque improvement over the previous 103. The new High Output 103 was only available in Touring and Trike models during its first year, then Softail and Dynas (except the Street Bob) for 2016.

944 The air-cooled Big Twin faithful nearly keeled over when The Motor Company announced its new Twin-Cooled Twin Cam engines in 2014. They discovered, after further reading, that the Twin-Cooled engine simply provides a single channel of liquid cooling around the exhaust valves of each head, which is the hottest part of any engine. Because emissions requirements keep increasing, Harley-Davidson has continuously leaned out fuel mixtures through the years, which results in hotter-running engines. Because Touring models already had an oil cooler, the only answer was to develop a system to handle basic cooling needs, but without a visible radiator or any visible alterations to the engine. The two small heat exchangers are hidden inside the fairing lowers while a small coolant bottle is located in the right lower fairing storage compartment. The Twin-Cooled engine benefits from a higher 10.1:1 compression ratio that enables it to put out 10 percent more torque than the previous Twin Cam 103. As of 2016, the Twin-Cooled Twin Cam is only found on a handful of premium models and Touring CVOs.

945 When Harley-Davidson unveiled its entirely new family of Streets in 2013, it based the powertrains on the V-Rod's liquid-cooled Revolution engine. Available in 750- and 500-cc displacements, the new Revolution X engines feature a 60-degree design with four-valve heads, single overhead cams (SOHC), and the welcome advantage of a 6-speed transmission. The 750-cc displacement is achieved by using a 3.35-inch bore with 2.6-inch stroke along with a 38-mm throttle body. The 500-cc version has a smaller 2.72-inch bore, identical 2.6-inch stroke, and a smaller 35-mm throttle body. Both entirely blacked-out powertrains use Mikuni throttle bodies, an 11:1 compression ratio, and get 41 combined mpg. The 750 is good for a claimed 44-1/2 ft-lbs of torque at 4,000 rpm while the 500 puts out 29-1/2 ft-lbs of torque at 3,500 rpm.

946 With the instant popularity of Harley-Davidson's Screamin' Eagle 120R race engine, the cry became so loud for a street-legal version of the crate engine that it only made sense to comply. In 2015, the 49-state street-legal 120ST engine was introduced for 2014-and-later Touring models without Twin Cooling. The only internal difference between the two is a milder set of cams with a .579-inch lift compared to the R's .658-inch lift. Externally, the 120ST uses a different tune; a new exhaust system was developed with the catalytic converters in the mufflers, instead of the headers, for sufficient flow.

947 To appease its power-hungry customers whose wallets can't or don't want to shell out for a CVO's price tag, Harley-Davidson introduced the all-new S Series of motorcycles in 2016. These Big Twins are built around the powerful 110-ci Twin Cam, which is found only in CVO models; this is the first offering of the 110 in non-CVO models. The first models introduced with the new package were the Fat Boy S, Softail Slim S, and Low Rider S. In addition to being fully optioned out, they feature unique styling components that set them apart from their base 103 siblings. The price difference between S Series models and base models is about $2,300, which more than covers the cost of a 110 kit, labor, and the additional features.

Here is 110 inches of Screamin' Eagle power stuffed into a lightweight Dyna frame with cartridge forks, premium emulsion rear shocks, mid controls, drag bars, and a sporty seat. All of this makes the 2016 Low Rider S one of the fastest Big Twins ever built. With the exposed air filter, gold wheels, and speed fairing, it even looks fast just standing still!

948 Regardless of the bike that you're riding, cruise control extends riding distances greatly on the highway, even if it's just to give your right arm a momentary stretch. Harley-Davidson brought the joy of electronic cruise control to its Softail line for the first time with the 2011 CVO Softail Convertible. Cruise control for the Softails was limited to the exotic CVOs until H-D announced that electronic cruise control would become standard on select Softails for 2016. For those other models, an easy upgrade kit was available from the parts and accessories catalog. When H-D launched the Dyna Low Rider S as a mid-year model, the electronic cruise control was part of its standard package; this marked the first appearance of cruise control on a Dyna.

949 In the Twin Cam era, Harley-Davidson has used several different cylinder head designs on Sportster models. The engineers really stepped up when it came to the heads on 2004 rubber-mounted 1200s. Actually, these heads first appeared in 2003 on Buells, for which they were nicknamed "Thunderstorm" heads, but the two are nearly identical. They use a 62-cc chamber, a 1.810-inch intake valve, and a 1.575-inch exhaust valve for more airflow and higher compression. However, the big advantage is the result of the reworked ports, which have a higher floor and more gradual radius. The new design greatly reduces port turbulence and, overall, they gave XBs and XL1200s an advantage of almost 5 hp over previous heads. This head design was used until 2006.

950 In 2007, XL1200 heads were changed again. This time, the intake port was actually made so that it flows slightly worse than the previous design, although it's only noticeable on highly modified engines. Either way, 2004-and-later XL1200 heads are a popular modification for XL883 owners looking for more factory-built horsepower. They make a difference particularly when upgrading with a 1,200-cc kit to get the most air in and out of the engine. Another popular modification is adding Buell Thunderstorm heads, but the difference is only negligible. However, don't be

The 2007-and-later 1,200-cc Sportster engine is powerhouse when placed into a 550-pound motorcycle. However, there's still a lot of room for performance improvements. A high-flowing intake and exhaust matched with a good set of cams will let an XL1200 easily outrun stock 103-ci Dynas.

surprised if you hop up your 883 and it still doesn't make as much power as your buddy's 1200.

PEOPLE AND POP CULTURE

951 Would you believe that one of the most expensive Harley-Davidsons ever sold at auction was a 2001 Dyna Low Rider that went for $360,200 on eBay? As you might guess, the motorcycle took on a special meaning when it was auctioned in September 2001, along with a 2001 Ford Harley-Davidson F-150, to raise money for the Twin Towers Fund to support victims of the 9/11 terrorist attacks. Jay Leno led the project. The Dyna was actually his; he had purchased it in July and had put only 200 miles on. Dozens of celebrities signed the motorcycle including notable gearheads Tim Allen, Tom Cruise, Arnold Schwarzenegger, and John Travolta.

952 In 2009, Harley-Davidson merged its long-running publication, *The Enthusiast*, with a newer publication in print since 1983, *HOG Tales*, to create a single magazine simply titled *HOG*, which is available in print and digitally. 2016 marks 100 consecutive years that The Motor Company has published its own consumer enthusiast publication. Harley owners look to *HOG* magazine for the latest information on their favorite brand and to stay up to date on what's going on with H-D riders from around the world.

953 In 2012, Harley-Davidson participated in an outreach program with Milwaukee public school students in grades five through eight. H-D stylists taught students about the art and science that goes into creating a motorcycle paint scheme. As part of the program, students painted their own gas tank based on what they learned from the stylists.

954 To celebrate The Motor Company's 100th anniversary, and commemorate those who build (and have built) the machines, employees signed a 100th anniversary edition Electra Glide Ultra Classic with sidecar. The motorcycle and sidecar are black, and the signatures were created with a silver Sharpie. Almost the entire package is covered in signatures: fenders, fairing, fairing lowers, gas tank, upper sidecar body, Tour-Pak, saddlebags, sidecovers, and sidecar seat. A black leather jacket was also signed; both now reside in the Harley-Davidson Museum.

955 If you're a Harley rider, and you've seen the movie, *Captain America: The First Avenger*, then you undoubtedly loved the parts when he's riding around on his military H-D saving the day. However, he wasn't actually riding a WLA Flathead that saw duty in World War II. Chris Evans was riding a brand-new Harley-Davidson Cross Bones that was customized to look like the original WLA. It's actually one of the better movie motorcycle transformations. The only thing that really stands out is the Twin Cam engine with its crossed pushrods unlike the 45's long cam cover with parallel pushrods. The builders also created finned, Flathead-style rocker covers for this bike.

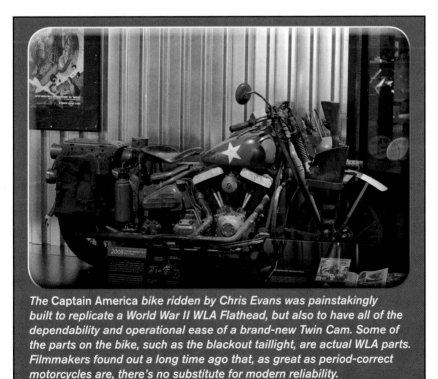

The **Captain America** *bike ridden by Chris Evans was painstakingly built to replicate a World War II WLA Flathead, but also to have all of the dependability and operational ease of a brand-new Twin Cam. Some of the parts on the bike, such as the blackout taillight, are actual WLA parts. Filmmakers found out a long time ago that, as great as period-correct motorcycles are, there's no substitute for modern reliability.*

956 The 2008 film, *Indiana Jones and the Kingdom of the Crystal Skull*, featured several great scenes with a modified 2006 Springer Softail made to look like a 1950s Panhead. Ridden by Mutt Williams (Shia LaBeouf) and Indiana Jones (Harrison Ford), the bike uses the 4-1/2 gallon late-model Sportster gas tank to replicate the styling and size of the older Panhead tanks. The rocker boxes and front disc brake are a giveaway, making the bike easily identifiable as a Twin Cam. Five versions of the Mutt Williams motorcycle were built for use by LaBeouf and Ford in the riding scenes and for stunt riders during the action sequences.

957 Sargento, the cheese producer based in Plymouth, Wisconsin, celebrated its 50th birthday in 2003, the same year Harley-Davidson celebrated its 100th. To recognize both well-known Wisconsin brands' milestones, Sargento commissioned a custom Anniversary edition Fat Boy. In addition to the full bolt-on custom treatment, the Fat Boy also received a custom sidecar made out of composite fiberglass and shaped like, what else, a wedge of cheese. The motorcycle and sidecar were painted yellow and had Swiss cheese–style holes airbrushed all over. The cheesy machine was featured prominently around Milwaukee during The Motor Company's 100th celebration, and was signed by numerous local celebrities on hand for the event. Sargento CEO Louis Gentine rode the motorcycle in the parade.

958 You've heard of the *Moo Glide*, the Heritage Softail that used cowhide inserts in the seat and saddlebag, but have you heard of a Harley built entirely from leather? A Japanese leather company called Red Moon spent two years building a reproduction Evolution-powered chopper entirely out of leather. The 6-foot-long motorcycle is so incredibly detailed, it almost looks like it could be filled with gas and started up! It even has a leather tool pouch filled with leather tools. Red Moon donated it to the Harley-Davidson Museum in 2001, after spending several days trying to get it through customs.

959 On August 27, 2003, noted Harley-Davidson restorer, expert, and enthusiast, Bruce Linsday arrived at the Juneau Avenue headquarters riding his 1905 Harley-Davidson, nicknamed *Tommy*. He had just ridden *Tommy* 462-1/2 miles from his home in Ohio to Milwaukee. Yes, you read that right. Bruce's 1905 is the oldest running, regularly ridden Harley in the world.

960 In 2014, an auction was held for what was claimed to be the *Captain America* chopper that was actually used in the movie *Easy Rider*. The owner supposedly had the bike rebuilt from the wrecked chopper ridden by Peter Fonda and claimed to have the authentication to prove it. In what is certainly one of the more curious, although, unfortunately, common, instances of a rare Harley-Davidson coming up for auction, the bike hammered down for a whopping $1.35 million, or $1.6 million with auction fees! However, the story took an interesting turn when it was discovered the same person who authenticated this chopper had previously authenticated another one, labeling both as the last remaining *Captain America*. Peter Fonda had voiced his concerns prior to the auction, saying that he hoped that it would be called off. Real or fake, that certainly didn't stop it from becoming the most expensive motorcycle ever sold at auction!

961 Who says you can't take it with you when you go? Billy Standley of Mechanicsburg, Ohio, had never heard that saying. When he died in 2014 at the age of 82, his dying wish of being buried with his Harley-Davidson was granted. But there's more to the story. He was buried astride his 1967 Electra Glide in a massive plexiglass coffin that his two sons had built for him. It took a team of five embalmers to outfit him in his leathers and white helmet, along with a metal back brace and straps to keep him upright while the see-through coffin was taken on a parade to his burial site. He had to buy three additional burial plots next to his wife to fit the massive coffin into the grave.

962 After the September 11, 2001, terrorist attacks in New York City, Washington, D.C., and Somerset County, Pennsylvania,

Harley-Davidson quickly rushed to the support of law enforcement and the victims' families. The Motor Company donated $1 million to the American Red Cross with that money earmarked to go directly to relief efforts. In addition, The Motor Company donated 30 motorcycles to the New York Police Department to replace motorcycles, squad cars, and other police vehicles that were destroyed in the World Trade Center attack.

963 Captain America is one of the best known silver screen Harley-Davidson riders of all time, but thanks to sponsorship from The Motor Company, Chris Evans' rendition of the superhero has brought the Bar & Shield into the spotlight in the 21st century. In fact, much of the promotional imagery for 2014's *Captain America: The Winter Soldier* included an image of him racing a brand-new Street 750 into action. Harley-Davidson sent out a press release saying so, along with the requisite image. Except, there was one problem. Captain America wasn't on a Street 750. He was riding a Sportster that was modified to look like a Street 750, which was immediately obvious to anyone who has spent time looking at both machines. The Sportster's signature battery sidecover and primary covers are immediate giveaways, but the smoking gun is the fact that the drive belt on the movie poster was on the right side (as on a Sportster) while the XG's drivebelt is on the left side. The most likely reason for the switch is that Chris Evans would have made the new Street look like a tiny kid's toy instead of a full-size motorcycle. He also rides the new Softail Breakout in the movie.

964 Harley-Davidson commissioned a 2014 study conducted by Kelton to survey women motorcyclists and the effects that motorcycling has on them. The study found that 12 percent of motorcycle owners were women, 30 percent more than in 2004 and that the top-selling brand among women was Harley-Davidson. Women riders are twice as likely to always feel happy as opposed to nonriders, and one-third of those questioned said they felt less stress after they started to ride. Men, take note here, women who ride motorcycles are four times as likely to always feel sexy and twice as likely to always feel confident!

965 In 2015, The Motor Company and the city of Sturgis agreed to a 75-year deal making Harley-Davidson the official motorcycle of the Sturgis Motorcycle Rally. The agreement also included the construction of the Harley-Davidson Rally Point plaza on Main Street and the renaming of part of Second Street to Harley-Davidson Way. Rally Point is open to the public all year and has become a popular destination for riders touring the area. The plaza was built using 75 original bricks pulled from the H-D headquarters on Juneau Avenue, and they're displayed prominently at the front of the concert stage. In March 2014, a handful of H-D execs, a few motojournalists, and I accompanied the bricks on motorcycles from Milwaukee to Sturgis on what was dubbed the BrickRide. We battled snowstorms, rain, freezing temperatures, and high winds on

Bricks used in the construction of Harley-Davidson's Rally Point plaza in Sturgis were pulled from the front entrance of the original Juneau Avenue factory building. These original bricks date back more than 100 years to the first brick factory at the site. Sturgis Mayor Mark Carstensen (left) came to Milwaukee for the occasion, led by Bill Davidson (right). (Photo Courtesy Harley-Davidson)

the 900-mile journey to Sturgis. We have all agreed that it was one of the best rides of our lives.

966 At the Sturgis Motorcycle Rally in 2015, daredevil Doug Danger achieved what the greatest motorcycle jumper of all time couldn't when he jumped over 22 cars at the Sturgis Buffalo Chip. Remember, Evel Knievel attempted his 22-car jump but ended up landing on the safety ramp, which was built over the last three cars at the last minute. Not only did Doug Danger accomplish this feat, but he actually did it on Evel Knievel's own XR-750! Supposedly, the difference between the two jumps was a better ramp design and different gearing and suspension tuning on the bike, although the suspension itself was still original.

967 In 2010, stunt rider Seth Enslow set the world record for the longest jump ever completed on a Harley-Davidson when he jumped a basically stock XR1200 183.7-feet in Sydney, Australia. Bubba Blackwell set the previous record of 157 feet in 1999. Seth Enslow reportedly broke the record twice on the same day when he had to make a second jump after it was discovered the video cameras weren't recording the first one. His initial jump was 175 feet, but he knew that he could go farther and had the crew widen the space. He hit the ramp at 95 mph to complete the jump.

968 In October 2012, as part of its 110th anniversary proceedings, Harley-Davidson sent a pair of Super Glide gas tanks, complete with anniversary trim, to the Vatican City to be blessed and signed by Pope Benedict XVI. Willie G. and Bill Davidson attended the official 110th kickoff ceremonies in Rome, which included a stop at the Vatican to meet the pope, and the signing of the special gas tanks. The tanks were then shipped back to Milwaukee where they were mounted on their respective motorcycles. One sits in the Harley-Davidson Museum and the other was auctioned off for charity at the 2014 Bonhams Paris auction. The Super Glide hammered for $280,000; it's believed that the pope never actually rode it.

969 Harley-Davidson tapped the motorcycle-riding supermodel Marisa Miller to be the face of the brand in 2008. She was actually the first official spokesperson in Harley-Davidson history! She starred in numerous videos aboard the V-Rod Muscle, Softail Cross Bones, and Sportster Nightster, which is her personal ride. Her best-known role was being featured on numerous posters, which likely hang in garages all over America to this day. She did military-themed pin-up-style posters as part of The Motor Company's first Military Appreciation Month and ended her run with the Bar & Shield in the Start Something campaign, which encouraged new riders to live out their dreams aboard a Harley-Davidson.

970 After years of distancing itself from the outlaw aspect of motorcycling, Harley-Davidson became a major sponsor of the hit TV show *Sons of Anarchy* on FX. The show revolved around a fictional Central California motorcycle club and its crazy, violent exploits. Naturally, all of the club members rode Harley-Davidsons, and had a preference for the Dyna family. This undoubtedly fueled sales of the high-performance Big Twin, and they began to pop up everywhere, modified just like the bikes in the TV series. H-D enthusiasts either loved the show for the great motorcycle scenes or hated it for the portrayal of Harley riders.

971 One of the most popular shows on television, and one that fueled the custom motorcycle craze of the early 2000s was Discovery Channel's *Biker Build-Off* which ran from 2002 to 2007. Suddenly, motorcycle builders became celebrities and custom bikes just got crazier and crazier. The show featured two top builders from different parts of the country, each known for his unique style. They competed head to head to build a complete, running motorcycle in ten days. Some of the biggest names in custom building competed over the years; the first build-off featured Billy Lane and Roger Bourget. Among the fans' favorite episodes were the three featuring Indian Larry, who built his second two bikes with Harley engines, except he used a Shovelhead front cylinder and rocker box with a Panhead rear cylinder and rocker box. This became his signature look.

972 The Discovery Channel built on its success with custom motorcycle programming when it launched one of its most popular shows ever, *American Chopper*, in 2003. The reality show featured the exploits and creations of Orange County Choppers (OCC) owner Paul Teutul Sr. and his son, Paul Teutul Jr. From 2003 to 2010, over the course of 165 episodes, the Teutuls built some of the wildest custom motorcycles ever for celebrities, corporate promotions, and real clients. Paul Jr. left OCC in 2008 to start Paul Jr. Designs, and many legal issues ensued. The final season of the show in 2010 was called "American Chopper: Senior versus Junior" and featured both shops and their builds. OCC's numerous Harley-based customs received so much national attention that The Motor Company even released chopper-style bikes such as the Rocker and the Breakout.

973 The Mixed Martial Arts ultimate fighter matches are about as tough, gritty, and raw as they come, just like Harley-Davidson motorcycles. Someone in H-D's marketing department thought so too. Beginning in 2008, The Motor Company became a core sponsor of the Ultimate Fighter Championship. As part of the sponsorship, the Bar & Shield logo appears prominently on the floor of the octagon-shaped fighting cage. The sponsorship was launched to epic proportions when H-D and the UFC announced the Hometown Throwdown, which took place in Milwaukee's Bradley Center. The winner, Chris Lytle, was awarded a Softail Blackline with 103-ci engine.

974 If *Easy Rider* was the ultimate motorcycle road trip movie of the 1960s, *Wild Hogs* may just be the ultimate motorcycle road trip movie of the 2000s. The movie follows Tim Allen, John Travolta, Martin Lawrence, and William H. Macy as they leave the worries and stress of their suburban family lives behind and hit the road on their Harleys. In addition to the requisite amount of hijinks and comedy in modern filmmaking, *Wild Hogs* did actually have some pretty decent, *Easy Rider*–type riding scenes that make it more than a stupid movie about the stereotyped middle-aged biker dudes.

975 On the 19th season of ABC's *The Bachelor*, of all places, the bachelor Chris Soules is shown frequently riding his brand-new Harley-Davidson Wide Glide. While I have no doubt that the Iowa farmer actually does ride a Harley, the motorcycle was primarily a prop to show the "regular" side of the reality TV star.

MILITARY, POLICE AND RACING

976 In 2007, Dale Walksler, the curator of the Wheels Through Time museum, led an attempt to break Fred Ham's record of 1,825 miles in 24 hours with a 1937 EL. The rider was Wayne Stanfield, five-time Great American Race winner. The team made the attempt at Talladega Speedway, which matched the size of the oval that Ham used, and the event was 70 years, almost to the day, after Ham's record run. Mechanical problems early on held the team back (they only managed 75 miles in the first 3½ hours), but Stanfield rode just over 1,350 miles over the course of 24 hours. Even though he didn't break Ham's record, he did manage a couple records of his own. These included the most consecutive laps at Talladega on any machine, the greatest distance ever covered at Talladega, and the most miles ever completed by a 70-year-old motorcycle in 24 hours. Stanfield is also the only person to ever run 24 hours straight at Talladega.

977 Harley-Davidson brought out the VRXSE V-Rod Destroyer in 2006, which was meant solely for drag-strip use and wasn't street-legal. Looks-wise, it wasn't a far departure from the showroom V-Rod, except, of course, for the included wheelie bar that stuck out 5 feet off the back and its special H-D paint scheme of black and orange with an orange frame. The real difference in this factory racer comes from within that Revolution engine. The techs at H-D HQ fitted it with a stroker flywheel, larger valves, high-compression pistons, hot cams, and a larger throttle body, making the Destroyer good for over 165 hp. Other necessary drag-race goodies included a lock-up clutch for those high-RPM takeoffs, a programmable shift light, and a DRZ 530 chain instead of the stock belt. Just like the factory-built racers that came before it, the

Destroyer was available at the local Harley-Davidson dealer; only 625 out of the total 646 built ever saw a showroom floor.

978 Riding the VRXSE Destroyer is nothing like firing up your Softail for a neighborhood jaunt, or even going stoplight to stoplight on a V-Rod. To start it, simply flick the kill switch to "run" and thumb the start button. Thanks to the high-performance lock-up clutch, takeoffs include pinning the throttle and throwing the clutch lever, which leads to 2-Gs of force on the rider. The digital tachometer and LED shift light tell the rider when it's time to shift, but, instead of using the left foot and left hand, all the rider has to do is to press what was formerly the turn-signal button. That kicks in the Pingel air shifter kit; it cuts spark to the engine momentarily to make a smooth shift without using the clutch. Advertised as a sub-10-second machine in the hands of a qualified rider, many non-pros have been able to land ETs well into the 9s.

979 At 17 years old, Harley-Davidson factory rider Jennifer Snyder became the first woman to win a national event in the Formula USA dirt track racing series. Her historic win came at Colonial Downs in New Kent, Virginia, in the first race of the 2001 season. Following that win, she moved up to compete in the AMA Pro Grand National Championship series for the next few years until an injury ended her career. The win at Colonial Downs was the only one of her career, but it paved the way for future women riders to compete in flat track racing.

980 In 2004, 21-year-old Screamin' Eagle/Harley-Davidson factory rider Andrew Hines won his first NHRA Pro Stock Motorcycle Championship, making him the youngest champion in NHRA history. Not only was it his first win, but it was also Harley-Davidson's first win with an NHRA team. Hines led the points standings for the entire season and earned the number-one qualifying position a record eight times. It was only a matter of time before he took home the big trophy; two years prior he qualified for every single event he entered. He was also one of six finalists for the Auto Club Road to the Future award, which is NHRA's Rookie of the Year honor.

981 Throughout his career, which is ongoing at the time of this writing, Andrew Hines has achieved five world championship titles, his most recent being in 2015. In his 13 years of professional NHRA racing with Harley-Davidson, he's earned 42 career wins out of 68 final round appearances. His career best ET currently stands at 6.728 seconds while his career best speed is 199.23 mph. Hines' career-best wins in a season was in 2012 when he took top honors 6 times out of 11 overall appearances. Strangely, he finished second in the championship points standings that year.

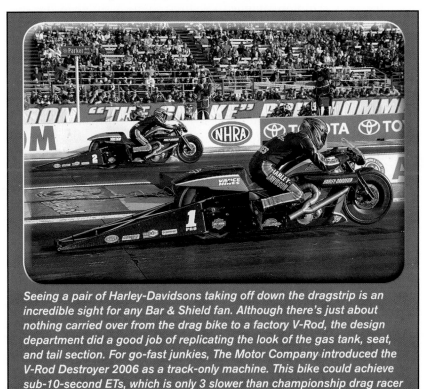

Seeing a pair of Harley-Davidsons taking off down the dragstrip is an incredible sight for any Bar & Shield fan. Although there's just about nothing carried over from the drag bike to a factory V-Rod, the design department did a good job of replicating the look of the gas tank, seat, and tail section. For go-fast junkies, The Motor Company introduced the V-Rod Destroyer 2006 as a track-only machine. This bike could achieve sub-10-second ETs, which is only 3 slower than championship drag racer Andrew Hines' best time. (Photo Courtesy Harley-Davidson)

982 In 2010 at Daytona, the AMA fittingly announced the launch of a new spec-bike racing series using the Harley-David-son XR1200. Vance & Hines sponsored the championship series and it provided Harley owners and dealers to finally see their favorite brand run at road courses all over the country. As fast as the XR1200 was in stock form, to race in the Vance & Hines XR1200 series, the bikes had to be equipped with a special $3,500 race package from, you guessed it, Vance & Hines. The kit included a competition-only exhaust system, Fuelpak, front number plate, single-seat tail section, belly pan, 17-inch front wheel and fender, steering dampener, oil cooler relocation kit, and racing decals. Beyond the basics, teams were allowed to upgrade their own suspension, controls, brakes, and gauges to break their XR away from the pack. Dunlop supplied the tires; Sunoco supplied the spec fuel. Perhaps the best part about the AMA Pro Vance & Hines XR1200 series was the fact that those required parts (and a few more) became available to ordinary XR1200 owners so that they could make one mean street machine.

983 Danny Eslick won the first XR1200 race, which was run on June 6, 2010, at Road America in Elkhart Lake, Wisconsin. As the reigning AMA Daytona Superbike champion, he was a road-racing expert, but still only managed a .055-second margin of victory over his teammate Jake Holden after 10 laps of neck and neck racing.

984 As part of the launch of the Street family of motorcycles, Harley-Davidson launched a campaign to make ice racing an official event at the X Games. The first XG750 ice race was held at the 2014 Aspen X Games as an exhibition race to gauge fan enthusiasm. Taking to the ice on the XG750 for the first time were AMA Pro Grand National champion Brad Baker, 2012 champion Jared Mees, and Jared's wife and fellow pro racer Nichole Mees. The Street 750s used in the exhibition race had special ice racing studs screwed into their tires for traction.

985 After the ice racing event at the Aspen X Games, Harley-Davidson once again sent its new Street 750 into the racing spotlight with an exhibition event at the 2014 Austin X Games. Brad Baker led the charge, this time in his more familiar dirt terrain in an attempt to make flat track racing a regular X Games medal sport.

It doesn't get a whole lot more extreme than racing Harley-Davidsons on the ice; that's just what The Motor Company did as part of an X Games exhibition race. As of this writing, ice racing isn't an official X Games sport. Flat track racing in the dirt was attempted in 2015 and then given medal-sport status going forward. (Photo Courtesy Harley-Davidson)

For Austin 2015, flat track racing did appear as a medal sport and drew fans in from around the world. Bryan Smith won the event aboard his Kawasaki, but he went home on a brand new Harley-Davidson Street 750, the winning prize.

986 Harley-Davidson factory rider Andrew Hines' 2015 NHRA Pro Stock Motorcycle world championship gave The Motor Company its eighth NHRA world Championship in 12 years. It was also the second year in a row that Hines and his teammate, Ed Krawiec, finished first and second in the season final standings.

987 In November 2015, Harley-Davidson Screamin' Eagle Wrecking Crew rider Jared Mees won his third AMA Pro flat track championship in only four years. His season shows how important it is to finish strong, regardless of position, when it comes to professional racing. He won only a single race during the 2015 season, but fought to the podium 9 times and only finished outside the top 10 twice out of 13 races.

988 Civilian motorcycles weren't the only ones to benefit from Project Rushmore updates; police Road Kings and Electra Glides also got in on the fun with most of the same changes in power and comfort, as well as a few additional upgrades. The Electra Glide received Daymaker LED lights up front while the Road King was fitted with dual halogens. With the new models, motor officers had more control over their emergency lights. They can control emergency lights independently to run front only or rear only, and a new accessory mode provides the ability to run emergency lights and sirens with the ignition off. One of the coolest updates was the new stealth mode, which can turn off all lights except for instruments and brake function, at the press of a button, and then turn everything back on again just as easily. Each version can also be ordered for fire department use, in which case it is painted Firefighter Red

989 The Motor Company doesn't just build motorcycles and then simply ship them to police departments. As with the Quartermaster's School during both World Wars, numerous training programs are available to motor officers. A class is available for every single aspect of maintaining a police bike from a general service course to more specific classes focused on powertrain, chassis, electrical, etc. Harley-Davidson, through the Northwestern University Center For Public Safety, offers nationwide courses that focus on riding skills and techniques unique to motor officers. To serve police departments nationwide in the same manner, a special trailer transports 21 training motorcycles to approximately 13 locations every year.

990 You might not see them as frequently as the Touring model of police bikes, but Harley-Davidson also makes a special, tricked-out police-issue Sportster XL883L. It differs little from the civilian version except for the color options of Birch White and Vivid Black, and optional accessories including a detachable windshield and front red and blue emergency lights. Special small police saddlebags and a mini Tour-Pak are also optional for the XL; they provide motor officers with greater storage capacity for their equipment.

991 In 2000, the California Highway Patrol (CHP) switched from Kawasaki to BMW after a comparison test between several brands, including Harley-Davidson. By 2013, service and maintenance for the BMWs had cost the famed police agency more than they had hoped. Then, Oakland Harley-Davidson stepped in to show off a custom-fitted police Electra Glide, which made it the ultimate police platform. Oakland H-D gave its version an upgraded suspension and rewired the electronics for easier access and add-on capability. The bikes were also given a Screamin' Eagle SE-255 cam upgrade for better torque and a more effective powerband. In addition, small items such as a gas tank–mounted clipboard were installed to make writing tickets and other daily police duties easier. The first order for 121 motorcycles was in 2013, but that was soon followed by additional orders to replace all 400-plus motorcycles. Each bike costs a little over $28,300 and, for the first time in 20 years, the Bar & Shield will rule the CHP's motorcycle corps.

992 Harley-Davidson created yet another worldwide jaw-drop phenomenon in 2011 when it unveiled the 120-ci Screamin' Eagle Pro 120R race engine. This race-ready monster Twin Cam marks the first time The Motor Company offered a race-only engine since the XR-750. The 120R uses a 4.06-inch bore and a 4-5/8-inch stroke with 10.5:1 compression nickel-plated pistons to deliver 135 hp and 137 ft-lbs of torque. To run the engine successfully, the customer needs to buy a Screamin' Eagle throttle body, high-flow injectors, and an upgraded clutch, exhaust system, air cleaner, and tuner. The 120R bolts right into any Big Twin in a Twin Cam frame. Even though the fine print clearly states that the engine is for competition use only and is not street-legal, it didn't take long before Harley enthusiasts in states without emissions requirements started dropping them into street bikes. The base price tag is around $7,000.

993 In the 1980s, it was the performance, comfort, and reliability that sold police departments around the world on the FXRP instead of the heavier, more costly Electra Glide variations. Harley-Davidson brought back that slim, trim crime-fighting ability with the FXDP Dyna Defender, which was based on the Super Glide Sport. The Defender had everything that the Police Road King had including large saddlebags, Tour-Pak, siren, emergency lights, and windshield. However, it did it all while being more than 100 pounds lighter, having sharper lean angles, and faster braking times.

994 You already know about the demise of the Harley-Davidson sidecar, but did you know that up until that time, police motorcycles could still be ordered with a matching sidehack? If a motor unit ordered a TLE sidecar, the factory matched its color options to the motorcycles that the department ordered.

995 In 2010, Harley-Davidson released several special first responder editions of the Fat Boy, Heritage Softail Classic, Road King, and Ultra Classic Electra Glide. Police edition H-Ds were available in Solid Dark Blue and Vivid Black while the firefighter edition was available in Fire Engine Red and Vivid Black. Special badges, unique to their models, read "PEACE OFFICER; SPECIAL EDITION" and "FIREFIGHTER; SPECIAL EDITION."

996 In 2015, on the flight deck of the U.S.S. *Yorktown*, Harley-Davidson announced that it would begin offering free Riding Academy training to all current and former U.S. military. The program was initially intended to run through the summer of that year, but it was so successful and was so well received by veterans (and the public) that Harley-Davidson decided to continue it through 2016. As is the case with both announcements, anyone who was deployed in 2015 could easily apply for a voucher good for the following year so that he or she could learn how to ride a Harley-Davidson.

997 To show further support for soldiers stationed overseas, Harley-Davidson sponsored Bikes Over Baghdad, an event that brings some of the top BMX athletes in the country to Iraq to put on a show. To give the troops the ultimate feeling of home, H-D displays covered the entire area; servicemen and women could immerse themselves completely in the Bar & Shield lifestyle, even if only for a few hours. Troops who hopped into the Jumpstart display received a $25 gift card and everyone present could enter to win a brand-new Blackline. All of the 2012 models were on display for viewing and sitting upon, and *Captain America* posters featuring the "WLA" motorcycle were handed out.

998 Army veteran Sergeant Noah Galloway lost his left arm above the elbow and his left leg above the knee from a roadside IED explosion in Iraq. Following his treatment and rehabilitation, he became a personal trainer and motivational speaker; he began competing in a variety of fitness competitions as well as becoming a model. His inspirational story has helped countless other injured servicemen and women return to their lives. When Harley-Davidson learned that the money he was saving for a motorcycle went instead for a wedding ring for his girlfriend, it stepped in to hook up the hero with the bike. The Motor Company offered to give him that motorcycle as well as modify it to suit his needs.

999 To support active-duty members of the military to get the most out of their time at home, Harley-Davidson initiated the Stateside Military Financing Program. This program allows servicemen and women to purchase a new Harley with reduced interest rates and flexible term options that take into account being on an overseas combat deployment for months at a time. Some can also qualify for a no-down-payment option so they don't have to worry about blowing their enlistment bonus all in one place!

1000 The U.S. military may have been using Harley-Davidson motorcycles long before 1998, but that's when the 883 Sportster became the preferred motorcycle of the Israeli Military Police Corps. The Israeli XL883L arrives fully equipped with the police package, as well as the addition of the Military Police Corps shield on the gas tank and saddlebags. This is the first time Israel's Military Police Corps has used a Harley-Davidson; it had previously used Moto Guzzis, BMWs, and Hondas.

1001 On March 3, 2016, Harley-Davidson announced that, for the first time since 2006, it would field two riders in the GNC1 flat track series. 18-year-old Davis Fisher was signed to run alongside previous champion Brad "The Bullet" Baker. In the 2015 season, Fisher raced in the AMA Pro GNC2 class for Parkinson Brothers Racing, where he won four events, had five second-place finishes, and won the overall championship.

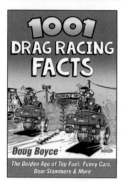
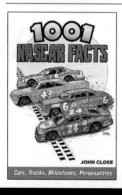